SOUL MUSIC

TRACKING POP

SERIES EDITORS: LORI BURNS, JOHN COVACH, AND ALBIN ZAK

In one form or another, the influence of popular music has permeated cultural activities and perception on a global scale. Interdisciplinary in nature, Tracking Pop is intended as a wide-ranging exploration of pop music and its cultural situation. In addition to providing resources for students and scholars working in the field of popular culture, the books in this series will appeal to general readers and music lovers, for whom pop has provided the soundtrack of their lives.

Listening to Popular Music: Or, How I Learned to Stop Worrying and Love Led Zeppelin
by Theodore Gracyk

Sounding Out Pop: Analytical Essays in Popular Music
edited by Mark Spicer and John Covach

I Don't Sound Like Nobody: Remaking Music in 1950s America
by Albin J. Zak III

Soul Music: Tracking the Spiritual Roots of Pop from Plato to Motown
by Joel Rudinow

Soul Music

Tracking the Spiritual Roots of Pop from Plato to Motown

Joel Rudinow

The University of Michigan Press ♪ *Ann Arbor*

Copyright © by the University of Michigan 2010
All rights reserved
Published in the United States of America by
The University of Michigan Press
Manufactured in the United States of America
⊗ Printed on acid-free paper

2013   2012   2011   2010   4   3   2   1

A CIP catalog record for this book is available from the British Library.

Library of Congress Cataloging-in-Publication Data

Rudinow, Joel.
    Soul music : tracking the spiritual roots of pop from Plato to
Motown / by Joel Rudinow.
        p. cm. — (Tracking pop)
    Includes bibliographical references and index.
    ISBN 978-0-472-07108-1 (cloth : alk. paper) — ISBN 978-0-472-
05108-3 (pbk. : alk. paper) — ISBN 978-0-472-02279-3 (e-book)
    1. African Americans—Music—History and criticism.   2. Soul
music—History and criticism.   3. Blues (Music)—History and
criticism.   4. Music—Religious aspects.   5. Music and philosophy
I. Title.
ML3479.R84   2010
781.6401—dc22   2010007915

♥ *For Jalen Jacob—when you're ready*

The superior man tries to promote music as a means to the perfection of human culture. When such music prevails, and people's minds are led towards the right ideals and aspirations, we may see the appearance of a great nation.

—CONFUCIUS

The inward and essential part of every being is composed of fine vibrations, and the external part is formed of gross ones. The finer part we call spirit and the grosser matter, the former being less subject to change and destruction and the latter more so. All that lives is spirit, and all that dies is matter; all that dies in spirit is matter, and all that lives in matter is spirit. All that is visible and perceptible appears to be living, although subject to death and decay, and is becoming every moment resolved into its finer element. But the sight of man is so deluded by its awareness of the seeming world that the spirit that really lives is covered under the garb of matter and its true being is hidden.

—HAZRAT INAYAT KHAN

Contents

Preface

It would be more than arrogant of me to suppose that I might have anything new and original to contribute to the literature on "soul," soul music, or on *the* soul. I doubt my capacity even to canvass this vast literature, let alone transform it. As I undertake to assay my topics I begin with this humbling realization. But I'm not going to let that stop me from working out what I have to say. For me, this book is a matter of inner necessity. There are some things I need to express about myself and my experience, and I need to clarify what those things are, for myself at least, whether or not they merit anyone else's attention. This essay is a project of work that I need to pursue in order to become more completely who I am. In this pursuit I suppose that I am engaged in what some people would call "soul searching."

I got into philosophy as an academic pursuit straight out of high school in 1964. In my freshman year I took my first formal course in the subject, declared philosophy as my major, and kept on going from there. For nearly forty years now I have been teaching the subject at the college and university level, presently back at the little community college in my hometown, where I took that first course. Music has been equally crucial to my life for an even longer period of time, a passion I inherited from my grandparents. From the time I was first initiated into the discourse of philosophy I have been striving to bring these two crucial interests of mine into close contact, and ultimately to integrate them. This book is a result of those efforts.

A word about the book's title, a compromise with the demands of contemporary search engine technology, which has no ear for poetry. I had long wanted the simpler title *Soul From Plato to Motown*, and that is still my nickname for it. Early drafts of what eventually became the prospectus for this book were presented at Sound Thinking: A Music and Philosophy Symposium at the University of Toronto in 1995, and at Music and Cross Cultural Understanding, the Twenty-fifth Richard R.

Baker Philosophy Colloquium at the University of Dayton in 1997. Portions of chapter 5 were presented to a joint meeting of the Canadian Society for Aesthetics and the Canadian University Music Society in Ottawa and to the American Society for Aesthetics in Denver in 2009. Portions of chapter 6 are derived from publications in the *Journal of Aesthetics and Art Criticism* in 1994 and 1995 and from talks given to the Society for the Advancement of American Philosophy in Seattle in 1996 and at the Pacific Division of the American Society for Aesthetics in 2001 and 2002. A portion of chapter 8 is derived from a presentation entitled "Parlor Professors of the Piano" given as part of the 2006 Arts and Lectures series at Santa Rosa Junior College. I am grateful to the editors, organizers, and audiences involved for their kind attention and conversation. My thanks also go to my colleagues and students at Santa Rosa Junior College, Sonoma State University, and Dartmouth College with whom I've enjoyed discussing these ideas.

It is a great pleasure to acknowledge with thanks the encouragement of series editor John Covach, the firm and patient guidance of pop music editor Chris Hebert, both at the University of Michigan Press, and the many colleagues and former teachers who have offered me helpful criticisms, support, guidance, and encouragement over the years: Phil Alperson, Mark Anderman, David Averbuck, Monroe Beardsley, Jonathan Bennett, Steve Bernstein, Bill Bossart, Lee Brown, Allen Carlson, Ted Cohen, John Fisher, George Freund, Stan Godlovitch, Ted Gracyk, Tony Graybosch, Kathy Higgins, Jennifer Judkins, Jill Kelly-Moore, Joe Margolis, Sean Martin, Ed Mooney, Teed Rockwell, Richard Sikora, Elizabeth Stillwaggon, Phil Temko, Everett Traverso, and Marx Wartofsky.

I am especially indebted to two anonymous colleagues who read the entire manuscript on behalf of the press and offered many very helpful suggestions, to David Evans and Ernest G. McClain, who read large portions of the manuscript and shared their crucial expertise with me in thoughtful and extensive commentary, and to my wife, Carolyn M. Carnell, for her love and support and for all she is teaching me about energy medicine. I am grateful to Carol Idler and Marjorie Grossman for research assistance, to Project Manager Marcia LaBrenz and copyeditor Jan Opdyke, who shepherded the text from word files and typescript into print, and to Mary Hashman, for preparing the index. I must also pay my debt of gratitude to the many musicians (far too many to mention by name) with whom I've been honored to share the stage, the studio, and rides in the equipment van for all they have taught me about the practice of music, without which this book could never have been conceived, and especially to Amy Lynn Treadwell, for introducing me to the world of gospel music.

Finally, my sincere thanks go to the Sabbatical Committee of the Academic Senate at Santa Rosa Junior College for a sabbatical leave, during which I was able to begin the manuscript, and to the Faculty Fund for Advanced Studies at Santa Rosa Junior College for the 2007 Randolph Newman Grant, supporting my travel to Memphis, the Mississippi Delta, and New Orleans.

—SONOMA, CALIFORNIA

Introduction

As I write this introduction, America (and the world) has just witnessed the inauguration of Barack Obama as the forty-fourth president of the United States, our first "president of color." Popular music was prominently used throughout the inaugural festivities and ceremonies, much of it representing the category known as "soul music," a style of popular music that originated in post–World War II America and flourished during the civil rights movement of the 1950s and 1960s. In widely circulated footage the soon to be first family was seen grooving to Stevie Wonder as he performed "Higher Ground" at the Lincoln Memorial. Two days later, at the inauguration ceremony, California senator Dianne Feinstein, who chaired the joint congressional inauguration committee, introduced Aretha Franklin, the Queen of Soul, to sing "My Country 'Tis of Thee." Struggling in the bitter cold wind to reach the high notes, Aretha nevertheless rose to the occasion, delivering a performance that still brings a lump to the throat. The next day, appearing on Larry King's CNN talk show, Aretha recalled her experience singing forty years earlier at the funeral services for Dr. Martin Luther King Jr. She went on to make apologies for her inauguration day performance as having not met her own standards, and remarked, with the assurance and humility of a churchgoing woman, "Yesterday, Mother Nature was not very kind to me. I'm going to deal with her when I get home." Other performances were deeply resonant as well. Soul survivor Bettye LaVette sang a duet with Jon Bon Jovi (!) on Sam Cooke's 1960s soul anthem "A Change Is Gonna Come." Bruce Springsteen performed "The Rising," with full gospel choir, and on and on.

I couldn't help but marvel in all of this at the vital role that music has played and continues to play in nourishing and healing the soul of a nation in crisis. This may sound like an extravagant thing to say. Many extravagant things, to be sure, were said in the inauguration coverage. But there were also deep and sober reflections along these same lines. Classical music critic Alex Ross likened Aretha's inaugural moment to Marian Anderson's 1939 Easter Sunday concert given on the steps of the Lincoln Memorial after the Daughters of the American Revolution had refused to house the performance in Constitution Hall due to the color of the performer's skin, prompting Eleanor Roosevelt to resign her membership in the DAR and her husband to authorize the concert on the Mall. The concert arguably awakened the nation, if only momentarily, to its racism.[1]

Anyway, whether or not it sounds extravagant, I think it can be said in all seriousness about soul music in particular that it has played a very important part in healing America's troubled soul. This book is about what it means to say something like this in all seriousness. We might begin by meditating briefly on the label "soul music." How does a style of popular music, *this* style in particular, come by such a name? Is it a mere coincidence that this music is called by a name evolved over millennia to point to the unfathomable spiritual dimensions of life and of consciousness both individual and collective? Is it happenstance, a mere matter of convenience, that *this* music in particular should be referenced and alluded to so frequently in discussions of our ongoing processes of collective and individual soul-searching? I doubt it. To those whose interest in this music is strong and deep enough to have read (or written) books about it, these connections will seem obvious, even routine. But understanding and explaining them remains a challenging and ephemeral goal—my goal in this book.

I am a philosopher and a musician, and this is a book of philosophy about music. The music I am writing about is popular music from the middle of the twentieth century—soul music, along with its vernacular antecedents: the spirituals, the blues, gospel music, and rock & roll. A book about Plato and these kinds of music is probably about as far outside the mainstream of philosophy as it is outside the mainstream of literature on popular culture. Forty years ago, when I first began to reflect on it, my topical agenda was considered quite marginal. Philosophy of music was a marginal category of philosophical aesthetics just as philosophical aesthetics (philosophy as applied to the arts) was a marginal discipline within philosophy. On top of that, popular and vernacular music were of marginal interest to philosophy of music. But that was then, and here we are now.

This book is about music, but this is also a book of philosophy, and so, like many philosophy books, it starts out with a puzzle. Here is the puzzle: soul music draws essentially upon sources that are said and sincerely believed by many to be "spiritually incompatible." Specifically, the spirituals and gospel music are widely held to be "spiritually at odds" with the blues and rock & roll. References to the blues as the "devil's music" are common to the point of cliché. And so were early condemnations of that "infernal" rock & roll music. I find this notion fascinating. One might think to write such commentary off as hyperbolic or merely figurative in some way if it weren't for the fact that so many of the folks who say this sort of thing are dead serious. Indeed, I myself sometimes think that certain music might really be "spiritually toxic," and I have already said (in all seriousness) that soul music in particular has helped to heal the soul of a nation in crisis. I nevertheless wonder what it can possibly mean for different styles of music to be "spiritually at odds" with each other—especially styles as closely and intimately related to each other as are gospel music and the blues. What substance can there be to such a claim? How does music work upon the soul? How does music work upon the "collective soul" (whatever that expression might mean)? Can music have "spiritually therapeutic" effects—both individually and collectively? Can music have "spiritually toxic" effects—individually and collectively? How is any of this to be understood and explained? What, if anything, is *really* going on here?

There are many ways to enter into such questions as these, ranging across the spectrum from the mystical to the skeptical. One can bring a great many scholarly disciplines and orientations to bear—music theory, musicology, ethnomusicology, cultural anthropology, neurobiology, psychology, mythology, theology, and so on and on. But ultimately such questions invite, and indeed call for, philosophical exploration. This book traces my own philosophical journey into them. It has proven to be, as I reflect on it now, a winding journey inward, like a labyrinth. Come to think of it, how else would one expect to approach answers to questions like these? I invite you now to go with me into these questions. Here is a brief sketch of the labyrinthine path ahead of us.

If we are to talk seriously about the soul in relation to music, we will sooner or later have to deal with what philosophy calls "metaphysics." And so, in chapter 1, as I bring the puzzles I find in the advent of soul music into focus in their social and historical context, I will also frame them in metaphysical terms, the better to open them up to philosophical investigation.

Among the many ways to explore the notions of the divine and the demonic in music, one can delve into their provenance. Where did such ideas originate and how did they evolve? In chapter 2 we look into one of the founding myths of American popular culture, the blues as the "devil's music." We examine the legend of delta bluesman Robert Johnson. A cipher dying in dark and mysterious obscurity in the 1930s, Robert Johnson emerged in the 1960s as one of popular music's most powerful and influential legends. According to legend, Robert Johnson made a midnight deal with the devil at a crossroads, trading his soul for the musical technique and inspiration he expressed in a voice that still haunts American and world music seventy years and more after it was first recorded. Is there a way to take this legend seriously without necessarily buying into its literal truth? I believe there is.

In chapter 3 our exploration of cultural history continues, as we trace the emergence of gospel music in the context of the evolving African American church. The blues, as it turns out, plays a central role in the story of one of gospel music's key founding figures, Thomas A. Dorsey, a role that ultimately belies the blues' mythological status as the devil's music. Here we come face-to-face with the theological problem of evil, and I will propose a way of understanding the blues as the expression of a crisis of faith in the collective soul of a people.

In all of philosophy there is no richer source of material to draw on for inspiration and insight, pretty much regardless of the subject matter, than Plato. It is especially true with my topics. In the *Republic,* the centerpiece of Plato's oeuvre and surely one of the most important and widely read works of philosophy ever written, we find several ideas of striking relevance to our themes. In *Republic* Book III there is a fascinating discussion of the uses of music in the cultivation of both desirable and undesirable character traits, followed in Book IV by Plato's distinctive "moral psychology"—or theory of the soul as pertains to moral consciousness. All of this is deeply informed by one of the important early advances in what we now know as music theory—harmonics and tuning theory as developed by the Pythagorean school of pre-Socratic philosophy. Music turns out also to be fundamental to Plato's most renowned philosophical legacy, formalism—a way of seeking understanding through an appreciation of abstract formal relationships. Plato's famous "Theory of Forms" as absolutely perfect and unchanging abstractions available only to contemplation by the rational mind has plausible applications in harmonics and tuning theory even as they illuminate it. Plato even uses harmonies to explain how awareness can be turned from the sensory (hearing a harmonic interval) through the contemplative (considering the arithmetic ratio between the pitches) to enlightened understanding (grasping the formal perfection of the harmonic relationship in the abstract).

In chapter 4 I will begin to explore these Platonic ideas as I address one of the most deeply challenging questions in philosophy of music: how to understand and account for music's apparent capacity to move emotional energy. Can a philosophical theory of the soul, coupled with a formal understanding of intonation and harmony in music, explain music's evident capacity to excite and direct emotional energy? Can they help us reliably distinguish spiritually healthy from spiritually unhealthy music? What light can these theoretical tools shed on blues tonality, in particular one of its more intriguing and important harmonic elements, the tritone or "devil's interval?"

Despite the obvious affinity between rhythm and arithmetic—beats are, after all, counted—rhythm has been surprisingly neglected by formalist philosophy of music. And indeed certain rhythmic concepts and phenomena crucial to an understanding and appreciation of soul music and other styles of popular and vernacular music—for example, groove, swing, syncopation, the backbeat—prove in the end to be beyond the comfortable reach of formalist analysis. Formalist analysis seems to aim at transcending, and result in denigrating, the physical. But as we turn our attention from harmony to rhythm we cannot so easily leave the body behind or out of account. Thus in chapter 5, following insights of the American philosophers John Dewey and Suzanne Langer and the contemporary pragmatist philosopher Richard Shusterman, we turn from the Platonic abstractions of formalism and mathematics and return to the body and biology for insight.

Soul music is obviously and inseparably entangled with the civil rights struggles of post–World War II America. This no doubt is symptomatic of an even deeper connection between race and popular music in America stretching over a much longer period of history. But in chapter 6 as I explore this connection I will focus on the period generally referred to as the rock & roll era, the period from the late 1940s and early 1950s when young white people became a major market for black music in America, the period during which soul music emerged and came into full flower, the period I grew up in and lived through. I will examine the dynamics of race and racism in popular music culture during this crucial period of American history, including some of the ways in which audiences were both segregated along and integrated across racial lines, the roles that race and music jointly played both in delineating and in transgressing cultural barriers, and the ethics of "authenticity." Plato's central analogy in the *Republic* between the individual and the collective soul will prove to be highly relevant here.

An ironic coincidence links the spirituals and the blues together: the prevalence of cryptic lyrical content—hidden and double meanings, messages communicated in code. By another odd coincidence, during a hiatus in my career I stumbled onto references to the work of a political philosopher whose ideas and theories about how to read and understand Plato's *Republic* now seem to me to explain these phenomena in popular music rather elegantly. By an even stranger coincidence these very ideas and theories are the focal point of an arcane intellectual controversy wrapped in a political scandal of global proportions. In chapter 7 I will explore the theories of irony and cryptic communication developed by Leo Strauss, a German Jew who taught political philosophy as a refugee in the United States from 1937 until his death in 1973 and whose legacy has been claimed in recent decades by a radical strain of "neoconservatism" in applied political philosophy. I will argue that the so-called Straussians in the neoconservative movement seriously misrepresent the insights of Leo Strauss, which when properly understood show irony to be an effective strategy of covert communication under conditions of political repression as well as an effective therapeutic strategy combining the cleansing effects of both comedy and tragedy—very much like the blues.

This brings us finally to the heart of the labyrinth, the metaphysics of music as a healing art. In chapter 8 I approach this topic by way of a critical examination of contemporary clinical applications of music in medicine. I argue that the prevailing psychopharmacological explanatory models assumed in the clinical and experimental practice of music therapy are inappropriate and should be replaced with a model informed by physics. Then, in an attempt to distinguish promising avenues of inquiry from dubious pseudo science, I explore the concepts of resonance and entrainment in acoustics and review the state of the science concerning these physical phenomena along with the emerging neuroscience of consciousness. Finally, I explore the medical distinction between therapeutic and palliative care modalities and review the clinical practice of music in end of life or hospice care.

I hope in this book to be addressing a diverse audience. As a philosopher, of course I am very interested in what my professional colleagues in the discipline of philosophy think about what I have to say in these pages. But I also hope to be understood by my fellow musicians and by music lovers who are not professional philosophers. Striking this balance has been perhaps the greatest challenge I have had to face in writing this book.

About ten years ago I ran across a volume entitled *Soul—An Archaeology: Readings from Socrates to Ray Charles,* an annotated compendium of quotations, some short and aphoristic, some longer and more discursive, arranged with commentary by one Phil Cousineau, a writer and speaker whose body of work is diverse and hard to categorize.[2] It was the first time I had encountered anyone working with what seemed to me to be the same set of conceptual coordinates as I was. It gave me pause to reflect on how remote from each other the various segments of my intended audience have been for so many generations and continue to be despite current trends. (Today philosophy of music is among the fastest-growing areas of interest in philosophical aesthetics, and there is a burgeoning interest in popular culture both inside and outside the academy.)

In the Middle Ages there were seven "liberal arts" subjects taught in the scholastic universities, organized into two levels: the elementary "trivium"—grammar, logic, and rhetoric; and the higher "quadrivium"—arithmetic, geometry, music, and astronomy. *Trivium* is where our word *trivial* comes from. The four subjects of the quadrivium were considered "higher" in large part because they were systematized mathematically. Above these stood the "metasubjects" of Philosophy and Theology. The medieval quadrivium reflected an ancient system of organization founded by the Pythagorean school of pre-Socratic philosophy. The Pythagoreans, who looked for numerical significance wherever they could find it, conceived of arithmetic as the study of number in itself, geometry as the study of number in space, music as the study of number in time, and astronomy (or cosmology) as the study of number in space and time together.

But then, during the Renaissance, music was dropped from the university curriculum entirely. As far as academic interest was concerned, music went from "quadrivial" all the way past "trivial" to "oblivial." During music's exile from the academic curriculum, it was studied ("practiced") mainly as a performance discipline. Thus music was assimilated into the crafts and vocations, and only later was it included in the fine arts. Composers and performers learned their crafts through apprenticeships and church choirs, while the general population took whatever music instruction was affordable privately in the home. Although this parting of the ways is interesting in and of itself, I call attention to it here as one reason why professional academic philosophy has only very recently begun to recognize philosophy of music as a specialized area of study within the discipline of philosophy. As a philosopher who is also a musician, it seems to me quite natural to focus on music. After all, philosophy is the most omnivorous of disciplines. Anything you can wonder about you can philosophize about. And music is about as wonderful a topic as you can find.

CHAPTER 1

What Is Soul?
(And What Is Soul Music?)

A person's soul is a person's essence, that part of our being which can soar to heaven. Gospel is the music of that essence, and the church is its home.

—STAX MUSEUM OF AMERICAN SOUL MUSIC

The basic thing is soul feeling. The same in blues as in spirituals. And also with gospel music. It is soul music.

—MAHALIA JACKSON

This sound was just pulled from the gospel roots and the blues roots . . . and they tagged it "soul music" because people just stood and sang from their guts, you know, whatever they felt, they just let it come out.

—CARLA THOMAS

What is "Soul"? What a question!

—DICK HEBDIGE

I've been a musician longer than I've been a philosopher. I started piano lessons at the age of seven. My teachers were all very serious and accomplished classical musicians, and I'm afraid I was something of a disappointment to them. I think the discipline required to perform the classical piano repertoire well was just too demanding and exacting for my youthful attention span and mischievous spirit. I stuck with it for about ten years, though I was clearly not going to make it as a classical pianist. But I had a good ear—good enough to get by without really developing much sight-reading ability—and anyway I was more interested in rock & roll and boogie-woogie, styles of piano playing that were developed and transmitted primarily as oral musical traditions (not essentially reliant on notation).

One of the earliest pieces I tried to learn off the radio was Ray Charles's "What'd I Say?" This was in 1959 when I was twelve years old. The tune is a simple repetitive 3-chord 12-bar blues, but it is not easy to play. On the record Ray's left hand holds down a Latin rhythmic figure, defining the chords, against which the right hand plays a second rhythmic figure, coloring the chords, and executes an ornate and exciting arpeggiated turnaround. Over the top of this Ray engages in a playful and passionate game of call-and-response with his group of female backup singers, the Raelettes. It was a real watershed record. Ray Charles was changing the musical landscape by bringing musical elements from the African American church together with the blues into what would soon become known as "soul music." The record was controversial, of course. Although it sold massively across the color line, becoming Ray's first million seller, it was banned in many regions as "too suggestive" in its thinly veiled celebration of sexual intercourse. Ray's deployment of gospel elements in combination with the blues was also at issue, as he recounts in his autobiography.

> I got letters accusing me of bastardizing God's work. A big-time preacher in New York scolded me before his congregation. Many folks saw my music as sacrilegious.[1]

I didn't know it at the time, but grappling with "What'd I Say?" as a twelve-year-old piano student gave me my first glimpse of one of the central puzzles of this book. It is a puzzle lurking at the heart of soul music—a puzzle bringing one of the most profound philosophical, spiritual, and religious mysteries (the soul) together with one of America's most deeply troubling ongoing social and political issues (racism) in the dynamic flux of vernacular popular culture. And, as I shall try to show, it goes also to the heart of philosophy of music.

"Defining" Soul Music

The word *soul* found its way into the discourse of American popular culture initially through music and spread out from there. African American essayist and playwright Amiri Baraka (LeRoi Jones) notes that in the 1950s the word was used by jazz musicians and critics alike to characterize a movement within jazz to reclaim and revitalize a musical tradition that had been repeatedly co-opted by mainstream and corporate culture. Baraka uses *soul* to name "an ingredient so essential to African American music that its absence would cause a knowledgeable listener to question the authenticity (as African American music) of what they were hearing."[2] As Baraka uses the term, *soul* denotes an essence: the necessary and sufficient condition of authentic blackness. In this application the word establishes, or honors, a lineage linking African American secular musical innovations with the work of the African American church. According to Baraka's analysis, the musicians about whom the term was first used in the 1950s—Horace Silver, Art Blakey, Max Roach, Clifford Brown, and John Coltrane—were drawing upon the distinctive call-and-response cadences of preacher and congregation and the frenzy of spirit possession characteristic of many African American church services. And they did so in conscious reaction and resistance to what they understood as the racist and therefore culturally and politically repressive conditions in 1950s America. Specifically they were aiming to restore vitality and authenticity to a music they felt had been "tamed," or "domesticated," and finally "stolen" for profitable mass distribution and consumption by a fundamentally racist culture industry, the music industry, serving a fundamentally racist society.[3]

Over the next decade the term became a potent signifier of solidarity within the African American community in the struggle for black power, and as such it was applied to all manner of cultural production and expression—from cuisine (soul food) to hairstyles (soul patch) and special recognition handshakes (soul brother). At the same time the term was also being taken up within the music industry, where it shifted from jazz to function first as a label for a distinctive style of pop music and later as a demographic (and racially specific) marketing category label, replacing the term *rhythm & blues,* which itself had replaced *race.*[4] It is ironic though predictable that the prevailing conventional usage of *soul* in the discourse of American popular culture, including the scholarly literature, reflects music industry practice over time and thus has by and large lost touch with the jazz references. Accordingly, what people generally understand, when they see references to "soul music," is a style or category of pop music dating from the late 1950s.

The earliest developments within this category of pop are generally agreed to be the crossover of Sam Cooke, lead singer in the gospel group the Soul Stirrers, to the pop charts in 1957 with the hit single "You Send Me." The style comes to full flower with the breakthrough work of Ray Charles, combining stylistic elements of gospel music with rhythm & blues and rock & roll. And it culminates, climactically, in the mid- and late-1960s in the monumental work of Aretha Franklin (the "Queen of Soul") and the still flowering genius of Stevie Wonder. Although it survives to this day as an identifiable style and marketing category in popular music (Mariah Carey, Beyonce Knowles, Mary J. Blige, Christina Aguilera, John Legend, Usher), it is widely regarded by scholars and critics to have passed through the prime of its creative artistic achievement, as well as its social and political relevance, certainly by the early 1980s. The central puzzles with which I will be concerned in this book arise within the frame defined by these prevailing conventions. But in chapter 6, when we return to the question of soul as the essence of authenticity, the jazz references will, as we should expect, provide crucial illumination.

The Origins of Soul Music

Like so many other musical categories ("jazz," "folk music"), the category "soul music" can be somewhat elusive under definitional or essentialist analysis. The difficulty stems in part from the fact that, as a cultural phenomenon, soul music is continuous and deeply entangled with a myriad of other cultural variables, all of which are inextricably bound up in dynamic struggle and evolution. And so soul music might reasonably be identified or defined in terms of any number of combinations of regional, historical, generational, ethnic, and racial factors, each of which has some bearing on our eventual interpretive understanding and assessment of the music. To illustrate, let me take as my example Peter Guralnick's 1986 landmark study *Sweet Soul Music,* which begins with a long and winding narrative of false starts and revisions in his own evolving definition.[5] How should we, for example, distinguish the music coming out of the American South—Memphis; Muscle Shoals, Alabama; and Macon, Georgia—from Berry Gordy's Detroit-based Motown sound or the music produced out of Philadelphia by Kenny Gamble and Leon Huff or Chicago's Curtis Mayfield and Jerry Butler? In the end, Guralnick draws a bright geographical line, emphasizing audience demographics as well as regional-cultural and musical-stylistic differences, and confines himself to the project of reconstructing the oral history of southern soul music. For Guralnick, Motown is not soul music. His argument for this is partly business-historic and partly stylistic. He writes:

> [W]hen I speak of soul music, I am not referring to Motown, a phenomenon almost exactly contemporaneous but appealing far more to a pop, white, and industry-slanted kind of audience.[6]

And he continues:

> Soul music is Southern by definition if not by actual geography. . . . [B]oth its birth and inspiration stem from the South.[7]

Crucial to the distinctive essential character of southern soul music are the racial and interracial dynamics of its inception. With soul music, not only were audiences integrating across long-hardened racial lines—lines that rock & roll had softened and transgressed—but the creative process was integrated as well. If the stars and singers of soul music were primarily African American, the creative teams upon whose collaborative energy soul music also depended—the songwriters, backing musicians, and producers—were not only racially mixed but racially integrated. A distinctive and quite remarkable kind of interracial collaborative creative partnership arose and flourished in the "southern soul triangle": Stax Records in Memphis, Muscle Shoals Recording Studios and Fame Records in Alabama, and the scene in and around Macon, Georgia, which would produce James Brown and Otis Redding as well as the southern blues-rock jam band the Allman Brothers. It was:

> Not so much the white man in the woodpile, or even the white businessman capitalizing on social placement and cultural advantage to plunder the resources of a captive people, as the white *partner* contributing as significantly as his more prominent—more visible certainly—black associate.[8]

Stax historian Rob Bowman confirms this assessment.

> While undeniably involved on a day-by-day basis in the crafting and marketing of African American culture, virtually from the beginning Stax Records was racially integrated in the studio, in the front office and, by the midway point of its history, at the level of ownership. All this took place in Memphis, Tennessee, a city that as late as 1971 elected to close its public swimming pools rather than allow black and white kids to swim side by side in the scorching heat.[9]

If such collaborations could theoretically have arisen in other places and times, Guralnick finds it unimaginable that they could have had the kinds of meanings they did, or produced the musical results they did, anywhere but in the American South at the precise historical moment they occurred.

> Unquestionably the racial turmoil of the South was a factor, and the rapid social upheaval which it foreshadowed; in fact the whole tangled racial history of the region, the intimate terms on which it lived with its passions and contradictions, played a decisive role in the forging of a new culture, one which the North's polite lip service to liberalism could never have achieved.[10]

Guralnick chooses to tell the story of a distinctive and important, but very tightly specified, musical movement—*Southern* soul music. As fascinating and illuminating as that story is, Guralnick's account remains quite puzzling and ultimately at loose ends, particularly in the lines he draws and the inclusions and exclusions they would seem to imply. For my purposes it just will not do to *define* soul music as Southern to the exclusion of not only Motown but Curtis Mayfield, Jerry Butler, the Philadelphia International label, and so on. Take, for example, the O'Jays' "Love Train" (Philadelphia International, 1973)—as pure an instance of soul music as you can find. And how can you possibly marginalize Curtis Mayfield from a discussion of the music of the mid- twentieth-century American civil rights struggle? Then, too, ruling out all of Motown would result in the exclusion of Stevie Wonder from the category of soul music—someone I regard as, well, a paradigm.

Both Ray Charles and Sam Cooke receive extensive treatment in Guralnick's book. They are the subject of a "prologue" and are treated as the two main progenitors of the style. But although Ray Charles was southern by birth (in Florida), he had relocated to Seattle and was already touring nationally with his own big band when he began recording for Atlantic Records, an upstart independent label at the time, based not in the South but in New York City. "What'd I Say?" (1959) reached #6 on the pop charts. But in the same year the Isley Brothers released "Shout (Parts 1 and 2)"—every bit as clear, as powerful, and as widely recognized an instance of African American gospel music penetrating into rhythm and blues and pop music. But the Isley Brothers came out of Cincinnati and recorded for the major label RCA. Sam Cooke made music history by crossing over from a successful career in gospel music as lead singer for the close harmony gospel group the Soul Stirrers. And he wrote the first soul music anthem of the civil rights struggle, "A Change Is Gonna Come," released posthumously in 1964, a year before passage of the 1965 Voting Rights Act. But if you see the essence of "soul singing" as the fully surrendered embodiment of spirit possession in the gospel music tradition, how do you categorize Sam Cooke stylistically? If Ray and Aretha would scream and shout, Sam Cooke was a controlled "crooner." You won't hear anything even close to a scream or a shout in "You Send Me," "Cupid," "Another Saturday Night," "Twistin' the Night Away," "Wonderful World," or any of Sam Cooke's recorded work. Stylistically, Sam Cooke is much closer to Marvin Gaye, a Motown artist who after all took Sam Cooke as a model. Gaye also delivered an anthem of the civil rights struggle, albeit at a later and less hopeful point in its history, "What's Going On?" (1971). Marvin Gaye doesn't even turn up in Guralnick's index. Aretha Franklin does, of necessity, and indeed Guralnick devotes an entire chapter to her arrival on the soul scene. Born in Memphis but raised in Detroit, where she blossomed as a singer in her father Reverend C. L. Franklin's church, she was first brought to the attention of John Hammond at Columbia Records in New York. There she recorded ten albums over an artistically and commercially frustrating six-year period, after which she, too, recorded for Atlantic Records, where she really came into her own. As Guralnick recounts it, Aretha made one fateful trip to the southern soul triangle as a recording artist. The recording sessions, organized by Atlantic Records' producer Jerry Wexler, were to take place at the Muscle Shoals studio in Alabama (Stax in Memphis having bowed out for financial reasons), and although they produced basic tracks for two well-known hit songs, they wound up in an ugly altercation on the first day and totally fell apart on the second. The two basic tracks that were produced ("Do Right Woman—Do Right Man" and "I Never Loved a Man") both had to be finished in New York.[11] So much for the southern connection in Aretha's case. So many exceptions and anomalies I suspect simply prove the rule that rigid essentialist definitions and classifications applied within the dynamic processes of culture formation run an ever increasing risk of being arbitrary.

Other critics and scholars approach soul music as a national phenomenon situated historically more than geographically. For Gene Santoro, jazz and popular music critic for the *Nation,* the story of soul music is primarily a tale of the rise and fall of a cultural movement, with music functioning at or near the center. Santoro's narrative revolves primarily around the success story of black entrepreneur Berry Gordy's conquest of the white pop music market with his Detroit-based Motown sound but with culturally parallel developments occurring simultaneously in other cities. The movement in question is of course the civil rights movement, which Santoro reads as progressing hopefully, as expressed in the crossover popularity of black music, until the late 1960s, when the political agenda of civil rights begins to fragment internally, while soul music becomes increasingly co-opted by commercial imperatives.[12]

Similarly, British scholar Brian Ward describes a complex national, though regionally differentiated, process of cultural formation—the simultaneous urbanization of Southern rural black music and the secularization of black church music. And he reads the history of post–World War II black popular music as a running record of changes in mass black (and white) consciousness during the peak years of the civil rights and black power movements.[13]

Similarly, ethnomusicology professor Portia Maultsby presents the story of soul music within the conceptual framework of the civil rights struggle, beginning with the sit-ins and freedom rides of the 1950s on through the black power movement of the mid-1960s, after which soul music succumbs to the commercial corruption of disco.[14]

For Nelson George, the black music editor at *Billboard,* soul music is where the black audience went when it gave up on rock & roll. On George's reading of America's cultural path, rock & roll was already the commercial co-optation of black music and of the dream of cultural integration. When black people saw what had happened by the early 1960s to the music of Chuck Berry, Fats Domino, and Little Richard, when they saw what the industry and the audience for rock & roll had become and had come to demand, black listeners turned elsewhere. So where Guralnick and Santoro find reason to celebrate the breakdown of racial segregation in soul music, George identifies soul music with the resegregation of popular music culture.[15]

The Originators of Soul Music

Geography, even if not definitive of the category, remains a key factor in understanding soul music, which is to say that distinctive regional stylistic variations are discernable and significant and that regional circumstances and peculiarities are important to history in all of its dimensions. There is good reason, for example, to consider Memphis, Tennessee, as an epicenter of the soul music explosion due in no small measure to its geographical location at one of America's most important crossroads. Memphis lies along the main route of northern migration on the eastern banks of the Mississippi River at the northern end of the Mississippi Delta where it intersects one of the main historical avenues of westward expansion, the present day route of Interstate Highway 40. Memphis was thus situated to become one of the major centers of emerging urban African American culture, easily on a par with the northern industrial destination cities of Chicago and Detroit. A number of innovations crucial to the history of American popular and vernacular music can be traced to this environment. These include jug band music, the first all black and the first all female radio formats, and of course rock & roll. Memphis' WDIA, the nation's first radio station to commit to a black audience with an all black on-air staff, not only established the economic viability of black-oriented radio, a model replicated nationwide, but thereby opened a crucial window for white listeners into black culture, especially black music. On the West Coast, for example, I listened regularly throughout the 1950s to Oakland's sister station KDIA. B. B. King began his career at WDIA, initially as host of a daily fifteen-minute broadcast and pitchman for the sponsor's product, in exchange for which he was allowed to use airtime to promote his local performances and eventually to perform and record his own material. Where else but in Memphis would a frustrated country fiddle player like Jim Stewart stumble onto the materials and means of recording what would become known as the Stax sound?

However, as much as these developments reflect geography, they were also as often as not the results of trial and error and blind serendipitous encounters between unanticipated circumstances and unique and forceful individual personalities. For example, Stewart had no idea that the location he leased for his recording studio, an abandoned movie theater at the corner of College and McLemore Avenue, was in a neighborhood that would go on to supply so much of the talent that wrote and recorded at Stax and created the Stax sound. Sam Phillips, the founder of Memphis' Sun Records, as well as of the nation's first radio station with an all female on-air staff, Memphis' WHER, is perhaps the best example of the kind of improvisational go-for-broke entrepreneurship that found and developed markets for American popular music after World War II. But much the same can be said of Motown founder and owner Berry Gordy. An aspiring African American songwriter, Gordy set Motown up as a factory to produce hit records. Indeed, it functioned very much on the model of an industrial assembly line. Hit records meant to Gordy records that the emerging audience of young suburban white people would want to hear over and over. Motown did indeed work out a sophisticated and highly successful formula for the production of music aimed at white American teenagers. Guralnick's argument that as a consequence Motown's music tended to be more emotionally restrained, even "repressed"—in any case, less open and expressive emotionally than *real* (southern) soul music—may work for Diana Ross and the Supremes. But it certainly doesn't do much justice to Gladys Knight and the Pips. Santoro, like Guralnick, disdains the "black cotton candy" sound of the Supremes. But he discerns other, more "soulful" elements in the Motown sound, particularly the "enormous horsepower" of the Funk Brothers rhythm section, driven by the bebop-influenced innovations of bassist James Jamerson. And if Booker T and the MGs (the house band at Stax) was integrated, so too were the Funk Brothers. It is also worth noting that, in much the same way that members of the Beatles and Beach Boys studied each other, the Stax production teams studied Motown music through the laboratory provided by Estelle Axton's Satellite Record Shop according to Booker T's testimony.[16]

The Meaning of Soul Music

The city of Memphis stood once again at the epicenter of the national movement when Dr. Martin Luther King Jr. was assassinated there in April of 1968, sparking violent uprisings in Detroit, Los Angeles, and other cities around the country and changing unalterably both the course of the civil rights struggle and the tone and content of soul music.

All five writers agree that stylistically soul music was a merger between gospel music and secular forms of popular music—blues, rhythm & blues, and rock & roll. All five agree that in terms of its social and political significance soul music transcended mere (disposable) pop fashion. It served as a kind of musical soundtrack to, and as such also as an integral part of, the American civil rights struggle of the 1950s and 1960s. Where the accounts differ, we find as much as anything else, differing understandings and assessments of the civil rights struggle itself and of this crucial period of American cultural and political history. This is only to be expected given the points of agreement just mentioned.

A Puzzle at the Heart of Soul Music

What intrigues me most as a philosopher about this otherwise obvious interpretive starting point is the strange tension inherent in the very notion of such a stylistic merger—a tension that manifested itself in a range of awkward responses to the music as it was being born. Was the birth of soul music a blessed event or an abomination? That depended on what you thought of the union of gospel music with rock & roll and rhythm & blues. And there were many strong feelings, not all of them favorable, especially among those best situated to recognize the gospel influences for what they were. Even stranger, as we shall see further in chapter 3, this same tension goes back to the birth of gospel music itself.

As an illustration, consider a passage from an essay entitled "Holy Blues: The Gospel Tradition," by Mark A. Humphrey, in which the author finds this tension in the early history of both blues and gospel music.

> "Holy blues" is an evident oxymoron. . . . Holy blues is oxymoronic if we believe blues to be "the devil's music," a tenet held by many "reformed" blues singers and the "saints" of some African-American churches. Blues is unholy, and sacred music unbluesy. Blues celebrates the pleasures of the flesh, while sacred music celebrates release from worldly bondage. One is oil to the other's holy water; [they are] unmixable."[17]

Those who subscribe to the view Humphrey is characterizing here presuppose some distinction between spiritually healthy music appropriate to the work of the church and depraved or demonic music. And they are concerned both to prevent corruption of the healthy kind and to discourage exposure, especially among the young and impressionable, to the demonic kind. On this view, soul music would be taboo. If blues is unholy then rock & roll must also be considered a corrupting influence. After all, rock & roll is the bastard offspring of the blues and hillbilly country music. A marriage between rhythm & blues or rock & roll, with its undistinguished lineage, and the music of the *church*?! It's unthinkable! Out of the question! And yet it's exactly what happened. It's exactly what soul music is historically and stylistically.

Now one might respond, "Where exactly is the puzzle here? The view that the blues and gospel music represent or express irreconcilable social forces is hardly refuted by deriving from it the observation that soul music breaks a taboo or two. The history of American popular music is in some ways a history of broken taboos (e.g., the taboo against interracial adolescent audiences). And so is the history of the American civil rights movement (e.g., the taboo against interracial marriage). So where exactly is this view in trouble?"

The view gets into interesting trouble, or perhaps I should say "exposes a conundrum," precisely where it is historically most accurate. It locates the origins of the taboo in the central institutions of African American culture, particularly in the African American church. Note the irony: there is no institution more central to the American civil rights movement of the mid–twentieth century than the African American church. According to this widespread view, again paraphrasing Humphrey, the twin populist voices of African American culture, blues and gospel music, lay on opposite sides of "a dualist divide crossed only *at peril to one's soul.*"[18] According to this view the choices available within African American culture were mutually exclusive: "either blues or gospel music, God or the Devil, Heaven or Hell."[19] So soul music, which *is*, after all, a mixture of gospel music and rhythm & blues or rock & roll, happens according to this view *in spite of* one of African American culture's most central institutions. Implausible though it may be on its face, there is a good deal of historical truth in this assessment, to which we shall return in chapter 3.

But notice above all that in dividing music into the categories of the divine and the demonic it seems to be presupposed that music has the power to affect the condition of the soul in both positive and negative ways. This is a commonplace idea. Most folks don't even blink when attention is drawn to it. They have long since accepted it. But it is nevertheless a very intriguing idea from the point of view of philosophy, meaning that a philosopher will find a lot to wonder about in it.

Metaphysics and the Soul

As a professional philosopher, I am dedicated to the pursuit of wisdom. In my academic training in the discipline of philosophy I was taught to be humble, and careful, but patient and tenacious in this pursuit. In practice the very first thing this means is that you need to develop a high tolerance for unanswered questions.

It is well said that philosophy begins in wonder. When it comes to the soul there is ever so much to wonder about—starting with consciousness. What *is* consciousness? How does what we call "consciousness" arise? What happens to me when I fall asleep? What will happen to me when I die? I like to think that most of us begin wondering about these things very early in life, long before we find out that there is an academic discipline called philosophy dedicated to pondering such questions. In any case, these are the kinds of questions that lead people to talk of the soul.

As a philosopher, I should point out that talking of the soul doesn't so much answer these questions as multiply them. What *is* the soul? If I "have" a soul, does that mean that "I" am somehow distinct from "it"? Or am I "identical with" my soul? In which case, what sense does it make for me to say that I *have* a soul or even to speak of *my* soul? I can point to my foot or my nose or my mustache. But where is my soul? Does my soul inhabit my body? Can it escape my body? Or does it animate my body by remote control? Is my soul something distinct from my mind (whatever that might be)? What is my soul up to while I'm sleeping? Will my soul survive my physical death? And so on and on indefinitely. I don't know the answers to any of these questions. But I've developed an above average tolerance for unanswered questions, which is a good thing because the soul ranks right up there among the oldest and most formidable problems of philosophy.

The philosophical problem of the soul encompasses a host of questions, each ranking in its own right among the classical problems of philosophy. In addition to those already mentioned or alluded to, there is the problem of freedom of the will. In what sense and to what extent do we freely choose any course of action we might take? For example, in my preface I said that for me this book is "a matter of inner necessity." Did I freely choose those words? And now I find myself sitting and staring at the computer screen, cursor blinking at me as I struggle for words. Am I freely choosing these words? Oh, and by the way, what difference does it make whether we freely choose our words or not? And why is there *so much struggle* involved in working out what I have to say?

Then there's the problem of personal identity: What is this "I" that survives from one moment to the next, throughout all of the evolving stages of life from birth to death, integrating all of this lived experience as "mine"? Is it the same "I" that keeps getting in the way of my writing, editing my composition even as I compose it, interrupting my flow with questions and objections and alternative phrasings, going off on tangents, till I have to rein myself back in? How many of "me" are there? Questions enough to make one dizzy!

Although I'm used to unanswered questions, the problem of the soul is an unusually deep bundle of them. One thing that deepens the problem is that at the outset both the reality status *and* the essential nature of the soul are up for grabs. When people talk or write about the soul, often they start from the assumption that what they are talking or writing about is *real*—and go on to say various things about it. As a philosopher, I cannot start from this assumption. My starting point is wonder. For me the reality of the soul is, at least at the beginning, another one of those unanswered questions. Is the soul something "real"?

Wondering about this question, it occurs to me that it would help if I knew how to identify or define the soul. Consulting a dictionary, I find an etymology tracing the word through the Middle English *soul* to the Old English *sawol* and the Germanic *saiwalo* to the Gothic *saiwala,* whose origin is uncertain. There is an interpretive tradition in which the word originally meant "coming from or belonging to the sea." This reading is based in part on mythology, according to which the soul's itinerary immediately before birth and after death is the sea, and on etymological convergence with the word *sea.*[20] It is apparent that in all of this the metaphysical reality of the soul as a spiritual entity that animates an individual human life, while being distinct from and existing independent of the person's body, is presupposed. This etymology is followed by a list of meanings to be found in conventional modern and contemporary usage.[21]

1) The animating principle, or actuating cause of an individual life, conceived of as an immaterial entity distinct from but temporally coexistent with the body

2) The spiritual principle embodied in human beings, regarded as immortal, separable from the body at death, and susceptible to happiness or misery in a future state

3) The spiritual principle embodied in all rational and spiritual beings, or the universe

4) A person's total self

5) A moving spirit

6) The disembodied spirit of a deceased person

7) The moral and emotional nature of the human being

8) Spiritual or moral force

These first eight meanings are given as conceptually primary.[22] In conventional usage, as in the etymology, the metaphysical reality of the soul as a spiritual entity animating an individual human life while being distinct from and existing independent of the body is presupposed.

Someone looking for shortcuts might be tempted by the notion that the meaning, now that we know what it is, settles both the question of the soul's essential nature and the question of its metaphysical reality status. (How can you coherently deny, or even question the reality of something whose reality is presupposed in the very meaning of the word?) There is a famous argument in the history of philosophy and theology that starts from the meaning of a word and arrives at the metaphysical reality of a spiritual entity. In the Ontological Argument the word(s) are "Supreme Being" and the spiritual entity is God.[23] From the moment it was presented by Saint Anselm in the eleventh century, it has confounded logic. Those who have found the argument persuasive can't seem to agree as to precisely how the argument goes, while those who find it unpersuasive can't seem to agree as to precisely what is wrong with it. If someone were to propose a similar argument from the meaning of the word *soul* as disclosed in the dictionary to the metaphysical reality of the soul, it would be easy enough to see how the argument goes. It goes in a circle. I should like to do better.

The Soul: A "Minimalist" Definition

If I go back to my own experience and start there, I am arrested by the following observations.

A. I am a conscious, or sentient, being. What I intend this to mean is that I am "aware of things both inside and outside of me"—and that I manifest this awareness in and through the use of my body.

B. I am aware that to some limited extent I am able to focus and direct my attention and awareness at will. If I cannot remember precisely how long I have been aware of this ability, I am quite sure that I have grown more acutely aware of it with age.

C. I am aware that to some limited extent I have been able to focus and direct my attention onto this process of focusing and directing my own attention and awareness. I am able, in other words, to reflect on my own awareness.

D. I am convinced that to some limited extent I have been able to develop, to cultivate and refine, these abilities.

So, if I may generalize from my own case, I shall assume that consciousness can be focused, directed, reflected upon, and developed to some extent at will.

E. Next, as I observed at the very beginning, I am driven to engage in this "soul-searching" enterprise—to exercise, reflect upon, and develop my awareness—by some sort of inner imperative.

F. Finally, I am aware also of resistance—of obstacles arising at times within me—obstructing this enterprise.

Taken together these last two observations indicate that from time to time I find myself "divided" internally and engaged in some form of inner struggle that must somehow be resolved in order for me to act.

What is it in me that is aware of these things? What is it in me that is driven to pursue these inquiries? What is the source in me of the inner imperative that drives me on? What is it in me that resists and obstructs? What is it that resolves these inner conflicts? Shall I call this my soul? Or am I being seduced and misled by these very questions—and the awkward way in which they are worded—into searching for and positing something (some *thing*) that has no inherent substantial reality? If I try to sneak up on my self and catch a glimpse of the "it," I meet with no success. If I try to get "above" or "behind" my own awareness to observe whatever "it" is that is aware, I am never "quick enough" to observe the observer. There is nowhere I can go and look outside of my own awareness—and there is always nothing there. Perhaps this is because *I am* the observer and I am always "here." If I reflect on my thinking and writing, again I am unable to maneuver myself into a position where I can directly observe the inner agent at work. Wherever you go, there you are. If I try to observe the observer, I am like a dog chasing its tail except that the dog can at least *see* the tail.

I am going to need the word *soul* to get anywhere in this essay. My topics would be utterly unintelligible without it. And the word will have to mean *something*. Suppose I adopt the expression "my soul" as a way of naming the locus of my awareness. This is, I take it, simply a way of talking about myself as a conscious, or sentient, being. My experience is constantly unfolding in time, and my awareness is always situated in the present. This is what is meant by "locus of awareness": a point moving through a continuum. And suppose I adopt the same expression "my soul" as a way of naming the agent of my voluntary behavior, assuming for the sake of the hypothesis that I am capable of voluntary action.

Notice that in calling both the locus of my awareness and the agent of my voluntary behavior by the same name I am implying that the agent of my voluntary behavior is identical to the locus of my awareness. Not that this implication strains intuition at all. I already call the locus of my awareness and the agent of my voluntary behavior by the same name. It is "I" who am aware of my experience and it is "I" who do the things I do. But this identity is crucial from the point of view of morality in that conscious awareness of oneself as a voluntary agent is a necessary condition of moral responsibility.

Some may wonder what this "moral responsibility" business is and where it came from all of a sudden? I find it in observation E above. When I look into the nature of the "inner imperative" that drives me (or anyone) to engage in "soul-searching," it is immediately apparent that the imperative is a "moral" one. Suppose someone asked: Why are you troubling yourself with this soul-searching? What does it matter whether you "know yourself" or not? Try to formulate a coherent response to such questions without a conceptual framework involving some such notion as moral responsibility. See how far you get.

Again, if I may generalize, I will use the expression "the soul" as a way of naming the locus of awareness and the agent of voluntary action in *any* conscious, or sentient, being. This way of speaking is roughly in line with conventional usage but with two important qualifications. First, it may strike some as remarkably inclusive in that it arguably applies to at least some nonhuman organisms. Second, and more important, it is also minimalist in that it leaves most of that swirling myriad of questions about consciousness and the soul unaddressed and unanswered.

Spiritualist Metaphysics

Let's go back to the metaphysical question of the soul's "reality status." Now most of the people I know, if they assign any meaning at all to the word *soul*, believe that there are such things as souls and that we each have one and that all of our individual souls are "real." Just because you can't *see* the soul, or find it in physical space, doesn't mean that there is no such thing or that such things are not real. The soul is a "spiritual"—not a physical—entity. For the moment let me call this the "popular view." If we needed a fancy name for it, we could call it metaphysical spiritualism. It is the view presupposed in the definitive etymologies and conventional idioms compiled in the dictionary. When people talk this way about their souls, they almost always have more in mind than simply a locus of awareness and an agency of voluntary action. Adopting the minimalist usage of the words *my soul* specified above might be understood as analogous to adopting the word *zero* to refer to "the additive identity of any integer."[24] Does defining the word *zero* in this way commit one to a belief in some "entity" corresponding to the word and existing in some ephemeral realm of being? Surely not without additional reasoning. So, although I'll carry on using the expressions "my soul" and "the soul" to refer to the locus of awareness and the voluntary agent in myself and other sentient beings, notice that I've not put my money down about any spiritual realms or entities yet. Why do I hold back? I hold back in deference to another side of the metaphysical issue and in particular to several movements and traditions within the history of philosophy, each of which, in its way, is at odds with metaphysical spiritualism.

Skeptical Empiricism

First, let me present the empiricist tradition in Western philosophy. Stated as simply as possible, empiricism is the view that sensory experience is the source of all knowledge. Empiricism must of course be refined and elaborated in various ways to accommodate and adapt to the limitations of everyday sensory experience. These include the apparent unreliability of the senses (the problem of illusion, etc.) and the fact that some important phenomena, such as causation, are inaccessible to direct sensory experience. So, for example, science investigates causation and other phenomena that cannot be verified directly in sensory experience by means of methodical experimentation. But the experimental method in science begins in experience, applies reasoning to generalize and extrapolate from experience, and then tests the products of that reasoning against experience, using instruments that extend and enhance human sensory capacity. Thus science, although it speculates and reaches far beyond ordinary sensory experience, is nevertheless fundamentally empirical. The empiricist tradition is basically skeptical of any claims that cannot in principle be tested in some such way. Thus, in the twentieth century a philosophical movement known as "scientific empiricism" (also known as "logical positivism") expounded a critique of all transcendental and speculative metaphysical ideas, saying in effect that even to talk about something that lies in principle beyond the reach of empirical science would be meaningless.

Eliminative Materialism

Following in this tradition is a contemporary theory known as eliminative materialism, which holds that all of our inner states of awareness and intention are really nothing but as yet inadequately understood brain chemistry in action. No need to posit a mental entity (a "mind") as separate and distinct from the body, much less a spiritual entity (or "soul"). Thus, even though I have held back from metaphysical spiritualism, eliminative materialists would no doubt be dismissing a lot of what I have offered as commonsense observations about my own experience (expressed as best I can in commonly understood terms). I talk about consciousness and freedom of the will because talking about them helps me express and make sense of my experience. But I don't have much in the way of theory to explain what awareness is or what volition might be or where they take place or to account for the mechanisms of their occurrence. Eliminative materialists believe in science. They count on the sciences, in this case neurology, neurobiology, neurochemistry, and other brain sciences, to eventually yield complete and satisfying explanations of all the things I observe in my own experience. The eventual emergence of mature scientific accounts of brain function would, in the hopeful view of the eliminative materialist, eliminate the need for us to talk about ourselves and our experiences in the familiar but ontologically cumbersome idioms of folk psychology, as I have been doing. "Ontologically cumbersome" means that our familiar ways of talking tempt us to believe in things that aren't real—like a soul or a locus of consciousness or a voluntary agent. And so, according to this way of looking at things, believing in the reality of the soul is like believing in unicorns or the tooth fairy.[25]

Buddhist Metaphysics

Then there is the Buddhist teaching known as Anatta, or the doctrine of "no soul," according to which we are encouraged to carefully examine our experience and notice that all phenomena are changing and ephemeral. We will therefore not find anything with which to identify the self or soul as a permanent and unchanging entity. This teaching contains striking similarities to elements in the Western philosophical tradition just discussed, with the interesting difference that where empiricism is primarily focused on the "outer" or "real" world of intersubjective experience, the Buddhist teaching is concerned primarily with introspection. This teaching also opens into a very important puzzle in Buddhism. The puzzle is how to reconcile the doctrine of no soul with the doctrines of karma and reincarnation. Karma is the doctrine that the consequences of one's actions will be revisited upon one, if not in this life then in a future life. But then, how are reincarnation and karma possible if there is no soul to pass from one lifetime to the next? In the accounts of the Buddha's teaching that are passed down, the Buddha kept his silence when he was asked "Is there a soul?" and also kept his silence when asked "Is there not a soul?" Evidently a high tolerance for unanswered questions is useful to one who is trying to progress along this path.

The Immortality Question

Thus far I have effectively ignored the elephant in the room by skirting the immortality question. Does the soul survive the death of the body? Generally speaking, metaphysical spiritualism responds to the immortality question with some version of the following story. Each individual soul entity passes through some indefinitely large number of lifetimes, of which the lifetime we're in now is but one, an "incarnation," meaning a lifetime spent in a physical body. There are many stories about what happens to an individual soul beyond the bounds of a given physical incarnation. All such stories offer answers to three of the questions that haunt mankind from birth to death: Where did I come from? What will happen to me when I die? And what is the meaning or purpose of this incarnation? Generally this last question is answered by saying something like this. An incarnation is an opportunity for self-expression and learning in preparation for the afterlife. What one does in the course of one's lifetime, and what one learns and accomplishes in the development of one's individual soul as a result of one's lifetime experience and actions, determines the course of one's life to come.

The philosophical problem that arises here is that, because what we are wondering about lies radically beyond the bounds of lived experience, it is essentially a matter of conjecture. What I mean by "radically beyond the bounds" is that the tools and procedures we would normally use to test and validate claims and conjectures about matters beyond our lived experience don't even begin to work here. If I were interested in the history of my birthplace before I was born, I could find out a great deal by going to the museum, the library, and other archives and by consulting my elders. If I wanted to check and verify the information I was getting, I could do that as well. Similarly, if I were planning to travel to an unfamiliar part of the world, I could find out a great deal about the geography, the seasonal weather, the local attractions and customs, the regional cuisine, the overnight accommodations, and so on and plan my journey well in advance. How can I find out about my soul's journey before and after its physical incarnation in me?

I should point out that a belief in the reality of the soul is not required in order to feel the weight of the immortality question. Nor does the question need to be worded in terms of the soul. Does awareness cease at the moment of death? And indeed, the questions that most deeply motivate the immortality question—Where did I come from? What will happen to me when I die? And what is the meaning or purpose of this incarnation?—are each and all agnostic about the soul. For the time being, I shall have to leave all of these questions open and unanswered, and simply resort to my "minimalist definition." This is a good time to remember the importance of a high tolerance for unanswered questions.

Philosophy of Music

The puzzles I find at the heart of soul music are based on the commonplace but philosophically intriguing notion that music has the power to affect the condition of the soul in both positive and negative ways. To get a sense of the philosophical intrigue, one good place to start is with the question of how we are supposed to determine what kinds or instances or performances of music are the demonic ones. Is death metal demonic? What about christian death metal? Or would that be as oxymoronic as "holy blues" is supposed to be? Or does music's demonic quotient depend on something other than such ill-defined music-marketing niche labels as these? Are there any criteria or objective standards we can appeal to in deciding controversial cases?

Also philosophically intriguing is the notion of a "collective soul." If the essential nature and metaphysical reality of the soul both remain open questions, what clear sense can we assign to such expressions as the "soul of a nation" or the "soul of a people?" And finally we must face the question of just how music works upon the soul, whatever the soul may be. How do music and the soul interact? What is it in us individually and collectively that is so profoundly affected by music? And what is it in the music that accounts for these effects?

That music should have elaborate and systematic implications reaching deep into the soul and its travails has proven to be an intuitively beguiling yet elusive notion shrouded in esoterica. And this is where Plato comes in. As we shall see in chapters 4 and 6, Plato's *Republic* is organized around a central analogy between the individual and the collective soul, it contains fascinating commentary about the crucial value and delicate nature of musical education in the cultivation of character, and it presents Plato's unique metaphysically based moral psychology as a "Harmonics of the Soul." But before we get to those parts of the labyrinth, we have other excursions on our agenda. First we go in search of the devil, and then we go to church.

CHAPTER 2

The "Devil's Music"
(Can Music Be Evil?)

Give me the making of the songs of a nation, and I care not who makes its laws.
                          —ANDREW FLETCHER

I adhere to the philosophy, "I don't care who writes the laws, let me write the songs."
    —CHUCK D, OF THE HIP-HOP GROUP PUBLIC ENEMY

Let me make the superstitions of a nation and I care not who makes its laws or its songs either.
                          —MARK TWAIN

An old Chinese proverb runs, "the music of a well-ordered age is calm and cheerful, and so is its government; the music of a restive age is excited and fierce, and its government is perverted." This invites the chicken-and-egg question: Is the music a cause or an effect of its cultural and political circumstances? Does the music direct the culture along its trajectory or does the music merely reflect and express the cultural conditions of its time? As a philosopher, I should point out the possibility that the chicken-and-egg question as just expressed presupposes a false dichotomy. In other words, it might turn out that music is *both* a cause *and* an effect of its cultural moment. Thus, exemplary of ancient wisdom, the proverb leaves the chicken-and-egg question unanswered.

There is a long tradition that worries about the spiritual effects of music—on the musician, on the listener as an individual, and on society as a whole. Too much hard rock at high volume can cause hearing loss. That's a physical effect. Focusing on the spiritual effects of music means identifying the soul as the locus of impact. Can the soul be damaged or harmed by exposure to music or to music of certain kinds? Often such worries are invested with the weight of philosophical authority. Perhaps the best example of this sort of appeal to philosophical authority is a fa-

mous extended rant against the cultural movements of the 1960s entitled *The Closing of the American Mind*. In that book classicist Allan Bloom
denounces rock musicians (exemplified by Mick Jagger, Prince, and
Michael Jackson) as depraved and wretched creatures of "the under-
world" and generally deplores rock music for its effects on the souls of
young listeners. In support of his dire warnings about the dangers of music, Bloom leans heavily on the texts of classical philosophy, as, for example, in the following passage.

> Plato's teaching about music is, put simply, that rhythm and melody, ac-
> companied by dance, are the barbarous expression of the soul. . . . Mu-
> sic is the soul's primitive and primary speech and it is *alogon,* without ar-
> ticulate speech or reason. It is not only not reasonable, it is hostile to
> reason.[1]

If one goes looking in weighty tomes for pithy quotes warning of the dangers of music, one will surely find them. Plato famously wrote:

> The introduction of novel fashions in music is a thing to beware of as
> endangering the whole of society, whose most important conventions
> are unsettled by any revolution in that quarter.[2]

The nineteenth-century Danish philosopher and theologian Søren
Kierkegaard wrote:

> Our age does offer many horrible proofs of the daemonic power with
> which music may lay hold upon an individual.[3]

But as we shall see, one must proceed with caution in these matters. Both
Plato and Kierkegaard composed enigmatic works, like the Chinese
proverb, designed to undermine the reader's reliance on the authority
of the text. Rather, in these essentially Socratic encounters, the reader is

> forced to take individual responsibility for knowing who s/he is and for
> knowing where s/he stands on the existential, ethical, and religious is-
> sues raised in the texts.[4]

Suffice it to say for present purposes that many people are firmly convinced of the power of music to affect the conditions of the individual
soul and the culture at large. Among the most vivid expressions of this
conviction are those concerned primarily about the negative effects and
capacities of music.

Can music be evil? The question calls up the myth of the "devil's music"—one of the founding myths of American popular culture around which has turned much of the controversy surrounding American popular music for many generations. I call this a "myth," and I mean to call it into question, but I don't propose to just throw it out. There's too much apparent truth in it for that. The "devil's music," music that has been assigned this designation, or "demonized" if you will, has been indeed notably associated throughout its history with hardship, vice, and violence. The history of rock & roll especially, but also of the blues, jazz, and soul music, can easily be read as a running narrative of spectacular overindulgence and self-destruction of all kinds. Consider the casualty list over the last forty-odd years: the suicide of Kurt Cobain, the stalking and assassination of John Lennon by an obsessive fan, the deaths by drug overdose of Janis Joplin, Michael Bloomfield, Lowell George, and Jimi Hendrix at the height of his creative powers. To these we may add the more or less violent deaths, under still mysterious circumstances, of Marvin Gaye, Sam Cooke, Sid Vicious and his girlfriend Nancy Spungen, and more recently Tupak Shakur and Biggie Smalls, as well as the deaths, and near deaths, by dissipation of Jim Morrison, Keith Moon, David Crosby, Jerry Garcia. One could go on and on and on. The list sounds like one Long Strange Tragically Fruitful Faustian-Bargain Hunt. Thus it is not surprising that what motivates and sustains the myth of the "devil's music" in recent and current cultural commentary has much to do with widespread and understandable horror at the spectacle of apparently avoidable human suffering regularly and flamboyantly enacted in certain sectors of popular music culture. Would it surprise anyone if Courtney Love or Amy Winehouse eventually destroyed herself?

But we must avoid jumping to conclusions as murky as they are facile about music's role in such all too human affairs. Music is hardly the only area of human cultural activity associated with extraordinarily high rates of substance abuse and other forms of disaffection. Look at the history of stand-up comedy for example. Nor can we simply assume that all of the incidents of misfortune in music listed above are of a piece. Clearly they're not. John Lennon's assassination can no more be assimilated to the death of Sid Vicious than can their respective bodies of work be equated. And if Keith Moon went down in flames at an early age, Keith Richards is still defying gravity. As tempting as it may be, the notion that music is particularly implicated in all of the decadence and pain that seems sometimes to surround it cannot be simply presupposed. The chicken-and-egg question applies here again. Does the music engender or merely reflect the decadence? Does the music cause or merely express the pain? To get a sense of the treacherous depths involved here, let us explore a paradigm case of the mythology of the devil's music.

I Went Down to the Crossroads

The myth of the "devil's music" finds one of its most complex, complete, and fully integrated examples in the legend of Robert Johnson—a pivotal and crucial figure in the history of American popular music and in American pop cultural mythology. Robert Johnson's relatively tiny output—some twenty-nine recorded songs—nevertheless looms as large in terms of influence on subsequent popular music in America and the world as many more prolific figures and prodigious bodies of work. The ethnomusicologist David Evans ranks Robert Johnson as "by far the most important" of the Mississippi bluesmen for his synthesis and consolidation of the delta country blues style.[5] Francis Davis, in *The History of the Blues*, ranks Robert Johnson as the "greatest of the Delta transcendentalists" and a "mystery as enduring as the blues itself."[6] In the large collaborative commemoration commissioned for the PBS documentary series *The Blues: A Musical Journey*, published in 2003's centenary "Year of the Blues," Robert Santelli calls Robert Johnson "the single most important artist of the country blues period and one of the most important blues artists of all time." He attributes "many of the myths and themes that helped give the blues its colorful story" to Johnson's murky biography, in which "fact and fiction are blurred."[7] Recalling his early exposure to the blues as a college freshman in the early 1960s, Peter Guralnick writes:

> Of all the figures who beckoned to us from a remote, mysterious, and foreign past—certainly it was a past that was not our own—Robert Johnson stood out, tantalized, really, in a way that no other myth or archetype has ever done. . . . Robert Johnson's music remains the touchstone against which the achievement of the blues is measured.[8]

Eric Clapton, for whom Robert Johnson's "Cross Road Blues" became a signature tune in the 1960s, calls him "the most important blues musician who ever lived." He goes on to testify that

> as deep as I have gotten into the music over the last 30 years, I have never found anything more deeply soulful than Robert Johnson. His music remains the most powerful cry that I think you can find in the human voice.[9]

As much as the scholars and musicians who came after him hold his music in awe for its deeply disturbing power, his life and the circumstances of his death remain shrouded in sinister mystery. According to some accounts he died in a knife fight (or perhaps was stabbed with an ice pick); according to others he died by poison at the hands of a jealous husband.[10] In any case it would appear that he lived fast and hard and died young; and the dark mystique enveloping his biography and work has been widely and romantically mythologized.

The legend of Robert Johnson's bargain with the devil is recounted and alluded to in countless discussions. According to the legend, Robert Johnson made a deal with the devil, trading his soul for the musical technique and inspiration he eventually brought forth in songs such as "If I Had Possession Over Judgement Day," "Me and the Devil Blues," "Hellhounds on My Trail," and "Cross Road Blues." Here is Greil Marcus's invocation of the legend.

> [C]ommitment is a tricky, Faustian word. When he first appeared Robert couldn't play guitar to save his life, Son House told Pete Welding; Johnson hung out with the older blues men, pestering them for a chance to try his hand, and after a time he went away. It was months later, on a Saturday night, when they saw him again, still looking to be heard. They tried to put him off, but he persisted; finally they let him play for a lull and left him alone with the tables and chairs. Outside, taking the air, House and the others heard a loud, devastating music of a brilliance and purity beyond anything in the memory of the Mississippi Delta. Johnson had nothing more to learn from *them*. "He sold his soul to the devil to get to play like that," House told Welding.[11]

This is typical legendary lore: a tall tale told at second-, third-, and fourthhand. Marcus attributes the story to music writer Pete Welding, who in turn attributes it to delta bluesman Son House. Central to the legend is the startling and seemingly unaccountable acquisition of instrumental virtuosity. Johnson first appears as an earnest but inept aspirant to the musical performance space, barely tolerated by the other musicians. After a short absence of some indefinite length, he reappears to deliver an awe-inspiring performance. A similar tale is told, at similar remove, by rock historian Ed Ward, who finds it in an interview with guitarist Michael Bloomfield taken by a radio producer named Tom Yates. Bloomfield in turn attributes the story to four bluesmen: Johnny Shines, Sunnyland Slim, Muddy Waters, and Elmore James.

Now, Robert was the thing that myths are made of. Here was a guy who hung around all the blues singers who were making the popular records of that time (like I did when I was his age), and he couldn't play worth a damn. He'd always try to sit in, and they'd say, "Sure, let him play." And he couldn't play. He was so painfully shy that he could barely get the request to sit in and play out, and then he'd get up there, and he couldn't do it. Well all these musicians were travelers, and they would leave the area where Robert lived, go away, come back a year later, and Robert would again ask to play, and again he couldn't do it. Two years passed—and I've heard this from four bluesmen who knew Robert Johnson intimately in their younger days—two years passed, and they came back and Robert could not only play, but he could outplay them. He could outplay guys that he could not even vaguely imitate two years prior. So, as it has been told to me—and I realize this sounds real strange, but a lot of Southern people believe this—they say that Robert sold his soul to the devil. He went to a fork in the road, to a crossroads, and he put his guitar down there and made a deal with the devil: that the devil would give him the ability to be good with women, good with gambling, and good with the guitar, and in exchange, he could take him at a young age and let him burn in hell. And the devil said that was a good deal. Now if you listen to songs like "Stagolee," they're usually moral tales about the devil making deals for a soul. Robert made that deal, and all the guys who told me this—Johnny Shines, Sunnyland Slim, Muddy Waters, and Elmore James—all of them distinctly told me that story about Robert selling his soul to the devil.[12]

Here we see a second important ingredient in the legend: the aspect of personality transformation—or transcendence. Johnson is reputed to have been "painfully shy"—a crippling if not uncommon trait for a musician, a liability that paradoxically haunts his recounted and recorded performances, although it is entirely belied by them. A third and related element is the notion that the performer acquires special musical powers of sexual allure and conquest. With the devil's patronage the musician becomes, in and around the performance space, the alpha male, the object of interest and desire of all the women in the vicinity.[13] A fourth crucial aspect is the whirlwind that the artist reaps. The artist who contracts with the devil is from that moment on tormented by the contract, its terms and significance, and by the holder of the note, the devil himself. Bloomfield continues:

Well, Robert got real good, amazingly good, and he had a chance to make some records, and he did, and some people say they're the greatest country blues records of all time. I don't know if I agree with that, but I do know that in them you can hear a young man, a young man with an amazing amount of energy, the kind of thing that you would find in the early Pete Townshend, or early Elvis, or in any young man who's just burning up his energy. You can hear this in Robert's records; it just leaps off at you from the turntable. But he was shy. There's a story about how shy he was. He was in a recording studio, and he couldn't face the engineer. There was a Mexican band, a band of Mexican musicians who had never heard blues or heard a black performer before, and they asked if they could watch him play. But he couldn't do it. He sat in the corner and they put the microphone in the corner with him. He sat with his back to the Mexicans, and they could hear him, but he was too shy to let them see him play. And that was the very opposite of the way he was when he was in front of a paying crowd in a honky-tonk or a nightclub, or at a fish fry. And he was even less shy around women. There're various arguments about how old he was, but everybody agrees that he didn't live past thirty. He was stabbed in the back with an ice pick in an argument over a lady, or maybe he was poisoned. Apparently—if you put credence in the idea of selling your soul to the devil— the devil collected his due pretty early. So maybe these musicians just know about him from the musical standpoint, but I know him as this mythic creature, terror-stricken, trying to run away from whatever is trying to get him.[14]

Reading the Legend of Robert Johnson

Robert Johnson is far from the only figure in the history of the blues about whom such legends circulate. Peter Guralnick recounts bluesman Johnny Shines's awe at his early encounter with Howlin' Wolf.

> People back then thought about magic and all such things as that. I did-n't know it at the time, but Wolf was a tractor driver. He could have crawled out of a cave, a place of solitude, after a full week's rest, to ser-enade us. I thought he was a magic man, he looked different than any-one I'd seen, and I come along and say a guy like Wolf, he'd sold his soul to the devil.[15]

It begins to look as if whenever one is bowled over and blown away by a musician with a distinctive style and high intensity one sees the work of the devil. Or perhaps such references to the devil are mere folk hyper-bole—a manner of speaking about "otherworldly" or "supernatural" mu-sical gifts or technical wizardry. In other cases the reference to the devil can appear somewhat more "self-promotional," as in the case of the stage persona of a 1930s blues singer named William Bunch, who called himself Peetie Wheatstraw, the Devil's Son-in-Law, and the High Sheriff from Hell.[16] Similarly, in the following passage Guralnick passes along from blues scholar David Evans the testimony of bluesman Tommy Johnson (no relation to Robert), as recounted by Tommy's brother LeDell.

> Now if Tom was living, he'd tell you. He said the reason he knowed so much, said he sold hisself to the devil. I asked him how. He said, "If you want to learn how to play anything you want to play and learn how to make songs yourself, you take your guitar and you go to where a road crossed that way, where a crossroad is. . . . [B]e sure to get there just a little 'fore 12:00 that night so you'll know you'll be there [in time]. You have your guitar and be playing a piece there by yourself. . . . A big black man will walk up there and take your guitar, and he'll tune it. And then he'll play a piece and hand it back to you. That's the way I learned to play anything I want.[17]

Nor are such legends confined to the region and period associated with the development of the blues. As we shall see, and as we should expect, the roots and branches of such legendary stuff as this reach deeply into and far beyond the Mississippi Delta of the early twentieth century.

In the legend of Robert Johnson, the myth of the devil's music finds unusually fertile ground due to a remarkable convergence of factors. Among these are his untimely death, along with its apparently violent but disputed and ill-documented causes; the degree of difficulty associated with his technique as an instrumentalist; the quality and effect of his voice; and the themes and lyrical content of his compositions. Each of these factors merits attention.

The Unsolved Mystery

The circumstances of Robert Johnson's death were the subject of speculation from the time in 1938 when John Hammond sought unsuccessfully to book him for his Carnegie Hall *From Spirituals to Swing* concert. For the next thirty years, the location of Johnson's death and final resting place, as well as the cause of death, were all matters of speculation, rumor, and more or less unreliable hearsay. This is not, in and of itself, terribly surprising for a young black musician in the Mississippi Delta region at the time. In one of my own early experiences in the music business, I was a member of a band that managed to book a two-week sit-down gig in a hotel lounge. It was a "union house," which meant that we all had to go down and sign up with the local musicians' union. There were initiation fees, monthly dues, and activity fees (a cut of the wages for the gig) to be paid. We were each handed a packet of papers, including a list of union benefits. At the very top of the list of benefits was a statement that the union would supply the paid-up member in good standing with a headstone. I immediately began to wonder what the statistical likelihood of a working musician dying in penniless obscurity might be. The Mississippi Delta blues musicians of the 1930s were of course not organized into a union. And, although there were official records and vital statistics kept at the time, there was and remains good reason to doubt the reliability of these processes as far as black people in the deep South were concerned. In subsequent years, as interest in recovering traces of the origins of blues music has grown, so have the efforts of a number of folklorists and researchers who have made careers out of attempting to reconstruct an accurate history of the blues. In 1968, after a three-year search throughout four states (Mississippi, Arkansas, Texas, and Tennessee), journalist and blues researcher Gayle Dean Wardlow was finally able to recover Robert Johnson's official death certificate, according to which he died on August 16, 1938, in or near Greenwood in LeFlore County, Mississippi. The cause of death is listed as "No Doctor."[18]

Sudden Awesome Virtuosity

What is most remarkable, and what seems to have most impressed listeners about Robert Johnson's guitar technique, is his use of the guitar in self-accompaniment, involving complex polyrhythmic figures and microtonality. His recorded performances are phenomenal displays of musical multitasking. Keith Richards recounts his first impression: "I was hearing two guitars, and it took me a long time to realize he was actually doing it all by himself. You know, you think you're getting a handle on playing the blues, and then you hear Robert Johnson—some of the rhythms he's doing, and playing and singing at the same time, you think, 'This guy must have three brains!' "[19] Francis Davis also notes Johnson's sophisticated guitar technique, enabling him to successfully emulate the complexity of a piano accompaniment, or even a whole rhythm section, as well as "utilizing his guitar as an equal contrapuntal voice." He reports the testimony of Johnny Shines: "His guitar seemed to talk—repeat and say words with him like no one else in the world could."[20] Robert Santelli observes:

No one, not back then, nor today, has been able to fully reproduce Johnson's gift to phrase guitar notes and chords so that they answered oh-so-artfully the lyrics he sang. The size of his hands may have had something to do with the way he played. Listening to Johnson you often swear two guitarists are playing, not one. His long fingers reached for notes other guitarists could only dream of, while his penchant for slide guitar and "walking" bass riffs gave his style a remarkably rich language of notes, tones, and sounds. No wonder people thought he made a deal with the devil.[21]

This, taken together with the fact that there is apparently no early indication of this virtuoso mastery anywhere in the oral histories, which portray an inept, aspiring guitarist, presents an anomaly, a phenomenon that seems to defy mundane explanation.

The Voice

Removed from the context of his self-accompaniment, and especially from his songs themselves, Robert Johnson's voice would probably not count as very remarkable. Greil Marcus is surely gushing when he says, "Robert Johnson had a beautiful high voice, a tragic voice when he meant it to be."[22] Nevertheless, like many popular singers with idiosyncratic voices (think of Louis Armstrong, Ray Charles, Joe Cocker, Dr. John, Bob Dylan, Nina Simone, or Tom Waits), what Johnson *did with* his voice is indeed remarkable. His music, as he sang it himself, continues to touch listeners deeply and move them powerfully. Contrast Marcus's assessment with that of Robert Santelli.

> Johnson's voice wasn't pretty or weathered; rather, it was whiny, but in a profound way. It ached, it reached out for comfort, it was dark and lonely, it could stop you in your tracks.[23]

David Evans describes his diction as "slightly muffled" and his voice as "passionate, agonized and sometimes strained"[24] or "clenched."[25] He says further:

> Johnson does not have an outstanding natural singing voice and sometimes strains excessively for high notes, but he invests his performances with so much feeling and intensity that one easily overlooks his limitations.[26]

Others describe Johnson as singing with "unusual tortured intensity,"[27] the voice of a wanderer.[28]

What stands out most in the commentaries are the descriptions of the effects on the listener when first exposed to Robert Johnson's recorded works. Here, for example, is Eric Clapton's account of his early listening experience.

> What struck me about the Robert Johnson album was that it seemed like he wasn't playing for an audience at all; it didn't obey the rules of time or harmony or anything—he was just playing for himself. It was almost as if he felt things so acutely he found it almost unbearable. . . . At first it was almost too painful [to listen to]. . . . It was as if I had been prepared to receive Robert Johnson, almost like a religious experience that started out with hearing Chuck Berry, then at each stage went further and deeper until I was ready for him. Even then I wasn't quite ready. It was still too powerful, and very frustrating for me, too, because I realized I couldn't play his music any more than I could play Muddy Waters' music. It was just too deep for me to be able to deal with.[29]

The Artist and the Art

In the final analysis it makes little sense to appraise Robert Johnson as a vocalist per se (as though he were auditioning for *American Idol*). It seems much more reasonable to appraise him as a singer-songwriter and to focus on his music as he delivered it in performance, as these performances may be retrievable now from the recorded versions. From the postwar folk-blues revival onward through the rock era, Robert Johnson's body of work has confounded the expectation that folk art generally, and African American folk art especially, must be "primitive" and "unsophisticated." A good many commentators treat Johnson as a literary figure of rarified stature. Greil Marcus, for example, compares the first verse of "Me and the Devil Blues" to a passage from *Moby Dick*.[30] Francis Davis's ranking of Johnson as "the greatest of the Delta transcendentalists" evokes Emerson and Thoreau,[31] and Dave Marsh ranks Johnson alongside F. Scott Fitzgerald in terms of creative sensitivity.[32] A persistent theme assimilates Robert Johnson to the Romantic poets of the nineteenth century.

> Today, many blues aficionados regard blues singers, especially the male blues singers of the Mississippi delta, as twentieth-century African-American analogues to the nineteenth-century Romantic poets, who rebelled against social convention, stole Promethean fire with their art, and died young of laudanum addiction, tuberculosis, syphilis, or suicide (choose one). The myth of the Byronic poet—brilliant, defiant,

and self-destructive—has sustained its great power and resonance for more than 150 years of Western culture. . . . The myth tells us that life and art are inseparable. For the Romantic artist, life and art must both defy taboos, roil with internal and external conflict, and ultimately martyr the artist.[33]

Such comparisons express genuine appreciation for Robert Johnson's music, but they arguably project alien aesthetic values onto the disembodied lyrical texts. But what shall we say about the demonic references and content? The songs of Robert Johnson, especially when approached as an integrated body of work, seem to many of his commentators to revolve around persistent themes of religious despair and pursuit by demons, which his performances reinforce and animate with a "brooding sense of torment and despair."[34] This appraisal is nicely summarized in David Evans's survey of delta blues in the *New Blackwell Guide to Recorded Blues*.

Like many of the greatest Mississippi bluesmen, [Johnson] was clearly worried about the condition of his soul, as is revealed in more than 20 percent of his songs. . . . Robert Johnson seems to have fallen into a state of utter spiritual despair, a state he describes vividly in "Cross Road Blues." In "Preaching the Blues" he equates the blues with the devil, who walks by his side in "Me and the Devil Blues." He challenges God in "If I Had Possession Over Judgement Day." His life seems jinxed in "Stones In My Passway," and he is just one step ahead of his doom in "Hellhound On My Trail." These images of despair and evil are complemented by other blues suggesting a life of compulsive wandering like some lost soul. . . . Other pieces suggest that he plunged himself into a life of hedonism, dissipation, and self-destruction in an attempt to avoid the demons that were pursuing him.[35]

As Evans notes, these themes are not peculiar to Johnson's music but have a much wider currency in early delta blues generally. However, by a more or less general consensus of posthumous scholarship and criticism, Robert Johnson would appear to have embraced and grappled with these themes more deeply, expressed them in a poetically more powerful and compelling way, and lived them more authentically than any of his contemporaries.[36]

It Might Be Superstition . . .

Well, what finally are we to make of the legend of Robert Johnson's midnight crossroads deal with the devil? How much of what kind of truth might there be in it? Greil Marcus, who has no doubt done more than any other writer to propagate the legend and the mythology that it supports, invites us to consider several possibilities.

> Well, they tell a lot of stories about Robert Johnson. You could call that one superstition, or you could call it sour grapes. Thinking of voodoo and gypsy women in the back country, or of the black man who used to walk the streets of Harlem with a briefcase full of contracts and a wallet full of cash, buying up souls at $100 a throw, you could even take it literally.[37]

Let us consider these in turn. What would it mean to classify the legend of Robert Johnson as an instance of "superstition"? What *is* a superstition? Let us suppose, with philosopher David Hume, that a superstition is a false and/or ill-founded belief in the supernatural.

> The mind of man is subject to certain unaccountable terrors and apprehensions, proceeding either from the unhappy situation of private or public affairs, from ill health, from a gloomy and melancholy disposition, or from the concurrence of all these circumstances. In such a state of mind, infinite unknown evils are dreaded from unknown agents; and where real objects of terror are wanting, the soul, active to its own prejudice, and fostering its predominant inclination, finds imaginary ones, to whose power and malevolence it sets no limits.[38]

A superstition may be a private matter or it may be more widespread and deeply rooted in a culture. Using essentially the above Humean conception, blues scholar Paul Oliver observes that superstition tends to flourish where standards of education are low, as they surely were in the 1930s Mississippi Delta.[39] The blues are full of references to charms and omens and conjures and potions and magic and animal spirits and the devil and the Lord. But we should be reminded by all of this that the blues are part of an oral tradition and that the conception of superstition we are assuming here arguably presupposes a scientific understanding of the world culturally alien to indigenous tribal beliefs and practices. If we view the blues through privileged lenses of skeptical empiricism many of its lyrical themes and references may strike us as "superstitious."

It is another question how such references actually function in the discourse of those who originally made and heard the music. Hume's description of the psychology supporting and surrounding superstition fits some of the details of Robert Johnson's life well enough. Certainly there were unhappy circumstances, both private and public, for him to contend with, and not just according to legend. But did these circumstances give rise in Robert Johnson's mind to exaggerated and imaginary objects of terror? Was Robert Johnson a witting and willing party, in his own understanding of things, to an exchange of advanced and accelerated development of his own musical talent for a lien on his soul? Did he believe that Satan came knocking on his door early one morning and then went walking with him side by side, perhaps inspiring in him the demonic urge "to beat my woman, until I get satisfied"? Did he believe himself to be pursued by hellhounds? Did any of his contemporaries believe any of these things about him?

. . . or You Could Call It Sour Grapes

Marcus's reference to sour grapes calls into question the testimony of Johnson's contemporaries, especially Son House. And there is indeed some evidence that Son House may have carried a grudge against Robert Johnson, who evidently stole (or copied or imitated) some of his licks and who certainly enjoyed greater posthumous fame than House did during his lifetime. Dick Waterman, who played a pivotal role in the folk-blues revival, bringing long forgotten delta bluesmen to college and festival audiences in the early and mid-1960s, narrates a telling encounter between Son House and Columbia Records executive John Hammond.

> After he resumed playing in 1964, Son House had the usual offers from smaller record labels. I could have settled for that, but I had hopes that he would be signed to a major label. Remembering that John Hammond had overseen the release of the Robert Johnson album on Columbia, I arranged a meeting to determine if John was interested in producing a Son House record. Son and I were waiting in his office when he came striding through the door, shook our hands quickly, and moved behind his desk. "I can't tell you what an honor it is to have the great Son House sitting in front of me. Your Paramount sides are some of the greatest recordings of all time. And, of course, Robert Johnson learned so much from you. You know that I tried to bring him to New York City for a concert?" I glanced at Son and he was looking out the window. This was not a good sign. I could tell that his attention was wandering. John, on the other hand was just getting started. His enthusiasm moved up a notch. "I was doing the Spirituals to Swing concert back in 1938 and I sent word down south that I wanted Robert to appear on the show and word came back that he was dead. Can you imagine how great it would have been to have had Robert Johnson on stage at Carnegie

Hall?" Son reached into his shirt pocket and took out a crumpled pack of cigarettes. Crossing one leg over the other, he lit one and looked back out the window. "Uh oh," I thought, "bad sign." I knew from this body language that Son had tuned out on this conversation and had gone into his own world. John continued with the Robert Johnson superlatives, raving about his incredible talent and what a loss it had been that he died so young. I couldn't get a word in, and I didn't want to interrupt, so I just waved my arm in the air until he stopped and looked at me. "Look, Mister Hammond," I said, "With all due respect to Robert Johnson being a great musician, you have to remember that Son only knows him in the context of being a snotty kid that hung around him and Willie Brown, copping their licks and breaking guitar strings whenever they let him sit in for a few songs. He just doesn't have the same appreciation of Robert that you do. Son is a great artist in his own right and it's a little insulting of you to bring us here and then talk about someone else." I nudged Son with my elbow to get his attention and we both looked up as John quickly moved around the desk and embraced Son. "Welcome to Columbia Records, Son House," he exclaimed. "We are honored to have you here and we are going to make a wonderful record together." After the meeting, Son and I went downstairs to the bar. I had a beer and ordered a double bourbon on the rocks for him. I lifted my glass and said, "Here's to John Hammond, . . . for bringing you to Columbia Records." Son held his glass aloft for a moment and said, "Here's to Robert Johnson, . . . for being dead."[40]

The Literal Truth?

Marcus also invites us to consider taking the legend "literally." It is by no means clear what this ought to mean precisely, but one possible point of departure would be the factual or historical record. Does Robert Johnson's legend correspond in any meaningful way with what is available or what can be reconstructed as a credible record of actual events? Of paramount interest in this regard is what happened during Johnson's absence from Robinsonville, Mississippi, the scene of his early encounters with Son House and of his impressive return. Stephen C. LaVere's account, published in the booklet accompanying the CD release of Robert Johnson's complete recordings, is much more mundane and correspondingly more plausible than the legend taken literally. According to LaVere, Johnson relocated from Robinsonville to Hazlehurst, some two hundred miles to the south, for an "extended sojourn" of two or more years, during which time he evidently devoted himself to the development of his music.

Robert realized that if he ever wanted to be anything other than a share-cropper, he needed to get himself and his music together. With that in mind, when wanderlust took hold of him, he decided to leave home and try to locate his real father. All he had to go on was his birthplace, the small, lush town some 210 miles to the south.[41]

Two years of serious woodshedding and performing yielded impressive results. That's basically all there was to it. Eventually:

A trip home was in order, and Robinsonville was made to stand up and take notice of Robert. Son House and Willie Brown were very surprised at his musical development since he'd been gone, and they openly ac-knowledged his improvements with acceptance and praise. They had to—both they and their audiences were acutely aware that Robert had been able to surpass them, both in abilities and appeal. He'd returned to Robinsonville to see his mother and kin as well as to show himself off to Willie and Son, and he stayed around for a couple of months playing on the street corners and in the jook joints.[42]

An "Urban Legend"

Legends often grow out of discrepancies and gaps in the fragmentary record. For example there is a legend of a lost thirtieth song, which ap-pears to have arisen in an undocumented reference (in Samuel Char-ters's 1959 book *The Country Blues*) to some unreleased masters de-stroyed in a billiard parlor fight. On the second of three days of recording sessions in San Antonio, only one of Johnson's songs ("32-20 Blues") was produced, and only one of two listed takes survives. The re-trievable discography indicates that eighteen alternate takes out of a to-tal of sixty-three listed takes of twenty-nine titles are currently lost and untraceable. What happened the rest of that day? What treasures may have been lost?[43]

Legends feed, and feed upon, the longings of those who receive them and pass them along, who trade and invest in them. Gayle Dean Wardlow has reconstructed the history of the Robert Johnson legend in the com-mentaries. He notes that, despite the demonic references and themes in Johnson's songs and lyrics, there is no reference anywhere in his music to any deal struck with the devil. Marcus says, "I have the feeling, at times, that the reason Johnson has remained so elusive is that no one has been willing to take him at his word."[44] But when Johnson sings about "a mortgage on my body and a lien on my soul," it is a barrelhouse woman with "front teeth crowned with gold" holding all that paper. Nor is there any reference to the legend in any of the published Robert Johnson lore until 1966, where it first appears in Pete Welding's article in *Down Beat,* the source of the testimony of Son House.[45] David Evans's study of Tommy Johnson (again, no relation to Robert) is the source of the LeDell Johnson quotation about Tommy's deal.[46] These elements were then combined and amplified by Marcus, Guralnick, and other enthusiasts during the 1960s blues revival period and its aftermath.[47] One wonders whether the story of Robert Johnson's deal with the devil might be nothing more than an overheated "urban legend" fabricated and sustained primarily to serve the personal, social, and commercial agendas of latter day enthusiasts and other latecomers.

Indeed, this is the persuasively argued thesis of three recent books that have altered the landscape of blues scholarship: Elijah Wald's *Escaping the Delta; Robert Johnson Lost and Found,* by Barry Lee Pearson and Bill McCulloch; and *In Search of the Blues,* by Marybeth Hamilton. Each of these books in its own way argues that not only the legend but the accumulated conventional wisdom about Robert Johnson and the blues is unreliable. Because it derives from sources that cannot be adequately documented, because it is often generated or at least filtered and amplified through media (such as album liner notes and entertainment journalism) with commercial and other conflicting interests, and because even the academic scholarship is methodologically questionable, everything we think we know as a culture about Robert Johnson is suspect.

This raises the question of the complex relationship between culture and history. Pearson and McCulloch concede that the Johnson legend "belongs to the people now, and the fact that the people embrace it as a part of American music history is as important as the question of whether it is true."[48] But they also note how the legend makes it "difficult for us to accept Johnson's simple humanity and artistic quality at face value."[49] And Wald stresses the point that the legend says less about its hero than about the culture that perpetuates it.

> Every culture has its legends—one could argue that this is what makes for a culture. The legend of Robert Johnson selling his soul at the crossroads is one of ours. The "us" being present-day, urban, literate, mostly white music fans. . . . It is a potent and intriguing legend, and says a great deal about our yearnings and dreams. . . . We are all romantics in our fashion.[50]

In an important sense, the question really goes to how authentic our collective cultural self-understanding is, a topic to which we shall return in chapter 6.

The Karate Kid Gets the Blues

An interesting example illustrating this position and reinforcing these arguments is presented in the 1986 feature film *Crossroads,* written by John Fusco and directed by Walter Hill. The movie tells a coming-of-age story about a white, teenage, classical guitar prodigy named Eugene Martone, played by Ralph Macchio. In many ways it is a simple variant of the story told in the *Karate Kid* series, for which Macchio is better known. As a student at the Juilliard School of Music, Eugene is nursing an interest, in spite of the active discouragement of his instructors, in modern rock guitar and its mysterious musical antecedent roots. We see him in his dormitory room poring over blues books and liner notes and listening to Robert Johnson's posthumously released recorded works. Already we recognize a story we have heard before. It is the story of Eric Clapton, the story of Mick Jagger and Keith Richards, the story of "our" generation in the history of popular music. Eugene is fascinated by the hints and indications in what he is studying of the existence of an as yet unrecorded Robert Johnson song—the legendary lost thirtieth blues song of Robert Johnson. If only he could track this song down, Eugene could record it, and this could put him in the company and position of the musicians he admires most, the guitar heroes of his age—the rock era. After a bit more research Eugene stumbles upon information leading him to an eighty-year-old Willie Brown, a contemporary and former road-dog buddy of Robert Johnson ("You can run, you can run, Tell my friend poor Willie Brown"), presently serving out a prison sentence in a minimum-security nursing home. Eugene manages to maneuver his way into the facility by taking a part-time job as a janitor, hoping to persuade Willie to teach him the song. But Willie has his own agenda. He'll teach Eugene the song if Eugene will help him escape his confinement and get back to the Crossroads, where he secretly hopes to renegotiate the deal *he* made with the devil long ago in exchange for mastery of *his* instrument, the harmonica. Thus begins their journey. Throughout the journey Eugene remains committed to his quest, although its naïveté is exposed to the challenge of various "harsh realities": about life on the road, about racial segregation, about playing the blues for a living, about sex and love. Eugene never comes to doubt that his talent and the sincerity of his quest to play the blues will see him through adversity. When they eventually reach the Crossroads, the devil is not about to renegotiate with Willie, whose career frustrations and disappointments are of no interest to the devil. What does interest him is another soul: Eugene's. And Eugene is just man enough, and naive enough, to agree to a wager. Eugene will enter into a head-cutting contest, a guitar duel with the devil's hottest guitar slinger. If Eugene wins, the devil will tear up Willie's contract; if he loses, the devil gets Eugene's soul. The film's climax is the guitar duel, which takes place onstage in the devil's own sizzling hot spot, a rock & roll nightclub. As we arrive, the devil's guitar slinger is slaying the room with hard rock. The duel follows the classic arc of heroic battle against evil. The hero must overcome an "unfair advantage" enjoyed by his opponent. In this case blues slide guitar technique (acted rather well by Macchio and performed by Ry Cooder) is pitted against the flashier arsenal of heavy metal guitar technique (acted and performed by guitarist Steve Vai). As the bar is raised, we are invited to wonder whether electric blues guitar, as "nasty and greasy" as that can be, can really be as demonically possessed as, say, Yngwie Malmstein? Finally, just as things appear to be tilting in the devil's favor (the devil's guitar slinger completes a long and blindingly fast run by sounding the dreaded tritone—the "devil's interval"), Eugene pulls out an extended recitation of Paganini (acted by Macchio, performed by Vai). The devil's guitar player tries in vain to recite the same selection. Eugene has won the duel and saved poor Willie's soul.

Legends and Mythology

Let us suppose that Robert Johnson's legend is by and large a puffed-up fan club fable ripe for skeptical deflation. Still, this hardly diminishes its mythological significance. For, as the skeptics especially have pointed out, legends speak volumes about the cultures they inform. Watching the movie *Crossroads,* we can see, as with any cultural narrative, numerous reflections of our own culture, which may of course appear different to differently situated observers, according to our diverse sets of cultural filters. (My own cultural filters will become more apparent as we go.) For the time being, let us set the legend of Robert Johnson to the side and return our focus to the larger myth of the "devil's music." Like any of the central and foundational myths of a culture as dynamic as our own, the myth of the "devil's music" continues to evolve while remaining crucial to a critical understanding and appreciation of American popular music, generation after generation. Let us note some additional cultural reference points for the myth of the "devil's music," beginning with those identified in the movie *Crossroads.*

The Devil's Playlist

The movie makes clear that in his musical preferences the devil is by no means a "blues purist." If he was buying up bluesmen in the 1930s, fifty years later he's investing in heavy metal. This would indicate that whatever else may be true of the mythology of the devil's music, it is a stylistically mobile mythology. And sure enough, we find that a good deal of the cultural debate surrounding heavy metal music has had to do, one way or another, with Satanism.[51] The identification of heavy metal as the "devil's music" goes back to the earliest prototypical heavy metal band, Led Zeppelin. Notice the close similarity and the explicit connection between the Led Zeppelin story and the legend of Robert Johnson in Mikal Gilmore's retrospective account of the band for *Rolling Stone*.

> Jimmy Page had an interest in the occult. By this point in Led Zeppelin's history [the 1971 release of their fourth album], that interest had transformed into an obsession with the British mystic and rogue Aleister Crowley, who messed in some pretty heavy juju, including an interest in Satanism, in the early 1900s. Page himself was never a Satanist, but he was attracted to Crowley's philosophy [a kind of "libertine self-actualizationism"]. Page admitted years later that his concentration on Crowley was unfortunate, but in the band's lifetime, occultism proved a source of both silly speculation and painful rumors. The most wearying—and trite—of these was that Page and the other members of Led Zeppelin had sold their souls to the devil in exchange for fame and success. Tales like this may hold a dark appeal for some—the soul-selling legend certainly didn't hurt Robert Johnson's stature over the years.[52]

Gilmore is skeptical of the notion that Led Zeppelin entered into a contract with the devil, and like Wald and Pearson and McCulloch, he doubts the Robert Johnson legend as well, at least as straightforward literal truth.

> [I]n the end it's all romantic know-nothingism. Johnson never met any devils at midnight crossroads for the same reason that Jimmy Page and Led Zeppelin could never have made a supernatural deal for fame had they wanted to: There's no devil to make deals with.[53]

And yet he hedges his skepticism in one interesting direction.

> Any bargains are bargains with the self—but that might be enough. Crowley's dictum "Do what thou wilt" would have a terrible effect on the life and death of Led Zeppelin.[54]

The Devil's Instrument and the Devil's Interval

Other important cultural reference points are centuries older. Nicolo Paganini, the nineteenth-century composer of the decisive selection in the guitar duel, is the subject of his own devil legend. Born in 1782, the child prodigy composed his first sonata at the age of eight. It was as a virtuoso violinist that he stood out most spectacularly. By thirteen he could find no teachers who had anything to offer to guide his further development. He began to tour Europe, giving concerts as a fifteen year old, reducing audiences to tears with his most tender passages and frightening them with his ferocious attack and furious velocity in others. Much of his work as a composer was written for his own inimitable performances, and his compositions for solo violin are among the most difficult pieces in the violin literature. It is this fiendish degree of difficulty, coupled with his corresponding virtuosity, that drove the legend of Paganini's pact with the devil. Nor is Paganini the earliest of such legendary figures; the eighteenth century Italian violinist Guiseppe Tartini also was the subject of such a legend. Indeed there is a still a living tradition as old as the violin itself linking it with the devil. In this tradition, the fiddle is the devil's own instrument of choice. The tradition survives, for example, in Charlie Daniels's 1979 Grammy-winning country song "The Devil Went Down to Georgia," in which the devil gets beaten in a fiddling contest, essentially similar to the head-cutting duel in the movie *Crossroads*.

As mentioned earlier, there is a musical reference in the film to the augmented fourth or flatted fifth, a harmonic relationship known historically in music theory as the "devil's interval." This reference reaches back through medieval church history to classical antiquity and the work of the pre-Socratic philosopher Pythagoras in harmonics and tuning theory. We will explore this in detail in chapter 4.

The Devil as Trickster

Finally, of paramount importance are the African references. At several points in the movie the devil is referred to by the name Legba—a shortened form of Eshu Elegbara, an important Yoruba deity. In Yoruba mythology the various *orisha*, or spirits under God, bring *ashe*, which denotes a spiritual command or "power to make things happen," understood as divine creativity accessible to humans. According to Yoruba mythology, all the *orisha* once met at a crossroads and undertook to find out who among them was supreme. So each of them made a journey to heaven bearing a rich sacrifice on his or her head, all except the trickster Eshu Elegbara, who wisely prayed in advance for guidance. Following that guidance Eshu Elegbara wore a single crimson parrot feather positioned on his forehead to symbolize that he was not to carry burdens on his head. God granted Eshu Elegbara the power to multiply *ashe*.[55] In early African American folklore, references to the devil and the cross-roads invoke this Yoruba deity, as, for example, in the following tale—a variant and perhaps a prototype of the Tommy Johnson legend.

> Sit down there and play your best piece, thinking of and wishing for the devil all the while. By and by you will hear music, dim at first but growing louder and louder as the musician approaches nearer. Do not look around; just keep on playing your guitar. The unseen musician will finally sit down by you and play in unison with you. After a time you will feel something tugging at your instrument. . . . Let the devil take it and keep thumping along with your fingers as if you still had a guitar in your hands. Then the devil will hand you his instrument to play and will accompany you on yours. After doing this for a time he will seize your fingers and trim the nails until they bleed, finally taking his guitar back and returning your own. Keep on playing; do not look around. His music will become fainter and fainter as he moves away. When all is quiet you may go home. You will be able to play any piece you desire on the guitar and you can do anything you want to do in this world, but you have sold your eternal soul to the devil and are his in the world to come.[56]

In light of the similarities between African American folk beliefs and Yoruba and other African mythologies, we should take care not to simply reduce the devil of the blues to Satan in any of Christianity's familiar characterizations. Interpretive alternatives begin to multiply at this juncture. Writers who have recognized and acknowledged references to Yoruba mythology in Johnson's lyrics have had to struggle mightily to forge a coherent interpretation linking Legba together with Satan in a cross-cultural interpretation of Johnson's work.[57]

The Soul at the Crossroads

As Mikal Gilmore suggests in his remarks about Led Zeppelin, bargains (and compromises) one makes with oneself—whether in pursuit of one's career or in pursuit of pleasure or in pursuit of power or in the service of one's art—are moral choices with practical moral consequences and implications. This brings us to yet another way of taking the legend of Robert Johnson seriously, if not simply "literally." This would be to take the legend on its own moral, spiritual, and theological terms, with the understanding that these are terms intended to capture the fundamental issues and struggles of a human life.

As he was dying of cancer, bluesman Skip James worried that his condition was somehow due to his blues playing. Similar worries prevented Reverend Ishmon Bracey and Robert Wilkins from resuming their careers as blues singers during the 1960s folk-blues revival. And Son House, who did return to the stage performing blues during the period, would often introduce his blues with chillingly severe homilies warning his audiences of the moral dangers inherent in the music.[58] Does a commitment to the blues, as an avenue of authentic artistic expression, as a way of life, encumber or put one's soul at risk in any way? Does it entail commitments, or risks and liabilities, that are morally problematic? These are serious and difficult questions. Did Robert Johnson have a "religious experience," perhaps associated with a breakthrough in his musical discipline? In the course of his wanderings as a musician did he make any commitments that caused him to wrestle with his conscience? Speaking in this way about momentous and often perilous moral choices as matters of the soul is certainly the most profound of the interpretive options Marcus invites us to consider.

> Let us say that Johnson . . . tried to sell his soul in exchange for the music he heard but could not make. Let us say he did this because he wanted to attract women; because he wanted to be treated with . . . awe . . . because music brought him a fierce joy, made him feel alive like nothing else in the world. Or let us say that . . . the devil gave Johnson a way of understanding the fears that overshadowed him. [Let us say] Johnson believed that . . . his desires and his crimes were simple proof . . . that his soul was not his own, and, looking at the disasters of his life and the evil of the world, drew the one conclusion as to whom it did belong.[59]

At the 2006 *Living Blues* symposium Blues: The Devil's Music? Jamaican-born bluesman Eddie Kirkland avowed his own crossroads experience. It was Kirkland's exposure to racist humiliation in the U.S. Army during World War II that prompted him to seek out the devil. After a series of humiliations Kirkland eventually retaliated against a second lieutenant, leading to a court-martial, six months in the stockade, and a dishonorable discharge, further humiliation too shameful for Kirkland to discuss frankly with friends and family when he returned home.

> So now, I want some power. And I heard the old peoples long time ago talkin' about people sellin' their souls to the devil, in order to make it up. I just wanted to come up in the world, you know. . . . So I made my mind up to sell my soul to the devil. Show you how young and foolish I was. But I found out that it was the wrong thing to ever do. I went through the whole confusion. But I couldn't finish.[60]

The black magic called for a "black cat bone." A black cat must be boiled alive and a bone selected by its magical tendency to float upstream.

> I found me a black cat, and then, went behind the market, found one of them lard cans they had throwed away in the garbage can. Got that can and took it back there in the alley, filled it full of water, picked me up some wood to put around it. Warmed that water scaldin' hot. Took that black cat, put him in that water. Cooked him till all the meat fell off him. And I'm listenin' to what people were sayin': say, now you take them bones and you drop 'em in runnin' water. One bone that don't go downstream, go upstream—that's the bone you get.[61]

That bone is then to be taken to a crossroads nine consecutive mornings. But by the third visit to the crossroads, Kirkland had had enough.

> It got tougher and tougher every time I went. . . . So I give up. I let it go. And I took that bone and I threw it back in the river. Then I bought me a Bible, and I prayed every day and every night. I betcha I prayed for about three months. I would be on my knees praying God to forgive me. You know, I've had such a rough time in my life, a lot of times I do believe to God that was some of the cause of it, takin' a innocent little animal and put him in a pot of water and boil it, you know. I thought about that many a day. I think that was a pretty terrible thing to do to an animal. And I love animals. I'm a Leo—I'm a cat, you know! Sometimes I felt like I boiled myself to death. But I asked the good Lord to forgive me, and I believe he did, because if He hadn't a' did it, I wouldn't be here today.[62]

"When you believe in things that you don't understand, then you suffer," wrote Stevie Wonder, "Superstition ain't the way."[63] What shall we say is the difference between a superstition and an article of faith? Is it superstitious to believe in the devil and black magic? Hume would surely have said so, on both counts, according to his definition. Because clearly to believe in the devil and black magic is to believe in the supernatural, and Hume would surely have regarded such beliefs as false or at least ill-founded. What about a belief in the Lord or in the efficacy of prayer or in divine forgiveness?

Kirkland thinks this through. And he reprimands himself for being "young and foolish" (for believing in a superstition and attempting to carry it out). And he prays to God for forgiveness over the animal sacrifice. Whether any or all of the beliefs involved are best categorized as superstitions or as beliefs of some other kind, clearly they exert a profound and powerful influence on the course and quality of one's life, on one's lived experience, on one's reality. Superstition or not, such notions surely play a crucial role in determining whatever truth is authentically expressed in a person's blues. This is a point made by rock historian Ed Ward (although he, too, assumes the concept of superstition as applicable).

> In the 1930s Robert Johnson lived in a Mississippi so alien to our times that it might as well have been Africa. The culture that produced him was laden with superstition. If superstition can instill enough fear in someone, its terror becomes reality. Robert Johnson sang of the hell-hounds on his trail, and it is not unlikely that he saw real dogs snapping at his heels, craving his flesh, waiting for the meal they knew was due them, from the contract.[64]

What can we know for certain about Robert Johnson's life and death? The growing mountain of speculative literature, so full of controversy and so much of it fueled by fanaticism of one sort or another, only adds to the uncertainty. If the crossroads story can be dismissed in literal terms as a fabulous construct, the question of its truth value as spiritual metaphor remains open. As to what Robert Johnson may have had in his mind as artist and man we can only speculate. In the end we are left, appropriately, with the music. In a private conversation David Evans explained to me why he remains convinced that Robert Johnson the man was indeed concerned about the state of his soul. For Evans, that is what is expressed in the music.

CHAPTER 3

Between Saturday Night and Sunday Morning
(The Dark Night of the Soul)

The God spoken about in the black songs is not the same one in the white songs. Though the words might look the same. (They are not even pronounced alike.) But it is a different quality of energy they summon.

—AMIRI BARAKA (LEROI JONES)

How many of y'all believe that it's gonna be alright? We gotta get together and make it alright. Everybody got to understand there's only one planet earth, and there's only one people livin' on it, and there's definitely only one God. And if we really believe that we are all God's children, and if we really believe that we were all made in God's image, then that means we are one family, one race, the human race.

—CYRIL NEVILLE

In creation where one's nature neither honors nor forgives—I and I—One says to the other, "No man sees my face and lives."

—BOB DYLAN

Music for "Mature" Audiences Only

Writing about the birth of soul music, Nelson George refocuses attention from the adolescent concerns of emerging youth culture of the early 1950s onto more adult concerns reflected in the music of the later 1950s. He writes:

> Most rock & roll historians, with their characteristic bias toward youth rebellion, claim that the last two years of the fifties were a musically fal-low period. But that claim only works if you're willing to ignore Ray Charles's brilliant work. In subject matter, the great "What'd I Say?" (1959) is rhythm & blues. In its use of piano, girl chorus, call-and-re-sponse structure, and plain old *feel,* it is devotional gospel. Though pos-sibly disturbed by Charles's gospel borrowings, such as his 1956 single "Hallelujah, I Love Her So", the secular black audience loved the com-

mitment of his vocals and the man-woman, love-conflict stories he told. This sound, not yet called soul, emphasized adult passion—the actions of people dealing with cars, kids, and sex. By breaking down the division between pulpit and bandstand, recharging blues concerns with transcendental fervor, unashamedly linking the spiritual and the sexual, Charles made pleasure (physical satisfaction) and joy (divine enlightenment) seem the same thing. By doing so he brought the realities of the Saturday-night sinner and Sunday-morning worshipper—so often one and the same—into a raucous harmony.[1]

The relationship between gospel music and the blues is not easily understood. George's observation that Ray Charles's gospel borrowings might be disturbing to a black audience, even a secular one, is telling. Not only was Ray criticized from the pulpit. Bluesman Big Bill Broonzy's reported reaction was similarly taken aback.

> He's got the blues, but he's crying sanctified. He's mixing the blues with the spirituals. I know that's wrong . . . he should be singing in a church.[2]

Apparently expressing irreconcilable social forces and values, yet inseparably linked, blues and gospel are like the poles of a single magnet. The stark dichotomies with which many have attempted to characterize this tangled relationship—God and the devil, the sacred and the secular, the spirit and the flesh, sin and salvation, good and evil—don't hold up under the weight of this puzzle. The main reason that they fail is that they shed no light whatsoever on the intimate connection between the two musical traditions. But it's not as if there is no credible testimony suggestive and supportive of such analyses. Mavis Staples provides an excellent example in narrating her own upbringing.

> I was about seven, eight years old. My mother and father had so many children, after a while there they couldn't keep us in shoes! So they would send Yvonne and I, the two youngest, down to Mound Bayou, Mississippi, with my grandmother. I was walking to school, walking down this gravel road every morning. And I'd hear this juke joint. They were playing this song, Buddy and Ella Johnson: "You, you made me leave my happy home . . ." ["Since I Fell for You"]. And I heard it so much I had learned it. I'd be singin' around school, so the kids at school knew I could sing. And we had a variety show. They pushed me on stage—I had never sung in front of people, but they pushed me on stage. I reared back, and that was the first thing that came out of my mouth. I looked around and I saw my uncle coming. He was like 16, 17 years old. Ham, we called him. He was real tall. I got happy! "Oh, Ham

comin' to pat me on the head!" I thought he was going to tell me I was doing a beautiful job, y'know? Man! He got on that stage, snatched me off! Pushed me off, he said, "You come on!" I kept lookin' up at him. I didn't know what to think. And he got me to my grandmother's house, he pushed me in the door, he told her, he said, "This young'n up at the schoolhouse singin' the *blues!*" And my grandmother said, "Singin' the blues, huh? You get on out there and cut me some switches! You don't sing blues in this family! You sing church songs in this family!"[3]

Led by the patriarch, Roebuck "Pops" Staples, with son Pervis and daughters Cleotha and Mavis, the Staples Singers were a family gospel group with Mississippi roots, based in Chicago from the 1930s, that starting recording commercially in 1953. At Stax in the late 1960s and throughout the 1970s, the Staples Singers became arguably the "First Family of Soul." As Mavis recalls it (above), the children were brought up with strict instructions to steer clear of the blues. But as a young man in Drew, Mississippi, Pops had learned to play the guitar from Charlie Patton.[4] What happened in that one generation? Here in the microcosm of the Staples family we see an ongoing dynamic of deep ambivalence, inside as much as outside the African American community, about the spiritual significance of the blues. The church has played a significant role in this process, seeming often to want not just to disavow but to "disown" the blues.

In Alice Walker's novel *The Color Purple,* this ambivalent dynamic revolves around the character Shug Avery, the blues singer who haunts, then intrudes and imposes upon the heroine Celie's domestic life, eventually to liberate her from her abusive husband's domination. Shug's relationship to the community is complex. Away on the road, and equally onstage in person, she is both glamorized and vilified. In the movie version of the story, Steven Spielberg embellishes the novel and resolves this dynamic with a scene in which Shug Avery leads a crowd of Saturday all-night revelers from the juke joint into her estranged father the minister's Sunday morning church service. The movie presents, in effect, a reconciliation of the tensions in African American culture between the blues and the gospel, a reconciliation scene that did not sit very well with Alice Walker herself.[5]

Renunciation of the Flesh

It is easy, perhaps even too easy, to hear just the reverberations of a spiritual ethic of renunciation in all of this. And blues scholarship has often taken it more or less for granted that rigid moral dichotomies of Christianity were embraced, or at least echoed, within black churches, laying the foundations for a blanket condemnation of the earthy and the worldly. All God's children were to avoid the sins of the flesh—the carnality and sexuality expressed and dealt with in the blues—as well as the more subtle and generalized work of the devil—the theatrical glitter, the illusions of the stage and of show business. Here, for example, is the dean of British blues scholarship, Paul Oliver.

> For the most part the blues is strictly secular in content. The old-time religion of the southern churches did not permit the singing of "devil songs" and "jumped up" songs as the blues were commonly termed. . . . Music and song . . . must be for the purpose of praising the Lord, and though "holy dancing" is permitted by many black churches, "sinful dancing" is strictly forbidden. To the outsider the distinction may be a fine one, but within the church it is clear enough: spontaneous dancing which is the result of religious ecstasy and in which the legs are not crossed, is the only form acceptable.[6]

But should one look more deeply into this distinction, and into its history, it appears to get murkier and murkier. For example, consider the account of the same prohibitive distinction given by folklorist Alan Lomax, beginning with a lengthy narrative description of early-twentieth-century black tenant farmers engaged in an erotic form of dance—"the blues" or "the slow drag." According to Lomax, when his father John, also a folklorist, first witnessed this dance he considered it so obscene that he couldn't bring himself to share the experience with his wife for years.

> The wooden floor of the shack was, so to speak, a drumhead, responding first of all to the double rhythm of the bluesman's feet as he stomped out an accompaniment to his playing. Then at his side a youngster was pulling the broom, dragging the head of a broom over the rough boards in a diagram of the beat, causing the floor to vibrate like a rub-board and the massed straws of the broom to rattle and swish like the swats in a rhythm section. This rhythmic source was reinforced by the feet of the couples who packed the steamy room and were performing the *blues,* also called the *slow drag,* a name that well describes it. The couples, glued together in a belly-to-belly, loin-to-loin embrace, approximated sexual intercourse as closely as their vertical posture, their clothing, and the crowd around them would allow.[7]

The carnality and sexuality of the dance is obvious. What is murky, to the point of being nearly incomprehensible, is the account Lomax gives of its prohibition by black clergy. First of all, it does not occur to Lomax that the judgment of obscenity is a projection onto the spectacle not shared by the dancers themselves. But Lomax immediately proceeds to assemble anthropological evidence to rationalize a black church-based prohibition.

> The slow drag was, I believe, an innovation at that time, and it may well have been the most erotic dance on earth. The Choreometric survey of dance style offers these facts. First, foot sliding with a wide stance is African. In the slow drag it combines with the mixed couple, which is largely European. We Westerners, culturally myopic about the rest of the species, tend to think the face-to-face mixed-couple dance is a human universal. In fact, it is rare in the world. In most cultures the sexes dance in segregated groups, or in mixed groups, but rarely as mixed couples. Only in West Africa and especially in Western Europe do the partners face each other, ready for action, so to speak.[8]

So, evidently there is, after all, an African precedent for the mixed couple dance form with partners facing each other. This exception ("only in West Africa," where of course many of the slaves originated) undermines Lomax's explanation as it continues to unfold, or should I say, unravel.

> Moreover, it is only in the waist-swinging courtship dances of Western Europe, our survey shows, that partners continuously hold on to or embrace each other. This expression of the singular importance of the nuclear family in Europe seems to have made a powerful impression on the black slaves when they encountered it.[9]

If the social ritual encourages or permits the changing of partners from one dance to the next, it is not entirely clear why an unbroken embrace, for example, in a waltz or polka, should be interpreted as an expression of the singular importance to Europeans of the nuclear family. If anything, it is even less clear why African American slaves should have found such an interpretive observation powerfully impressive other than as evidence of unfathomable hypocrisy. But Lomax forges ahead to make his two main explanatory points.

> In the first place, black ministers, perhaps reacting to the shock that their followers must have felt at the untoward eroticism of the waist swings their masters were performing, ruled against the dance even more strongly than their Calvinist preceptors. They condemned everything to do with dancing as totally out-of-bounds for the godly. Dancing was defined, not only by the facing waist swing, but by another Eurasian

feature—*foot crossing.* Your African heritage was to shuffle or slide your feet, but if you crossed your feet, you were hell-bound.[10]

The reference to foot crossing by Lomax, Oliver, and others is a fascinating curiosity. But it seems also to be something of a red herring. First of all, foot crossing does not occur in the slow drag. Try it. You and your partner will fall to the floor. Furthermore, nowhere in any of these accounts can I find anything even hinting at an explanation as to why crossing one's feet should count as a particularly sinful dance move. Intertwining one's legs with those of one's partner has obvious erotic connotations and effects. But crossing one's own feet? Nevertheless, Lomax goes on to derive from this

> an anomalous and confusing sacred/sinful dichotomy that has painfully split the black community ever since—into those who gave up dancing (the European foot-crossing type) and all secular music and those who would not.[11]

The sacred/sinful dichotomy that has split the black community is anomalous and confusing, indeed! But the attempted explanations that begin and end with foot crossing leave the confusion and anomaly, as far as I can see, untouched. Historical references to foot crossing as a dance taboo do also call for some explanation. But in this connection a story with more modest explanatory ambition and correspondingly greater straightforward plausibility might go something like this. African Americans (like human beings generally, by the way) find that dancing helps you get into higher, healthier, happier conditions of consciousness than the ones normally associated with hard labor.[12] So naturally they like to dance on the weekend, including in church on Sunday. Christian missionaries found this behavior unmanageable and unbecoming to their standards of decorum in church and made efforts to suppress it. In reaction to this, European foot crossing might have become a convenient dodge, a relatively low-cost prohibition that left room for other sorts of bodily movement and expression.[13]

Proper Decorum

We are still confronted with an "anomalous and confusing dichotomy" between the sacred and the sinful in music and dance. What are the sources of the divisions within the black community over the "spiritual compatibility" of the blues and gospel? Some portion of the problem must be traced to friction over standards for the liturgical use of song

and dance in the African American church. An important instance was
the establishment in eighteenth-century Philadelphia of an independent
African Methodist Episcopal Church under the direction of Richard
Allen, who replaced the standard Methodist hymnal with one he compiled himself, choosing material he felt better suited to appeal to a black
congregation. Mellonee Burnim writes:

> Allen's goal was to generate congregational participation. . . . Non-
> Black observers of Allen's worship were frequently struck by the high
> level of congregational involvement in spirited singing. Not surpris-
> ingly, such early commentators did not hesitate to register their dis-
> pleasure at the A.M.E. song style.[14]

This evidently became a sore point in American Methodism lasting
decades. White Methodist clergy from church founder John Wesley on
down were apparently offended by the "profanities" of musical repetition and bodily involvement characteristic of communal celebration that
were practiced in Allen's church and linked his worship practices to
those of the rural South. John F. Watson, in a critique of "undesirable
practices of Blacks in Methodism" entitled "Methodist Error" (1819),
notes that Wesley himself expelled three ministers from the Methodist
Church

> for singing "poor, bald, flat, disjointed hymns" and . . . singing the same
> verse over and over again with all their might 30 or 40 times, to the ut-
> ter discredit of all sober christianity."[15]

He expressed even more vehement displeasure at the evident enjoyment
on the part of the singers and at the overt and audible rhythmic use of
the body to reinforce the music. Other writers confirm that during this
period African Americans were sometimes

> not permitted to enter Methodist church buildings at all since they dis-
> turbed quiet and dignified worship by beating out the rhythm of songs
> with feet patting and hands clapping.[16]

It is apparent that the disapproval originated from within the hierarchy
of the white Methodist establishment. But black clergy were also accom-
modating to these strictures. A century after its founding, the leader of
the African Methodist Episcopal Church, Bishop Daniel Alexander
Payne, wrote of his encounter with a black congregation still practicing
the ring shout.

> After the sermon [the congregation] formed a ring, and with coats off sung, clapped their hands and stamped their feet in a most ridiculous and heathenish way. I requested the pastor to go and stop their dancing. At his request they stopped their dancing and clapping of hands, but remained singing and rocking their bodies to and fro. This they did for about fifteen minutes. I then went, and taking their leader by the arm requested him to desist and to sit down and sing in a rational manner. I told him also that it was a heathenish way to worship and disgraceful to themselves, the race, and the Christian name. In that instance they broke up their ring but would not sit down, and walked sullenly away.[17]

A pattern is visible here: A strict ethos of bodily renunciation, of European derivation, is imposed as a matter of liturgical discipline through the hierarchy of the established white Protestant churches. An effort is made to incorporate at least some vestigial expressions of traditional African and African American communal worship within the thus prescribed liturgical practices or, failing that, to adapt some workable African American variation or hybrid. An accommodation is made, endorsed by African American clergy, bringing the African American liturgy "up to" the European standard.

What are we to make of such accommodation on the part of black clergy? No doubt, many among the black clergy sincerely believed that the social, economic, and political progress of black people in America would be enabled and accelerated by coming into conformity with white expectations and patterns of behavior. Accommodations to the demands of white clergy and conformity to European cultural standards may have been rationalized as tactics or as part of an overall strategy of social mobility. Certain elements of this strategy we may suppose were essentially sound. Raising the rate of literacy and the level of education in letters and science among African Americans were part of the work undertaken by the established churches, especially during Reconstruction. Another related factor, especially during Reconstruction, may have been a strong reluctance on the part of African Americans, as they took up leadership positions in the churches, to be reminded of or to "look back" to the days (and ways) of slavery in charting a course forward. It should be clear, however, that in thus turning away from the days, and music, of slavery African American clergy were turning away from the communal performance practices associated with the *spirituals* and not the blues. They could not have been repudiating the blues directly because the blues were not the music of slavery. The blues were just beginning to emerge during Reconstruction.

The Flesh and the Spirit

However, the blues do become implicated indirectly. At the heart of this struggle over liturgical practice is an issue of profound metaphysical and theological significance. Lurking behind all of the fretting and fussing over foot crossing and foot stomping and swaying and hand clapping is the question, what really *is* the relationship between the flesh and the spirit? Are they really so neatly and thoroughly divisible as would be required or presupposed by an ethic of bodily renunciation? Looking back over the historical theological discussions surrounding and informing this struggle over liturgy, African American theologian James H. Cone makes an arresting point

> [W]hite oppressors do not know how to come to terms with the essential *spiritual* function of the human body. But for black people the body is sacred and they know how to use it in the expression of love.[18]

Cone thus calls into question the very dichotomies on which the historical, theological, liturgical discussions seem to hinge. For Cone, conditions of oppression create radically distinct understandings of spirituality and radically distinct theologies. Where the oppressor may afford to sharply distinguish between the spirit and the flesh, the divine and the human, the sacred and the secular, the oppressed are in a position to fully appreciate and celebrate "the power inherent in bodily expressions of love."[19]

In her landmark study *Blues Legacies and Black Feminism,* Angela Davis makes a complementary argument. To the extent that black clergy did take up and reinforce traditional Christian moral dichotomies about sexuality and call for a general renunciation of the carnal and the sexual, they in effect undercut one of the most significant gains of emancipation: the freedom to choose one's sexual partner. For Davis this becomes, whether so intended or not, instrumental in the development of a persistent theme in backlash racist ideology according to which black sexuality is associated with spiritual inferiority or backwardness.[20] And we see another reason why the blues, which by all accounts deal more openly and honestly with the liberated sexuality of the former slave than most any sermon, may come in for criticism from the pulpit.

The Wages of Upward Mobility

Although the cultural struggles surrounding American popular and vernacular music have often found expression in theological terms, Davis also notes how considerations of social advancement led some African Americans to dissociate themselves from the blues as "primitive," "inferior," or "too country" for upward social mobility in twentieth-century America. Although the blues had its champions in Langston Hughes, Zora Neal Hurston, and others, Davis argues that during the Harlem Renaissance there were those who sought to marginalize the blues from the effort to articulate a uniquely black aesthetic. In effect, then, the African American community is fractured by divisive class consciousness on its journey toward justice and equality.[21] In this division we can see something of what W. E. B. DuBois had in mind when he wrote:

> This waste of double aims, this seeking to satisfy two unreconciled ideals, has wrought sad havoc with the courage and faith and deeds of ten thousand thousand people,—has sent them often wooing false gods and invoking false means of salvation, and at times has even seemed about to make them ashamed of themselves.[22]

From the Spirituals through the Blues to Gospel

Let us look at the history of three related musical movements: spirituals, the blues, and gospel music, starting with the historical order in which they appear. Spirituals are older than the blues, but the blues are older than gospel music. Situating them in their historical context will help elucidate their interrelationships. The spirituals were first brought out of the fields and arranged for presentation to white audiences by the Fisk Jubilee Singers, a choral ensemble of eleven students at the fledgling Fisk University, under the direction of the university treasurer, George White, in 1871. White conceived of the group as a fund-raising ambassador for the then debt-ridden school. In musical terms this meant "grooming" the ensemble and the material for performance in concert. Following the pattern we saw earlier in the African Methodist Episcopal experience, performance practices were brought into line with the expectations of audiences who regularly patronized the arts. Indefinite repetition and variation gave way to composed arrangements. Bodily involvement (hand claps, dancing, etc.) was purged. Heterophony (the interplay of spontaneous melodic variation by the participating voices) gave way to stable and clearly defined harmonies. Selections from the European classical repertoire and from such popular secular composers as Stephen Foster were interpolated into the program. Twenty years later Harry Thacker Burleigh began transcribing and arranging spirituals for solo voice, paving the way for concert presentation of programs of spirituals by the great operatically trained voices of the twentieth century, most notably Marian Anderson and Paul Robeson. Burleigh, who was highly advanced in his musical training and accomplished on several instruments, including voice, taught Antonín Dvořák the melodies from spirituals that Dvořák eventually used in his New World Symphony. In these various ways the spirituals were made more and more "respectable" on their cultural journey toward the mainstream. When he published his arrangements of the spirituals for solo voice in 1917, Burleigh felt the need to safeguard them from misunderstanding and misrepresentation in performance, offering the following guidance.

> The plantation songs known as "spirituals" are the spontaneous outbursts of intense religious fervor, and had their origin chiefly in camp meetings, revivals and other religious exercises. They were never "composed," but sprang into life, ready made, from the white heat of religious fervor during some protracted meeting in camp or church, as the simple, ecstatic utterance of wholly untutored minds, and are practically the only music in America which meets the scientific definition of Folk Song. Success in singing these Folk Songs is primarily dependent upon deep spiritual feeling. The voice is not nearly so important as the spirit; and then rhythm, for the Negro's soul is linked with rhythm, and it is an essential characteristic of most all the Folk Songs. It is a serious misconception of their meaning and value to treat them as "minstrel" songs, or to try to make them funny by a too literal attempt to imitate the manner of the Negro in singing them, by swaying the body, clapping the hands, or striving to make the peculiar inflections of voice that are natural with the colored people. Their worth is weakened unless they are done impressively, for through all these songs there breathes a hope, a faith in the ultimate justice and brotherhood of man. The cadences of sorrow invariably turn to joy, and the message is ever manifest that eventually deliverance from all that hinders and oppresses the soul will come, and man—every man—will be free.[23]

W. E. B. DuBois heard in the spirituals as they were thus evolving the deep inner struggle within the souls of black folk to integrate the double consciousness of being black in America. For DuBois, the spirituals—the "Sorrow Songs"—were the musical expression of African Americans living in exile under slavery. They were, as he put it, the "articulate message of the slave to the world."[24] They were "the music of an unhappy people, of the children of disappointment," and they told of "death and suffering and unvoiced longing for a truer world."[25] But, as sorrowful as they were, they were also *hopeful.*

Through all the sorrow of the Sorrow Songs there breathes a hope—a
faith in the ultimate justice of things.[26]

Thus another crucial theological point about the liturgical turn away
from the performance practices of communal worship associated with
the spirituals: the theology of the oppressed is a liberation theology. It
celebrates a faith in a just, mighty, and merciful Supreme Being with do-
minion over human affairs, moving through unfolding historical events
to lead His people out of bondage. Although they were receiving instruction in Christian theology at the hands of slave masters, the black
slaves surely heard in the verses of the Old Testament a narrative of liberation—a liberation theology they would celebrate under the cover of
the brush arbor in the plantation fields. Using the spirituals to lift spirits
and communicate practical strategies of escape and resistance, they were
surely practicing a religion at odds with that of their masters, who found
many strange and disgraceful ways of ministering to their chattel in the
name of the Lord. It was reasonable within the framework of a liberation
theology to understand the Civil War and the Emancipation Proclama-
tion as the fulfillment of God's promise of deliverance.

A Crisis of Faith

But this faith was shaken and the hope running through all the sorrow
songs was dashed, at least for a significant segment of the African American population, after Emancipation. Writing at the turn of the twentieth
century, DuBois was well aware of the disillusionment of Reconstruction.
"Few men ever worshipped Freedom with half such unquestioning faith
as did the American Negro for two centuries," he wrote.

> Emancipation was the key to a promised land. . . . Years have passed
> away since then,—ten, twenty, forty years of national life, forty years of
> renewal and development, and yet . . . the freedman has not found free-
> dom in his promised land.[27]

James H. Cone neatly summarizes the series of disappointments that followed for the former slaves in the wake of the Civil War.

> The Hayes Compromise of 1877 led to the withdrawal of federal troops
> from the South and ended the hopes of black people becoming au-
> thentic participants in the political processes of America. In 1883 the
> United States Supreme Court declared the Civil Rights Act of 1875 as

unconstitutional; and in 1896 it upheld the doctrine of "separate but equal" (Plessy vs. Ferguson), giving legal sanction to the dehumanizing aspects of white supremacy. By the end of the nineteenth century the political disfranchisement of black people was complete.[28]

If exile and bondage were the conditions that produced the spirituals, the conditions that produced the blues were the conditions under post–Civil War Reconstruction. Although both the spirituals and the blues spoke to the harsh conditions of life in the New World, Cone notes two important differences in their responses. First, the blues are characterized by "a stubborn refusal to go beyond the existential problem and substitute other-worldly answers."[29] Where the spirituals looked hopefully toward salvation in a promised land, the blues seem to have abandoned all hope and lost all faith in divine salvation from the trials and tribulations of this world. Alan Young makes the same point about the blues in differentiating their outlook from the outlook characteristic of gospel music.

> Where the gospel singer uses "The Lord woke me up this morning" as a prelude to a catalog of blessings, the blues singer says, "I woke up this morning," following it with an observation or a declaration—"I woke up this morning/Blues all around my bed;" "I woke up this morning/Looking 'round for my shoes;" "I woke up this morning/Feeling so bad." The two expressions are similar, but their philosophies are quite different. While the gospel singer's "He woke me up this morning" affirms belief in a higher being and his dominion over every aspect of human existence, the blues singer's "I woke up this morning" characterizes a bleaker outlook in which the singer is troubled and knows—and accepts—that nobody except he or she can (or will) do anything to alleviate the problem. Whatever points of similarity may exist between gospel music and blues, the differing ways of waking up illustrate one vast difference. Gospel singers know they are not alone; blues singers know they are.[30]

This also highlights Cone's second point of distinction: "In contrast to the group singing of the spirituals, the blues are intensely personal and individualistic."[31] The bluesman emerges as a lone self-accompanied voice, well represented by Robert Johnson, in whose music and murky biography many continue to hear solitude and deep spiritual despair.

Dark Night of the Soul

If we follow DuBois and Cone in seeking out the meaning of the blues in the spiritual strivings of the people who expressed themselves in this music, a striking similarity between the blues and a certain monastic no-tion—"the Dark Night of the Soul"—is noticeable. Here we must recog-nize an aspect of "spirituality" as distinct from "religion." It seems to me that religion is always fundamentally a communal practice—a matter of belonging to a community of worship.[32] By contrast, it seems to me that even when pursued in the company of others a spiritual quest is in some ways at its heart a solitary and individual personal pursuit. The idea is that real spiritual progress requires radical *self*-transformation, at least until one has achieved some such goal as the annihilation, or enlight-ened transcendence or radical enlargement, of the "self." Thus, typically a monk must forgo or abandon the community of worship and go it alone. Under church auspices, a monastic brotherhood is a "commu-nity" only in some sense radically enough attenuated to reflect the es-sential nature of monastic living: "living alone." Monastic vows commit the spiritual seeker to a path of profound solitude—dedicated to radical self-transformation in preparation for divine enlightenment. The expe-rience can be terrifying. Only poetry can begin to express it, as when Bob Dylan sings:

> In creation where one's nature neither honors nor forgives
> I and I
> One says to the other, "No man sees my face and lives."[33]

In the tradition of Roman Catholic mysticism, the experience is charac-terized as "the Dark Night of the Soul."[34] The expression derives from the title of a sixteenth-century poem composed with commentary by the Spanish poet and mystic Saint John of the Cross. The poem and com-mentary describe the terrors and depression associated with the monas-tic ordeal, during which the spiritual seeker must grapple with the utter collapse of faith.

We may find in this comparison a way of understanding the darkness in the blues without consigning it to the flames, as it were.[35] The blues, as they emerged during Reconstruction, may be interpreted as an ex-pression of a deep and understandable crisis of faith within the African American community. How could an omnipotent, omniscient, and benevolent God so forsake and betray his faithful people? Rhetorical questions like this express what theologians and philosophers of religion refer to as the "problem of evil." How is it logically possible for injustice to prevail in a world created and overseen by a benevolent Supreme Be-ing—a God with omniscient awareness of injustice and unlimited power to correct it? An attempt to rationalize the existence of evil within a theological framework is called a "theodicy." Jon Michael Spencer is alone in arguing that the blues attempt to reconcile the unjust evils suffered by African Americans with a continued faith in God. In effect Spencer argues that there are several characteristic "blues theodicies," not just in occasional idiosyncratic instances but running throughout the blues as a genre.[36] I won't attempt to rebut Spencer's argument in detail, but I think it is prima facie much more reasonable to understand the blues as *posing*, rather than answering, the problem of evil. So do most commentators, including Cone.[37]

With hindsight it remains possible to view Christian faith as a means by which the slaves were cynically tricked into believing in a false promise of freedom—the position taken explicitly by Amiri Baraka in a BBC documentary on the history of gospel music.[38] He has not been alone in this assessment.

> As one delegate to the 1900 National Negro Business League put it, "I am one of those who believe the Negro must do something besides praying all the time. [Applause.] We started out directly after the surrender praying, 'Lord, give me Jesus and you can have all the world.' The white man in the South took us at our word and we got all the Jesus and he got all the world. [Laughter and applause.]"[39]

So complete is the loss of faith in some cases as to suggest a radically *anti-theistic* assessment of the blues. Generalizing even beyond Angela Davis's argument about the church's function as an agency of repression and control, Paul Garon writes:

> The blues critique, emphatically materialist, is directed not against heavenly abstractions (God, Jesus, the Holy Ghost) but against the hypocrisy and pretension of the pompous self-appointed "representatives" of God on earth. Nothing would be more false, however, than to suggest that the blues is therefore not opposed to religion as such, but only to this or that organized religious institution. . . . The blues is uncompromisingly atheistic. It has no interest in the systems of divine reward and punishment: it holds out for "paradise now."[40]

And yet, despite all of this and the prevailing mythology of the "devil's music," the blues and gospel music are intimately linked. The blues are every bit as integral to gospel music as gospel music is to soul music.[41] How can this be?

Notice how the issue of the spiritual compatibility of the ingredients of soul music has shifted in orientation over time. In the eighteenth and nineteenth centuries the issue was about musical liturgy. That is, it was essentially about what kind of music to admit into the sanctuary. In the twentieth century the issue was about sacred music "crossing over" into pop. That is, it is essentially an objection to the removal of sacred music from the sanctuary into profane and sinful settings (where it no longer serves the Lord's purposes but does serve the devil's). But notice also how African American sacred music has evolved over the same period of time. By the time soul music emerges, the influence of the blues and other secular music has been thoroughly absorbed into gospel. Of the major African American denominations, the churches in the Pentecostal Holiness movement have taken and kept the most vigilant position opposing gospel crossover. But these churches have also been most open and enthusiastic in incorporating secular musical styles, influences, and instruments into their musical liturgy. For example, the Church of God in Christ (COGIC) takes scriptural support from Psalm 150.

150:1   Praise the Lord! Praise God in His sanctuary;
        Praise Him in His mighty firmament!
150:2   Praise Him for His mighty acts;
        Praise Him according to His excellent greatness!
150:3   Praise Him with the sound of the trumpet;
        Praise Him with the lute and harp!
150:4   Praise Him with the timbrel and dance;
        Praise Him with stringed instruments and flutes!
150:5   Praise Him with loud cymbals;
        Praise Him with crashing cymbals!
150:6   Let everything that has breath praise the Lord.
        Praise the Lord!

The musical ministry of COGIC will use anything that helps the Holy Spirit come into the church and typically incorporates a full band with amplified instruments and drums supporting the preacher and choir. The band typically rocks harder than anything you're likely to hear in any nightclub. Another Pentecostal Holiness denomination, the Church of the Living God the Pillar and Ground of the Truth without Controversy, founded in 1903, developed a unique tradition of musical ministry using lap and pedal steel guitars. This "Sacred Steel" tradition, which began in the 1930s, absorbed influences ranging from early-twentieth-century Hawaiian lap steel to postwar Nashville pedal steel. Listen to the Campbell Brothers playing "Don't Let the Devil Ride" and tell me you don't hear the blues![42] Robert Randolph, who represents the current generation in the Sacred Steel tradition, has taken inspiration from Duane Allman and Stevie Ray Vaughan.[43]

The Blues Had a Baby

Muddy Waters sings, "The blues had a baby and they named the baby rock & roll."[44] It is interesting that so many (not to say all) of the issues attending musical innovation in the United States have found expression in terms of the "illegitimacy of offspring." In the case of rock & roll the issue arises with an unmistakable tinge of racism. The "genetic traces" of two secular musical traditions, one white and one black, are recognizable in the newborn music. In the cases of both soul and gospel music, it is the chastity of sacred music and the comingling with the secular at issue. We might say that the spirituals gave birth to gospel, raising the question of paternity.

The "Father of Gospel Music": Bluesman Thomas Dorsey

The leading claimant to the title "Father of Gospel Music" would be one Thomas Andrew Dorsey, and the seminal element he contributed to gospel music is arguably the blues.[45] Of course Dorsey did not innovate gospel music alone. He was accompanied and preceded by other composers of hymns and praise music, including Charles A. Tindley and Lucie Campbell, and by a cadre of street preachers and religious songsters such as Blind Reverend Gary Davis. But Dorsey's story is an important one for a number of reasons. As a composer Dorsey left a large and definitive body of work, including perhaps two of the most enduringly famous of all gospel songs, "Peace in the Valley" and "Precious Lord, Take My Hand." He was among the pioneers in the publication of gospel songs as sheet music and thus in the development of gospel music as a commercial enterprise. His songs were debuted by the greatest voices in early gospel music, including Mahalia Jackson, who worked as his song demonstrator at the start of her own career. Most important is that he led a movement to bring gospel music into the center of the worship service in large, urban, African American churches, overcoming vigorous and entrenched opposition from within the church hierarchy. Dorsey was also a bluesman—just one in a long line of musicians who have "straddled the fence," working on both sides of the divide between African American sacred and secular music. This line stretches from "blues elders" Charlie Patton and Son House through "guitar evangelists" Reverend Gary Davis and Sister Rosetta Tharpe to "rock and holy roller" "Little Richard" Penniman, as well as the outrageous "Esquerita," on whom Little Richard evidently based his act, and the still active Memphis soul giant, Reverend Al Green.[46]

Born into a religious household in rural Georgia, the son of an itinerant Baptist minister and his church organist wife, Dorsey's first exposure was to keyboard instruments. When Dorsey was eight or nine years old, the family moved to Atlanta, where he took as musical role models the piano players who provided musical accompaniment to silent movies playing in the city's theaters. From them he learned how to complement as an accompanist, how to set and alter the mood, how to improvise, and the rudiments and importance of notation, skills that would serve him well when at the age of seventeen he would join the migration northward. In Chicago Dorsey pursued a career in music with ingenuity and determination, developing whatever skills he thought might be useful and following whatever opportunities presented themselves. He played in whatever contexts he could, sometimes substituting for other pianists. He wrote and published original compositions and learned the treacherous ways of the recording and publishing businesses by writing arrangements for other recording artists. By 1923, in his early twenties, he was at or near the top of the game. One of his copyrighted works, "Riverside Blues," was recorded by King Oliver, and as the commercial recording industry was taking interest in the blues, Dorsey's versatility won him the position of pianist and bandleader behind Paramount Records recording artist Gertrude "Ma" Rainey, a position he found both exciting and lucrative. Dorsey was traveling in style, performing to packed houses in the largest and most opulent venues for musical entertainment of the day. He was able even to arrange for his bride, Nettie Harris, to travel with him on tour as Ma Rainey's wardrobe mistress.

Dorsey's story incorporates a fascinating conversion or "turning point" narrative according to which he loses the Ma Rainey gig due to a mysterious and debilitating illness, which is eventually cured by means of an "exorcism" performed by one Bishop H. H. Haley, who said,

> Brother Dorsey, there is no reason for you to be looking so poorly and feeling so badly. The Lord has too much work for you to do to let you die,

and proceeded to "pull a live serpent out of his throat,"[47] whereupon the illness lifts and Dorsey commits to composing religious material. It was as natural for him to use in his compositions what he had witnessed and learned on the vaudeville blues circuit as it was for him to publish his compositions as sheet music. That he brought both the blues and showmanship into his gospel compositions and their presentation, that he did so deliberately for musical and theatrical effect, and that he thought this was entirely appropriate to the work he was doing for the Lord are all quite clear throughout the record of his recollections.[48]

But of course he encountered resistance. The music he was writing would make the congregation want to get up out of their seats and stomp their feet and clap their hands and sing and shout. This was unacceptable to those in charge of services in the established old-line black churches of northern migration cities like Chicago, where Dorsey was living in the 1920s and 1930s. These old-line, or, as they were sometimes called, "silk stocking," churches at the time were trying to outdo each other in presenting highly polished programs of European classical religious music.[49] A continuation of a pervasive pattern noted earlier, this was part and parcel of the central mission of these institutions—to "elevate" African Americans to levels commensurate with the highest European cultural standards. Dorsey was up against Mendelssohn and Haydn and Bach.

A musician needs to generate income just as much as a doctor or a mechanic or a preacher does, and Dorsey's blues-inflected gospel music was not paying the rent. Dorsey's career as bluesman "Georgia Tom" continued until at least 1934, as he wrote and arranged for the Brunswick Recording Company. He is credited on over sixty recordings, with Bertha "Chippie" Hill (1928–29), Kansas City Kitty (1930–34), the Famous Hokum Boys, and most notably in a duo with Tampa Red. Georgia Tom and Tampa Red specialized in a kind of sexual double-entendre blues that came to be known as "hokum," for which there proved to be a more than adequate market.[50] Although his wife Nettie reportedly remonstrated with him over his "fence straddling," Dorsey kept up his blues activities until sometime after the deaths of both his wife during childbirth and their newborn son, Thomas Jr., in 1932. Dorsey was on the road at a concert in Saint Louis when his wife went into labor. In his grief he composed "Precious Lord, Take My Hand," which would become his best-known gospel composition. There are those, including Dorsey himself, who see in this chapter of his life the workings of a providential hand.[51] But to read Nettie's and Thomas Jr.'s deaths as divine punishment for Dorsey's "backsliding into the devil's music" would be a naive and facile mistake, and it would attribute to that hand a terrible clumsiness. Dorsey was just arriving at the threshold of his breakthrough in gospel, had just been installed as president of the newly formed National Convention of Gospel Choirs and Choruses, and had gone to Saint Louis to perform not blues or hokum but a series of gospel concerts on the organization's behalf.

It's Just Business—as Usual

What Dorsey brought into African American sacred music was the blues. So crucial is this ingredient that when you challenge people to make the moral distinction between the "devil's music" and African American gospel music, many will fall back immediately on the lyrical differences (as being the only differences even discernible). But the opposition to Dorsey's gospel music was not and could not have been due to their lyrical texts. Thus, considerations of the lyrical content of the blues is quite beside the point. It was the showmanship Dorsey brought from his experience on the vaudeville blues circuit, and the music itself—the fact that it swung and it rocked—that offended the church authorities and threatened some of the ministers and choir directors who stood in Dorsey's path. The reaction of Edward H. Boatman, director of music at Chicago's Ebenezer Baptist Church, to the prospect of Dorsey's gospel chorus performing at Sunday services illustrates.

> If you're in a club downtown, a nightclub, that's all right. That's where it belongs. But how can you associate that with God's word? It's a desecration. The only people who think it isn't a desecration are the people who haven't had any training, any musical training—people who haven't heard fine religious anthems, cantatas, oratorios.[52]

It is also apparent that the showmanship and feel of the music were the very elements to which the congregations responded with such enthusiasm as to overwhelm the opposition. Thus when church authorities finally did embrace Dorsey's gospel music it was due not to any softening or reassessment of their initial criticisms but to business considerations. A church, like a musician, must function as an accountable entity in the material world. With assets and liabilities and revenues and expenses, a church measures its fortunes in many ways, some of which (membership and attendance) are closely analogous to those prevalent in the entertainment industry. Dorsey's bluesy gospel was ultimately successful in overcoming entrenched opposition when it became apparent to the church hierarchy that congregations wanted to hear more of it and that it would grow the church. In other words, it was a hit.

This should serve as a useful reminder to us not to overlook the business angle in attempting to understand the controversy a generation later over crossovers from gospel to pop. As Nelson George observes:

> [W]hen the Soul Stirrers' lead singer, Sam Cooke, at the urging of black adviser Bumps Blackwell and James Woody (J. W.) Alexander, at-

tempted to forsake gospel for pop with "You Send Me" in 1957, Specialty owner Art Rupe was outraged, not out of any real concern for the music but because a backlash by churchgoers could endanger his company's gospel sales. The gospel catalogue was the backbone of his profit, and the last thing he wanted to do was anger a loyal audience (and proven source of income).[53]

Why were Dorsey's gospel blues such a hit? The most reasonable answer is that they restored to the African American church what its congregations were most hungry for, and what had been systematically eliminated from the old-line church services, the musical support for fully engaged congregational participation in the service.

A Rift Yet Unresolved

Looking back over this history we may appreciate the challenges involved in coming to terms with the black church in America—an institution (if that is not already too sweeping a generalization) developing under the conflicting and shifting pressures of America's most troubled past. From the colonial period and slavery through the Civil War and Reconstruction to the civil rights struggle of the 1950s and 1960s, the mission of the church might perhaps best be described as contested from within. As black and white clergy with often conflicting agendas struggled to minister to their flocks in ways that would speak meaningfully to their lives and aspirations, the double consciousness of which DuBois wrote was manifested and deepened. Not the least significant among these manifestations was the opposition that grew up between the blues and gospel music.

In 1937, just as Thomas Dorsey's gospel blues were finding a place in the old-line religion, a young Willie Dixon arrived in Chicago as part of the great migration. Thirty or more years later he reflected on his career in music.

> I was raised up on blues and spirituals, but after you wake up to a lot of facts about life, you know, the spiritual thing starts to look kind of phony in places. So this is one of the reasons I guess I took off to the blues. I liked the blues and I stick to the blues because the blues gives you a chance to express your feelings. And it's wrote on facts—not phony.[54]

Attributing the faith that his mother kept in deliverance and salvation awaiting in a "heavenly promised land across the River of Jordan" to the results of "brainwashing by white slave-owners," Dixon goes on to recount his own experience in the Holy Land.

> [A]fter I came to Chicago, I went to Israel with a music tour, and I brought back a Bible and some letters with postmarks from there. And my mother couldn't understand how in the devil did I go to Israel, you know, and Jerusalem. Especially Jerusalem! Because the Bible had a lot of Jerusalem stuff in there. When I got back from the tour, I told Mama, "There really is a Jerusalem and a River of Jordan, because I *been* there. And they have more gambling in Jerusalem than in the United States; and most of the crooks they can't find in the States, they're over there!" And she just couldn't understand it.[55]

The deep ambivalence over the spiritual compatibility of the blues and gospel remains unresolved, despite the significant recent work of such contemporary "blues redeemers" as Corey Harris, Keb' Mo' (Kevin Moore), and Eric Bibb. But the emergence of soul music as an accompaniment to the civil rights movement of the 1950s and 1960s did go a long way toward a reconciliation, thereby contributing significantly to healing the nation's troubled soul.[56] Willie Dixon's contemporary, Roebuck "Pops" Staples,[57] who had forsaken the blues to sing for the Lord, was radicalized by the preaching of Dr. Martin Luther King Jr. and began for the first time to perform and record protest songs. For the patriarch of the "First Family of Soul Music," the thought of using his music as a way to engage in the struggle over worldly affairs became a realistic possibility when he took encouragement in that direction from the pulpit. The Staples Singers began to adapt traditional spirituals and gospel material to the struggle and later expanded their repertoire by composing positive "message songs" (like "Respect Yourself") with a broader secular appeal. Today Mavis Staples continues this healing work. Recently on tour with blues harmonica legend Charlie Musselwhite and the North Mississippi Allstars, her 2004 release *Have A Little Faith* on the blues-oriented Alligator Records label was less a case of fence straddling than a confirmation or reaffirmation of her own long-term spiritual path. In 2007 she released *We'll Never Look Back,* an album of music from the civil rights struggle. In the liner notes to the album she writes:

> When we started our family group, the Staple Singers, we started out mostly singing in churches in the South. Pops saw Dr. Martin Luther King speak in 1963 and from there we started to broaden our musical vision beyond just gospel songs. Pops told us, "I like this man. I like his message. And, if he can preach it, we can sing it." So we started to sing

"freedom songs," like "Why Am I Treated So Bad?" "When Will We Be Paid for the Work We've Done?" "Long Walk to DC," and many others. Like many in the civil rights movement, we drew on the spirituality and the strength from the church to help gain social justice and to try to achieve equal rights. . . . Here it is, 2007, and there are still so many problems and social injustices in the world. Well, I tell you we need a change now more than ever, and I'm turning to the church again for strength. With this record, I hope to get across the same feeling, the same spirit and the same message as we did with the Staple Singers— and to hopefully continue to make positive changes. We've got to keep pushing to make the world a better place.[58]

CHAPTER 4

Blue Notes and Greek Philosophy
(Pythagoras, Plato, and Spiritual Intonation)

Aesthetics is for the artist as ornithology is for the birds.
—BARNETT NEWMAN

Writing about music is like dancing about architecture.
—ELVIS COSTELLO

A song is a poem that can walk by itself.
—BOB DYLAN

Intercultural Aesthetics

Searching out the roots of soul music leads quickly into areas of deep theoretical uncertainty. In the blues and the spirituals we encounter musical materials that challenge readily available theoretical frameworks. What theoretical apparatus is best suited to comprehending and illuminating these materials? A recognition and appreciation of this problem should come before any attempt to resolve it. The problem is how to properly "theorize" the art of an "alien" culture. By "alien" I mean simply a culture other than our own. This might well include a "subculture" within our own contemporary local community or the culture of our very own ancestors. But in any case I mean a culture we don't understand well enough from within to call our own on its own terms. But this problem is easily overlooked even at the most basic level of recognition. Notice, for example, that in calling the blues and the spirituals *musical* materials I am *already* assuming a theoretical framework. Still the problem is easily missed: What might possibly be mistaken or misleading about identifying the blues and the spirituals as music?

To answer this question and to illustrate what I mean by "theorize" let me present an analogous, if somewhat controversial, case. In a fascinating study entitled *Hidden in Plain View,* Jacqueline L. Tobin and Raymond G. Dobard present a quilting tradition in which, according to their account, directions and instructions guiding runaway slaves along the Underground Railroad were encoded into geometric quilting patterns developed and passed down by African American women from generation to generation.[1] Assuming their research and analysis to be correct, what would be the proper analytical framework to bring to an understanding and appreciation of such artifacts? With what set of conceptual categories should we approach them? To approach them as exemplars of a particular tradition in the decorative or fabric arts or as antiques or as bedding, although they are all of these things, would underemphasize or perhaps even overlook one or more of their most important functions. The quilts, according to Tobin and Dobard, belong also to the history of covert communication systems. Hence cryptography and linguistics would be appropriate conceptual frameworks to bring into play as well. By analogy, with what additional sets of concepts and bodies of knowledge do we need to inform our musicology in order to comprehend the blues and the spirituals? We shall return to this question in chapter 7.

Ethnomusicology has emerged over the last two centuries as a discipline aimed at understanding music in its cultural context. As such it represents an attempt to overcome the limitations of more traditional academic approaches based in Western music theory and musicology as applied to indigenous music from around the world. A good example of the added value of an ethnomusicological approach as applied to the blues is the analysis of "blue notes." In traditional Western musicological terms, the blue notes are the flatted third, seventh, and to a lesser extent fifth degrees of the standard Western twelve-tone or "diatonic" scale. To conceptualize the blue notes in these terms represents an attempt to comprehend some of the distinctive characteristics of blues tonality within the framework of Western harmonic theory. But as cultural anthropologist and ethnomusicologist Gerhard Kubik points out, from the point of view of cultural anthropology and ethnomusicology, such an analytical approach is doomed to distortion.

> [O]ne could with equal justification try to describe the blues in Chinese with the terminology of classical Chinese music theory. The results would be comparable in kind.[2]

Point taken. But cultural anthropology and ethnomusicology may admit of their own limitations as well, especially when the cultural context in question is as unstable and is evolving as radically and rapidly as

African American culture surely has from the moment slaves arrived in the Americas. Under such circumstances the identification or establishment of cultural reference points and benchmarks for comparison, especially for an oral culture, can become extremely difficult. Then, too, as the preeminent ethnomusicologist Bruno Nettl has pointed out, ethnomusicology is itself a product of Western thought.[3]

Once taken as a subject of scholarly analysis in any academic discipline, an artifact generally ceases performing its originally intended function(s). On display in a university museum of art or anthropology, a quilt no longer functions as bedding. Presented along with interpretive commentary explaining its supposedly covert communicative functions, it can no longer serve those functions. Transcribed and enumerated as data points in a comparison study relating early Mississippi Delta melodic patterns with those of tribal West Africa, blues music is no longer functioning "in its element" either. When it comes to folk art, all such scholarly frameworks—of cultural anthropology, ethnomusicology, art history, linguistics, or philosophical aesthetics—are essentially alien to the cultures under examination. The problem, once recognized, may thus seem absolute and insurmountable. Is there in principle *any* way to arrive at a deep and sensitive scholarly appreciation of the art of an alien culture? Is a "learned" approach to the blues and the spirituals essentially and irreducibly alienated from its subject matter?

The great American pragmatist philosopher John Dewey confronts this problem in his book on the arts, *Art as Experience*. The concluding chapter presents Dewey's lecture entitled "Art and Civilization," in which he explores the role and function of the arts in the life of a culture. For Dewey the arts of a given culture are more than mere cultural artifacts, the products or behavioral manifestations of a particular people of a particular time and place. They also function to express that culture's "collective individuality." Thus the arts of a given culture are its most deeply revealing "face," although this face is "veiled" by every degree of our alienation from that culture. One comes to know a culture by its arts. Thus again the problem of how to approach the art of an alien culture comes front and center.[4]

What is meant by the "collective individuality" of a culture? We could characterize it as a culture's soul or essence. It is whatever it is that members of a given culture share in common with each other identifying them as members of that culture. Dewey explains this concept on the basis of an analogy to an individual's "personality." This analogy enables Dewey both to appreciate the problem deeply and resolve it rather neatly. The problem of approaching the art of an alien culture, like the analogous problem of coming to know the personality of a stranger, must overcome an obstacle: the strangeness of the other. To the extent we fail to understand the experience of those culturally remote from us, we cannot adequately understand or appreciate their art. The problem of intercultural art appreciation is thus a species of the more general and fundamentally human problem of communication.[5]

So what is communication? Think of the root of the word. For Dewey, communication, the making of community, is essentially the sharing of experience, sharing in common what is originally private. This may not be easy, yet we know it is in principle possible because we do it. However difficult and mysterious or incomplete the process may seem at times, interpersonal communication is a fact of human life. Thus intercultural understanding must also be achievable, as indeed our experience, notably with the arts, confirms.[6] So, just as interpersonal communication depends on trust and therefore mutual vulnerability, what is required to unveil, understand and appreciate the art of an alien culture or subculture is an "essentially disorienting and re-orienting" experience. We must work to approach the alien cultural material from within its own experiential and conceptual framework, which requires an expansion of our own. We have to "go through" the strangeness to "get over and beyond" it. As Dewey describes it:

> We understand [the art of an alien culture] in the degree to which we make it a part of our own attitudes. . . . [W]e install ourselves in modes of apprehending . . . that at first are strange to us. To some degree we become artists ourselves as we undertake this integration, and, by bringing it to pass, our own experience is reoriented.[7]

Dewey's insight—the importance of an insider's perspective to an understanding of any cultural phenomenon—which now generally informs cultural anthropology, is deceptively simple. Simple in that it is rather obvious on its face, deceptively so in that the obstacle to achieving that perspective with regard to any alien culture is ever present and easily overlooked.

Ethnomusicology and Blues Tonality

Let us return to the blue notes to see how this is so. Kubik observes how musicology has historically approached the blue notes consistently as "deviations from" or "inflections of" certain degrees of the standard diatonic scale. The blue notes "seem to be notoriously unstable and somewhat superimposed on the Western major scale like 'aliens.'"[8]

In very early delta blues a more appropriate model might be one in which the lyrical text is primary. In an oral tradition one of the most prevalent means by which the lyrical text is transmitted while retaining its integrity is by presenting it as an incantation, as a sung text. Traditionally, what was necessary in order to accomplish this was a drone (providing a tonal reference point) and a rhythmic pulse.[9] The lyric is then chanted over this accompaniment (which can be as minimal as a stomping foot or absent altogether), rising and falling melodically (and phrased and accented rhythmically) as best supports the meaning and emotional content the singer wishes to convey. John Lee Hooker presents a good example of this approach. As for pitch intervals relative to the reference tone, Kubik's point is that it would be presumptuous to automatically assume the diatonic scale as the model. Thus the blue notes, which occur especially and most clearly in the vocal lines, when studied in the context of their traceable African antecedents, appear to Kubik to be more fundamental. And the European scale degrees from which they "deviate" and the three common chords generally understood by Western musicology as the harmonic matrix for the melody "appear to be the real 'aliens.'"[10]

And yet, as Kubik also notes, the blues is not African music. The song text is sung in a dialect of English, and the accompaniment, especially as the blues evolves, is accomplished on instruments of largely European derivation. More on this shortly. Thus, because it is, as Kubik notes, "natural for everyone to interpret a sound event in terms of the culture with which they are familiar," it is not just Western musicology that may require a Deweyan reorientation.[11] However, that the challenge—the strangeness of the other—is an elusive yet ever present obstacle does not make it an insurmountable one; it just means that constant vigilance about it is advisable.

Whose Music Theoretical Framework?

As Kubik and others have argued, the conceptual frameworks of Western music theory and musicology by themselves fail to comprehend blues tonality without significant distortion. Similar arguments can be made regarding the spirituals and were made, for example, by Zora Neal Hurston and others during the Harlem Renaissance, objecting to the transcriptions and arrangements using conventional Western notation by Burleigh and others as distortions of the music.[12] But it would also distort matters to ignore or exclude conventional Western music theory as irrelevant. Western music theory remains crucial to an understanding of the blues and the spirituals for several reasons.

First, it would be impossible to understand and appreciate the points Kubik, Hurston, and the others make about theoretical and musical distortion absent some understanding of conventional Western music theory. Because so much of the extant analytical literature and critical commentary about the blues has been and continues to be conceptualized in terms of Western music theory, understanding something of this theory remains relevant, however handicapped it may be in its ability to account for how the music actually works.

Beyond this negative reason, the spirituals and to an even greater extent the blues are, as noted by Kubik, not purely African. They are African American, and as such they incorporate musical elements that do indeed reflect the influence of Western harmony. Thus, for example, a narrowly confined focus on early Mississippi blues combined with an Africanist perspective will result ironically in a distortion in another direction.

Significantly omitted from such analyses is any account of a blues piano tradition. There is no significant blues piano tradition to be found in early blues of the plantation and subsistence farming areas of the old South.[13] But certainly by the time blues is first recorded, the piano is well represented. Besides Georgia Tom (Dorsey), important figures include Little Brother Montgomery, Leroy Carr, Cow Cow Davenport, Pinetop Smith, and so on. The piano is first of all a bulky instrument. It takes a truck and a gang of teamsters to move one. Also pianos are expensive and relatively high maintenance. So there might have been a piano in a railroad or levee camp or a sawmill company town if the work gang was large enough to support a barrelhouse or brothel. Itinerant piano players with colorful names like Game Kid, Papa Lord God, and No-Leg Kenny traveled this circuit, but with few exceptions (e.g., Roosevelt Sykes) their music is undocumented.[14] Otherwise pianos were mostly confined to the cities. The piano was a fundamental and dominant instrument in the urban recording studios, as well as in the ensembles supporting the blues divas of the early twentieth century, Mamie Smith, Ma Rainey, Bessie Smith, Alberta Hunter, and others. The striking thing about the piano, as distinct from the guitar, is its nearly absolute inflexibility with regard to intonation. The piano player goes to where the piano is and plays it as is. There are no idiosyncratic tunings available nor technical workarounds (such as bottleneck slides) to enable the exploitation of microtonality. Certainly the great stride and boogie-woogie pianists stretched the boundaries of piano music and developed strikingly innovative playing techniques using the piano as a tuned percussion instrument and so on. But the brute fact is that a piano is tuned (or out of tune) to a tempered diatonic scale. Moreover, the roots of the blues piano tradition clearly reach back into music that was not just transcribed but *composed for piano* in European notation—by Scott Joplin, Ferdinand "Jelly Roll" Morton, Thomas Dorsey, and others.

The most important reason to bring Western music theory into consideration, however, has to do with the purpose of theory altogether. We would have little or no interest in theory apart from an interest in understanding music and its effects. Remember that dividing music into the categories of the divine and the demonic or diabolical seemed to presuppose that music has the power to affect the condition of the soul in both positive and negative ways. How do music and the soul interact? What is it in the soul that is so profoundly affected by music? And what is it in the music that accounts for these effects? These are the questions we posed at the end of chapter 1. To put these questions even more plainly and situate them squarely within the discussion of soul music and its roots, we want to understand how it is that music can effectively harm and alternatively heal the soul. This brings us to the threshold of what is arguably the deepest puzzle in philosophy of music, and certainly one of the most widely discussed, the problem of music's emotional power. If any theory of music, Western or otherwise, can shed light there, that light should be most welcome.

How Does Music Move Us?

Music's capacity to move listeners emotionally, and to do so in an apparently direct way, seemingly without any rational mediation, is widely acknowledged, but as a puzzle. At the movies everyone knows the difference, for example, between "villain music" and the music of romantic consummation. The Muzak Corporation, which began its business life in the 1930s producing elevator music (music programmed to calm the nerves of people riding up and down tall buildings in small and rickety enclosed capsules) and piping music into factories and other work environments to improve workplace morale and increase worker productivity, now offers to "Bring Your Business to Life with the Emotional Power of Music" through its proprietary service called "Audio Architecture." According to the company's literature:

> Audio Architecture is emotion by design. Its power lies in its subtlety. It bypasses the resistance of the mind and targets the receptiveness of the heart.

Take a field trip to any contemporary shopping center and listen to the programmed shopping music. At the gymnasium, hear the programmed exercise music (in the weight room what else but . . . heavy metal!). At restaurants in the dining room there is dinner music and in the bar lounge music. It is a commonplace that the music sets the mood. But this is also one of the central and perennial puzzles about music. How does the music do it?

Philosophers and Wild Geese

This problem—of explaining how music arouses and otherwise influences emotional energy—has been so vexing and a consensus solution to it has been so elusive that some philosophers of music have basically given up and turned their efforts instead to "articulating the experience of music," which they do by analyzing or critiquing the language in which that experience is expressed. What might we "really be referring to," and what might we "legitimately be taken to mean," when we find ourselves talking about music in emotional terms?[15] Gradually the theory has emerged and taken shape that the emotional language we use to talk about the experience of music is really about (or would better be understood to be about) "expressive properties" inherent in the music rather than our own inner emotional states and experiences. Thus for about two hundred years now Western philosophy of music has taken a circuitous excursion around the explanatory problem of accounting for music's emotional power and replaced it with the problem of explaining music's emotional "expressiveness." In addressing and discussing the problem of musical expressiveness, philosophers are fond of pointing out that recognizing a passage of music, or a work in any other of the expressive arts, as emotionally expressive is independent of actually *feeling* the emotions expressed.[16] Thus we are admonished, speaking theoretically, to get over ourselves (and our private emotional lives) and pay our philosophical attention rather to the music "itself."[17] The new problem, then, is how to explain and account for the emotionally expressive properties of music. Not that the new problem has been any easier to resolve than the old one but worth a try at least.[18]

The leading contemporary exponent of this approach is philosopher of music Peter Kivy, who says in one place:

> Accounts of how music is supposed to arouse the garden-variety emotions invariably give us ponderous or bafflingly intricate Rube Goldberg machinery that, like Ptolemy's epicycles, it is just impossible to believe

have any reality in nature, and yet cannot be refuted because of the notorious impossibility of proving the negative.[19]

What Kivy refers to as Rube Goldberg machinery are various apparently failed emotional arousal theories in which, for example, feelings were correlated with musical patterns such that the feelings

> aroused in the listener when the tonal pattern to which they were correlated produced analogous motions in the corporeal fluids, or "vital spirits."[20]

However embarrassing such failures may appear to be in retrospect, the explanatory problem has not gone away quietly. Rather it has haunted and continues to reverberate throughout the discussion of the problem of music's emotional expressiveness. Some philosophers have even gone back to emotional arousal as a way of explaining how music is recognized as emotionally expressive.[21]

Tracing the history of his approach, Kivy credits Arthur Schopenhauer as

> the first thinker of major stature to see clearly that musical expressiveness belongs *in* the *music*.[22]

But he notes also that

> in so doing [Schopenhauer] strongly affirmed, nevertheless, music's power to move the listener deeply. In other words Schopenhauer separated off, in his theory of musical expression, the question of music's expressiveness from that of music's emotional effect for the first time.[23]

The next major figure in this shift of emphasis was the nineteenth-century music critic Eduard Hanslick, whose essay *On the Beautiful in Music* made a trenchant and sustained, if somewhat polemical, philosophical argument that the embodiment, representation, or expression of specific emotional content is beyond the power of music as an art consisting essentially of organized sound. Hanslick's argument is admired to this day for its forward-looking account of human emotion as having essential cognitive elements and for its commonsense skepticism. As Kivy put it:

> Hanslick's healthy skepticism with regard to the extravagant claims made for music's vaunted emotive powers, including Schopenhauer's, brought the subject of musical expression down to earth.[24]

But, as Kivy also notes, even Hanslick, for all his hardheaded skepticism as a theorist, can't help talking about music in emotional terms in his writings as a music critic.[25]

Kivy's own theory, among the most fully developed in this line, is that music has emotionally expressive properties that we recognize intellectually as a result of our understanding and appreciation of music's formal structures. When we describe music in emotional terms we are in effect making claims about its objectively verifiable properties, just as when we describe music as slow or fast or loud. Music has emotionally expressive properties (i.e., there is sad music and joyful music and angry music) not because it arouses the relevant emotions in us as listeners (making us feel sad or joyful or angry) but because it resembles other vocal, facial, and behavioral expressions of these and other emotions. Put simply, music is emotionally expressive because it sounds like what sad or joyful or angry faces look like, or more broadly because it sounds the way sad or joyful or angry people behave. However, when we focus past these rather broad emotional categories (sad, joyful, angry) and get into the intricate nuances of emotion that we ascribe to music and that come over us as we listen, then, as Hanslick famously argued, a problem arises for the theory of musical expressiveness every bit as deep and troublesome as the explanatory problem facing arousal theory: by what standard do we validate conflicting claims about precisely what the music expresses?

Kivy battles gamely against this and other objections to his theory. But I won't follow these objections and replies out any further than we have already come. We have already strayed far enough from the questions on my agenda. To get back on track, I want to make just two points about the attempted end run around arousal theory and its nagging explanatory problem. The first point is that we keep coming back to arousal, problematic or not. Even Kivy returns to the problem of explaining music's emotional power. Because Kivy, like all music lovers, is deeply moved emotionally when listening to the music he loves, he recognizes and acknowledges the need to account in his own theory for music's capacity to arouse emotional energy. This is how he identifies and situates the problem.

> [W]ith the emergence of pure, textless, instrumental music as a major art form . . . the special claim of music on the affective life became . . . a "philosophical problem.". . . Without a text, music lost its conceptual, representational, and narrative content. What seemed left to it, for "content," was its *affective* content alone. . . . [I]t was agreed, on all hands, that listening to instrumental music, absolute music as the nine-

teenth century came to call it, can be, at its best, a deeply moving experience. But in the absence of a text—which is to say, in the absence of the conceptual, representational, and narrative content—pure instrumental music seems to lack all those components that give the other arts their power over the affective life. It thus became, and remains, a philosophical as well as music-theoretical problem to provide an explanation for how pure instrumental music, sans conceptual, representational, and narrative content, *can,* nevertheless, arouse affective states in its audiences.[26]

In this way of stating the problem Kivy illustrates the second point I want to make about this two-hundred-year-long excursion. It effectively excludes, or at least ignores, soul music, as well as its crucial antecedents— the blues and gospel music. Kivy's theory of musical expressiveness is strictly confined in its range of application to a particular narrowly circumscribed musical tradition. He writes:

> In the mid–eighteenth century two obviously related musical phenomena occurred: the institution of the public concert and the rise, both in social status and production, of pure instrumental music—what the nineteenth century called "absolute music," and what I have become in the habit of calling "music alone." It is, I am sure, no accident that the public concert and its setting, the modern concert hall, came into being at about the same time as another great public institution devoted to the propagation of the fine arts, namely, the museum. And it seems altogether appropriate, upon observing this far from coincidental set of events, to think of the concert hall as a kind of "sonic museum." It is absolute music, in the setting of the sonic museum, that is, and always has been the sole object of my enquiry and over which my theory of music and the emotions ranges. I make no claims for other musics, in other settings."[27]

Well, alright. We may as well suppose then that Kivy has articulated the experience of attending to pure instrumental classical music in the museumlike setting of the modern concert hall with all the clarity and precision that it deserves. But we cannot expect his theory of musical expressiveness to shed much light on the experience of the blues or gospel music or soul music because the settings, performance practices, audience expectations and so on characteristic of these musical traditions are so different from those on which Kivy has focused.[28] In particular, the music with which I'm concerned has typically got words in it, and the audience does not sit as silently as it possibly can during the performance of the music, the better to contemplate its formal compositional structures, but is generally fully engaged and taking active part in the energetic exchange as the music is made. These are crucial differences, both of which pertain to the music's emotional effects. They each complicate the explanatory problem for arousal theory, because now, in addition to explaining the mechanism whereby the emotion gets aroused, we face the theoretical challenge of isolating what the strictly musical element contributes to the overall emotional effect from the contributions made by the words and by the experience, for example, of singing and clapping hands and "getting in the spirit" in church.

This, then, is what I find most frustrating about this whole quest in philosophy of music after a theory of expressiveness and about Kivy's theory of expressiveness in particular. If we were hoping to learn something from a philosopher of music about the emotions and music per se, what we get instead is some very detailed analysis of one exceedingly specialized variety of music and of the specialized use of emotional metaphor to describe the experience of listening to it, or something like that, which we're then told has nothing to say about any other sort of music or musical experience. What Kivy means by "music alone" is not music per se or music isolated from other emotionally potent variables for purposes of orderly experimentation. We should remember that what set philosophy of music off in this direction was frustration at being unable to solve the problem of music's emotional power, the fruitless search for the missing explanatory link in arousal theory. If the emergence of pure textless instrumental music as a major art form is what it took to isolate or reenergize the problem or to bring it to the attention of nineteenth-century philosophy, the problem has nevertheless been there all along.

There. I have "expressed" my own frustration. I said it in words. I got it out. And now I can see more clearly that, in my frustration, I was perhaps being unfair to Kivy and the topic of musical expressiveness in the philosophy of music. For even though it has not addressed itself directly to music in which the *arousal* of emotion as distinct from its contemplation as an aesthetic property of a work of art is what matters most, this long philosophical discussion, and Kivy's contribution to it in particular, may yet have something to offer to arousal theory and an understanding of music's emotional power. So I'll be returning to this discussion in the next chapter. But for now I do want to refocus on music in which the *arousal* and *movement of emotional energy in the audience* is where the action is (and where the explanatory problem therefore arises).

Music and Emotional Energy

Who can forget a childhood experience of Sergey Prokofiev's *Peter and the Wolf*—a narrative set to music, originally composed as a piece of educational children's music (to introduce young listeners to the distinctive sounds of various orchestral instruments)? In the narrative, the young hero, Peter (represented by the strings), against the instructions of his grandfather (represented by the bassoon), ventures off into the wild meadow, accompanied by a cat (the clarinet), a bird (the flute), and a duck (the oboe). There they encounter mortal danger in the form of a wolf (the horns), which they overcome through natural cunning before the arrival of adult assistance (a band of hunters represented by the tympani).[29] There is action and considerable suspense. There are thrills. The bird narrowly escapes the predatory advances of the cat. There is tragic disappointment. The duck does not escape the predatory advances of the wolf. The surviving adventurers struggle and strive successfully to trick and capture the wolf. There is triumphant exultation tinged with mourning. Now, here's the problem: the music is as indispensable to the work as is the narrative. It's the music—including the tonal ranges and timbres of the representative instruments but also the themes and motifs, the melodies and harmonies as scored and orchestrated by the composer—that conveys the narrative's essential emotional force. We *feel* the emotional energy in large part *because of the music*. Of course the music doesn't do it alone. The narrative is there helping it along. But the music is helping the narrative along, too. How does the music do it?

The problem also arises in song. It arises at the heart of the question of music's contribution and suitability to the message of a sung text. Think of Ray Charles's classic version of "Georgia On My Mind." Where would that song—and Ray's performance of it—have been able to go emotionally without the changes and the melody Hoagy Carmichael wrote for it?

Similarly in cinema, music can be used to imply psychological nuances even more effectively than the dialogue it accompanies or underpins. Aaron Copland observed that music

> can play upon the emotions of the spectator, sometimes counterpointing the thing seen with an aural image that implies the contrary of the thing seen.[30]

In other words, music can even be used to complicate a cinematic narrative by *contradicting* other cinematic elements, implying something emotionally at odds with either the visual image on the screen or the verbal text or both. How does the music do it? What is it in us that responds to music in these ways and what is it in the music that accounts for these responses?

And so I return to the problem of music's emotional power. And I look to the Greeks, as thinkers with older and wider ambitions than the articulation of the experience of appreciating the pure instrumental musical traditions of eighteenth- and nineteenth-century Europe, for clues. As I shall argue, the Greek philosopher Plato and his predecessor Pythagoras have something of immense historical importance to contribute to this inquiry, even though, as I shall go on to explain, their contributions leave many crucial questions unanswered.

Pythagorean Harmonics: The Theory

Pythagoras is best known today as the source of the famous Pythagorean Theorem in Euclidean geometry.

> In a right-angled triangle the square described on the hypotenuse is equal to the sum of the squares described on the other two sides.

But for Pythagoras and his followers geometry was but a small part of a much broader and more ambitious theoretical undertaking. Like their philosophical contemporaries in ancient Greece,[31] the Pythagoreans were trying to comprehend the cosmos (all of reality) in a single, all-encompassing explanatory theory. Whereas most of his contemporaries looked for explanations in nature—for example, Thales ("all is water") and Anaximenes ("all is air")—Pythagoras was the first of the Greek philosophers to turn to something purely abstract and formal—number—as the basis for his cosmology. The Pythagoreans looked for, and found, numerical values and relationships, which they posited as fundamental organizing principles, not only in space (geometry) but also in time (music), where their discoveries and theories remain as influential today, if not as widely recognized, as their contributions to geometry.

Perhaps the most important musical idea attributed to Pythagoras is the octave, arguably the most fundamental and important of all musical intervals and thus recognized in all of the world's tuning systems. To produce the octave, and to appreciate the place of number in this relationship, try this with any handy stringed instrument such as a guitar or violin. Pluck any string, and the tone you hear we will call the "reference tone" or "tonic." Now stop the string at exactly half its length and pluck again. The tone you hear is one octave above the tonic. Notice how "powerful"—how "clear and distinct" to use Cartesian terminology—the octave is to the ear as a relation between distinct pitches. Most people, on hearing and recognizing this harmonic relationship, describe it as "the same tone—only higher." Now consider that the interval corresponds in physical terms of string length, and frequency of vibration or pitch, to a very simple arithmetic ratio, 1:2, the ratio produced by comparing the unit (1) with the result of adding the unit to itself (2). At one half the length, the string vibrates at exactly twice the frequency.

Consonance and Dissonance

Pythagoras found other interesting correspondences between number and tone. According to one account of the original discovery, Pythagoras noticed when passing a forge that different anvils sounded different tones when struck with a hammer. When he determined that the weights of the anvils stood in mathematical proportion to each other corresponding to the differences in pitch, he began experimenting with other vibrating media—with weights suspended on strings, with strings of different lengths, with pipes of different lengths and diameters, and so on. In this manner he came to recognize a series of tonal relationships corresponding to arithmetic ratios that survive as a theoretical foundation of Western harmony and tuning theory and of the harmonic concepts "consonance" and "dissonance" still in use today.

As the numbers in the ratio defining the pitch interval become smaller (i.e., the arithmetically simpler the ratio) the more "consonant" the interval. The higher the numbers in the ratio defining the interval (i.e., the more arithmetically complex the ratio) the more "dissonant" the interval. Dissonance and consonance are generally understood to contribute to the buildup and release of tension in music. Dissonant intervals are used harmonically and/or melodically to create musical tension, making the music feel like it needs to "go somewhere else for resolution." Consonant intervals impart an "at rest" feel. More recent speculation in music theory posits consonance as easier to hear, or "comprehend aurally," than dissonance because of the difference in complexity and corresponding difference in information load. As dissonance (complexity or amount of information to process) increases, so does the difficulty of aural comprehension and the aversion associated with it.[32] In any case, the octave (1:2) is the simplest and most consonant interval, the pure fifth (2:3) and fourth (3:4) and the major third (4:5) and minor third (5:6) are decreasingly but still relatively simple arithmetically and thus also highly consonant and appealing to the ear. The half-step interval (15:16), or "semitone," is by contrast rather dissonant and, for some listeners, unpleasant to hear.

It is hard to overestimate the theoretical appeal of these ideas. The facts that Pythagoras was a Greek philosopher and that the European diatonic scale is traceable to Pythagorean harmonics do not constitute an adequate reason to ignore Pythagorean concepts in the analysis of blues tonality. That Pythagorean harmonic relationships are explicated in terms of measurable transcultural formal abstractions gives them an attractively universal range of application. Although the basic insight is called Pythagorean, because Pythagoras and his followers made such an extensive and systematic study of it, meaningful correspondences between number and tone were also evidently known to the ancients in Babylon, Sumeria, Egypt, Mesopotamia, India, and Islam.[33] And they are readily demonstrable empirically to any observer at fundamental levels of application. To continue the earlier demonstration, now stop the string at exactly one-quarter of its tonic length and pluck, letting three-quarters of its length vibrate. The tone you hear is one musical fourth above the tonic. This interval, the pure fourth, corresponding to the arithmetic ratio 3:4, is also quite powerful, though not quite as powerful as the octave. Now stop the string at exactly one-third of its tonic length and pluck, letting two-thirds of its length vibrate. The tone you hear is one musical fifth above the tonic. This interval, the pure fifth, corresponding to the ratio 2:3, is again not quite as powerful as the octave, but it is noticeably "stronger" than the fourth. This high degree of consonance, by the way, is surely the main reason why parallel fifths play such a prominent role in rock music—especially the "harder" or "heavier" varieties.

The Promise of the Theory

An important measure of theoretical value is explanatory power. A theory holds forth the promise of improved understanding based upon some system of rules and regularities. As the range of phenomena to be understood increases relative to the size and complexity of the system of rules and regularities, so does the explanatory power of the theory. Pythagorean harmonics as originally conceived was thus an immensely powerful theory, easily on a par with Aristotle's syllogistic logic, at least so Pythagoras and his followers must have thought. They understood the harmonies they heard and demonstrated to be manifestations of abstract formal relationships between numbers themselves. They thought that the cosmos was ordered harmoniously and that an understanding of the beautiful harmony of the cosmos could be achieved by studying numerical relationships as such. Furthermore, they thought that the theoretical apparatus needed to fully grasp and appreciate cosmic order could be generated out of the first four arithmetic integers: 1, 2, 3, and 4. Audible musical harmony was for Pythagoras and his followers welcomed as empirical confirmation of their system.

As we shall see, however, the theory shortly ran up against its own limitations. Even so, this does not thoroughly invalidate it. There is no question whatsoever that geometry and trigonometry work. All subsequent engineering depends upon and confirms their validity. Similarly, Pythagorean harmonics continues to illuminate tuning and harmony theory generally, and the concepts of dissonance and consonance continue to function at the heart of composition theory and are considered especially relevant to the programming and composition of music for films, video games, casino environments, and other ambient applications. What Pythagoras contributed to music theory in his harmonics, then, is a formal and thus rationally appealing theoretical apparatus, applicable in theory across the full range of human emotion, to at least begin to explain how music can, independent of any accompanying text, arouse affective states in listeners.

Plato's Pythagorean Moral Psychology

Although it is not as much examined in the philosophical literature as it might be, the influence of Pythagorean harmonics on Plato's philosophy is profound.[34] References to Pythagorean harmonics turn up in interesting connections throughout Plato's work. Here are but a few examples. In the *Republic* when Socrates calculates the life of the just man to be 729 times happier than the life of the unjust man, he is following a Pythagorean formula.[35] Plato's "sovereign number," according to which political regimes degenerate in the direction of tyranny, arithmetically baffling to most Platonic scholarship, is a reference to a "Pythagorean comma" (explained further later).[36] In the passages describing the dialectic as a path to philosophical enlightenment, music is assigned the pivotal position at the threshold between the realm we can experience with our senses and the higher realm of abstract form available only to rational contemplation, with explicit reference to Pythagoras and the Pythagoreans.[37] In describing the political and personal virtues of moderation and justice Plato uses explicitly Pythagorean metaphors of tuning an entire scale from top to bottom and of harmonizing three voices in a chord.[38] The thoroughgoing interpretation of Plato's Pythagorean references would be a vast undertaking of considerable value to philosophy but beyond the scope of my topics in this book.

What Plato adds to Pythagorean harmonics that is of special interest for our present concerns is a "moral psychology"—a theoretical model of the soul crafted to illuminate morality. On Plato's model a person's soul is like an organized community, a city, in which three basic "psychic agencies" or "kinds of energy"—the rational, the passionate, and the appetitive—must work together. Each has its own proper function and role to play in the life of the soul. The rational agency (or reason—the part of the soul capable of calculation), like the deliberative institutions of a government, has the role of deliberation and decision making within the soul. The passionate agency (the emotional energies—fear, grief, anger), like the emergency response teams and security forces in a city, functions to motivate and activate the soul under duress, that is, when there is no time for deliberation. The appetites (hunger, thirst, sex drive), like the commercial economy of a city, function to address the basic biological needs and imperatives of the organism. Each agency is ranked within a hierarchy of moral purpose expressed in Plato's Allegory of the Metals—gold above silver above bronze. The highest and most important agency is reason (gold), followed by the passions (silver) and the appetites (bronze). In a mature, healthy, and well-ordered soul, each agency is dutifully devoted to its proper function. No agency meddles in the roles and functions of any of the others. Each performs its proper function in support of the others and the whole. Thus, despite the fact that the passions and appetites each represent much more powerful energy than reason, they both take direction from reason.[39] With his or her soul in this well-tuned and harmonized condition, which Plato defines as "justice," the just person lives in a state of grace, manifesting virtuous conduct in any and all circumstances, and is truly happy.

We may project from within this model that whatever moves the soul toward this healthy condition of harmonious balance is a healthy influence. Whatever moves the soul away from this healthy condition is harmful. And whatever restores the soul to a more healthy condition after it has suffered harm is a healing influence. Thus, following Plato's model we may reframe the question of music's healing and harmful effects on the soul as follows: how does music enhance and contribute to, or undermine and detract from, the soul's healthy condition of balanced intonation and inner harmony?

In chapter 2 we noted a long tradition of worry over damage to the soul as a result of exposure to music or more narrowly to "diabolical" music. The classicist Allan Bloom, based on his reading of Plato, seems on the one hand to take the more sweeping position that music is inherently dangerous to the soul.

> It is Plato's teaching that music, by its nature, encompasses all that is today most resistant to philosophy. So it may well be that through the thicket of our greatest corruption runs the path to awareness of the oldest truths. Plato's teaching about music is, put simply, that rhythm and melody, accompanied by dance, are the barbarous expression of the soul. Barbarous, not animal. Music is the medium of the human soul in its most ecstatic condition of wonder and terror. Nietzsche, who in large measure agrees with Plato's analysis, says in *The Birth of Tragedy* (not to be forgotten is the rest of the title, *Out of the Spirit of Music*) that a mixture of cruelty and coarse sensuality characterized this state, which of course was religious, in the service of the gods. Music is the soul's primitive and primary speech and it is alogon, without articulate speech or reason. It is not only not reasonable, it is hostile to reason. Even when articulate speech is added, it is utterly subordinate to and determined by the music and the passions it expresses.[40]

This position reflects the observation that music, purified of any representational, narrative or other meaningful textual accompaniment, as Kivy puts it, or *independent of* any such accompaniment, as I would prefer to put it, nevertheless exerts a mysterious yet powerful influence upon the affective or emotional life of the listener. Music appears, then, to play upon our emotions without rational mediation of any kind, bypassing and thus effectively silencing reason entirely. Bloom thus seems to be aligning himself, and attempting to align Plato, with the more musically repressive traditions associated with some varieties of religious fundamentalism.

On the other hand, Bloom also longs for a departed era when college students came from backgrounds in which they were exposed at an early age to European classical music, and he testifies to frequently giving his better students the gift of exposure to Mozart.[41] This would indicate that Bloom considers some music to be nourishing to the soul while other, "degenerate" music is harmful. In explaining the difference, however, Bloom says nothing about harmonics but focuses entirely on two elements. The first is the lyrical, theatrical, and other references to the lower order pleasures he finds most offensive, where in effect he is paying attention to the accompanying text and imagery rather than the music. And second is the powerful and insistent beat of the music he abhors. We'll talk about rhythm in chapter 5.

Taken altogether this treatment of the Platonic texts of which Bloom speaks with such authority seems on its face to be stunningly out of touch with his own translations of them. Bloom, the neoconservative critic of pop culture, is also the author of one of the more widely studied translations of Plato's *Republic,* about which he says in his preface:

> This is intended to be a literal translation. My goal—unattained—was the accuracy of William of Moerbeke's Latin translations of Aristotle. These versions are so faithful to Aristotle's text that they are the authorities for the correction of Greek manuscripts, and they enabled Thomas Aquinas to become a supreme interpreter of Aristotle without knowing Greek.[42]

Surely Bloom knows therefore the passages in Plato's *Republic* where education in music is ranked first in order of the primary curriculum for the education of the guardians of the model city.

> "Gymnastic for bodies and music for the soul." And "Music must be taken up before gymnastic" because "The beginning is the most important part of every work and this is especially so with anything young and tender, for at that stage it's most plastic."[43]

And where education in music is ranked generally as

> most sovereign, because rhythm and harmony most of all insinuate themselves into the inmost part of the soul and most vigorously lay hold of it in bringing grace with them, and they make a man graceful if he is correctly reared, if not, the opposite.[44]

Bloom must also be aware of the extended discussion in *Republic* Book III of the harmonic modes and their suitability or unsuitability to the cultivation of desirable character traits.[45] Most important of all, Bloom is surely aware of Plato's moral psychology, in which the soul's moral condition is explained and accounted for in terms of intonation and harmony. Since he must know that Plato's account of virtue is presented as essentially a matter of "tuning the soul," why does Bloom leave harmonics (tuning theory) entirely out of account in his critique of contemporary "diabolical" music? I'll come back to this question below and again in chapter 7.

The "Devil's Interval"

Bloom's applications or misapplications notwithstanding, Pythagorean harmonics and Plato's Pythagorean moral psychology remain interesting insofar as we are trying to understand the role of music in the health care of the soul. In light of Plato's moral psychology it would seem to make sense to inquire into the harmonic dimensions of the music. In this connection it is especially interesting to consider the unfortunate career of one particular musical interval—the tritone—also known infamously as the "devil's interval."

The term *tritone* derives from the fact that it comprises three whole tones. So, for example, the interval between the fourth and seventh degrees of the diatonic major scale (comprising three whole tones) is a tritone. But this is only one of several distinct ways to find or generate the interval. One might say there are several theoretically distinct musical intervals (formal or arithmetic relationships such as the "augmented fourth" or "flatted fifth") all gathered together under the name tritone.

In Western ecclesiastical music the tritone is expressly forbidden as the "devil's interval" (*diabolus in musica* or "the devil in music"), and it is generally frowned on in strict counterpoint. In the teaching of composition it is still widely discouraged, although in the rebellious twentieth century this has had more or less the force of a dare, and important composers have used it quite prominently and pointedly. For example, Leonard Bernstein used the tritone as the basis for the lead melodic motif in "Maria" in *West Side Story*. As he sings the name "Maria," the romantic lead, "Tony," begins on the tonic ("Ma"), then sounds the tritone ("ri"), resolving the aching tension thus produced by sliding up to the fifth ("a"). Danny Elfman uses the very same musical phrase as the opening fanfare in *The Simpsons* theme song (sing "The Simpsons"). Another prominent example of the tritone would be the chiming guitar chords in the opening bar of Jimi Hendrix's "Purple Haze."

The Tritone in Blues Tonality

The tritone plays a crucial and powerful role in evolving blues idioms, although its analysis continues to baffle blues scholarship. In his analysis of blues tonality, Gerhard Kubik devotes a chapter to the "flatted fifth," which stands out for him as something of an anomaly. He notes that it receives little attention as a "blue note" in the literature of musicology before the 1940s, although it appears in earlier recordings. Where does it come from and how does it function? In keeping with his general reluctance to carelessly superimpose Western tuning theory onto blues practices, Kubik says that the so-called flatted fifth is better understood as an independent component of a distinctive pentatonic blues scale. Kubik confines his analysis to its melodic use in vocal lines, observing that it occurs primarily in descending phrases. In such contexts Kubik locates it within a pentatonic scale or mode—descending from the tonic, through the flatted seventh, the pure fifth, the tritone, then the flatted third, and returning to the tonic—which he traces speculatively to multiple African sources with possible links to Arabic and Islamic origins. But the tritone also turns up occasionally in ascending vocal lines. In such cases Kubik seems inclined to follow David Evans's speculation that it may function in such ascending phrases as a blue third above a blue third. But he says, "There is probably no unitary theory to 'explain' the 'flatted fifth.' "[46]

If we look beyond its deployment in melody, we find the tritone also playing an important role in blues harmony and modulation. Consider the definitive blues chord formed by the tonic plus the major third and the flatted seventh. The interval between the major third and the flatted seventh is a tritone. It is this tritone that "colors the chord blue." Now move that tritone interval down chromatically one half step while moving the root from the tonic to the fourth or subdominant. A wonderful thing happens: the identical blue chord is produced but with the voices "inverted" as the subdominant or IV chord. Once this movement principle has been understood, it can be reproduced quite mechanically all the way around the "circle of fourths" (C, F, B♭, E♭, . . .), shifting the tritone down chromatically for each modulation. The same principle applies in reverse. Move the tritone up chromatically by half steps while moving the root from the tonic to the fifth or dominant and continue modulating through the "circle of fifths" (C, G, D, A, . . .). Now a corollary: hold the tritone interval between the third and flatted seventh steady while shifting the root from the tonic to the tritone either above or below it (i.e., to either the augmented fourth or the flatted fifth). Again, the same chord "inverted" is produced but now as a "passing chord" with ambiguous harmonic implications or leanings toward *either* the V (sliding everything up a half step) or the IV (sliding everything down a half step). Early blues applications of these harmonic principles can be found in guitar accompaniment. The effect can be accomplished on guitar by sliding the tritone up or down chromatically against a fixed drone. This movement is also the basis for what is surely among the most frequently used final resolutions in the blues, in which the blue chord is sounded one half step above the tonic (implying the V) and then resolved to the tonic (Ta daa!). An interval with so much harmonic energy and inherent flexibility is a very powerful tool, and it is used accordingly throughout modern blues in horn arrangements and other ensemble applications. If the pentatonic blues scale were a harmonic basketball team, the tritone would be the post.

The Tritone Demonized

How, then, did the tritone come to be "demonized" as "the devil's interval"? The answer to this question begins to emerge from an account of the history of Pythagorean tuning theory and from an understanding of its inherent limitations. Let us now recall that the Pythagoreans recognized correspondences between number and tone in the form of identifiable harmonic intervals and numerical ratios between the integers. The octave = 1:2, the pure fifth = 2:3, the pure fourth = 3:4, the major and minor thirds = 4:5 and 5:6, and so on. As beautifully systematic as this appears to be on first discovery, problems very quickly rise to attention. As the Pythagoreans discovered, to their dismay, the "pure" intervals, produced by the series of integer ratios, are not commensurate within the octave series. The pure intervals "add up" very closely, but not *precisely*, to the octave. The interval between the pure fourth and the octave above tonic is approximately, but not *precisely*, a pure fifth. And the interval between the pure fifth and the octave above tonic is approximately, but not *precisely*, a pure fourth. These and other similar discrepancies are generally so small as to be for practical purposes imperceptible to the ear, but they do accumulate. Over a series of several octaves the discrepancy *does become* audible so that a circle of pure fourths (or pure fifths) will return to a tone nearly, but audibly off tonic. Such discrepancies were termed "commas." It is because of these discrepancies that the pure intervals must be "stretched," or "tempered," or we might suggestively say "deformed" (de-formed), to fit evenly and consistently within the octave series from bottom to top (of the keyboard, for instance). It turns out that one can demonstrate the inevitability of this problem by a rigorous numerical proof.

> The integer ratios Plato knew are either slightly too large or too small to generate such a "closed" system; they lead, in fact, toward the musical chaos of an infinite number of tones. An intimation of the problems which Plato dramatizes can be seen in the fact that the powers of 2 (4, 8, etc.) defining octaves are *even* numbers which never coincide with powers of 3 (9, 27, 81, etc.) defining fifths and fourths by *odd* numbers, and neither of these series agrees with the powers of 5 (25,125, etc.) defining musical thirds. Tuning a 12-tone system is something of an art, then, for we must orient ourselves by the few "pure" intervals which we can hear accurately and then slightly deform them—we call it "tempering"—to insure cyclic agreement.[47]

The fourth and fifth intervals seem *almost* to divide the octave. In effect, they divide the octave in two arithmetically distinct ways, each of which is oddly asymmetrical, although interesting symmetries exist between the two of them. The fourth lies at what is called the "arithmetic mean" between the tonic and its first octave. However, the remainder is not another fourth but a fifth (approximately). The fifth lies at what is called the "harmonic mean" between the tonic and its first octave, leaving a remainder of not another fifth but a fourth (approximately). The distance between the arithmetic and harmonic means, corresponding to the audible interval between the fourth and fifth, is defined as one "whole tone."

All of this naturally engenders a question. Is there no way to divide the octave symmetrically—into equal segments or intervals that *would be* commensurate within the framework of the octave series? And, indeed, there is such a way, namely, the tritone, the "augmented fourth / diminished fifth," which lies at the so-called geometric mean, and the "aural midpoint" between the tonic and its first octave.[48] The tritone was earlier defined as three whole tones, or six semitones, that is, half of an octave in a twelve-tone system. The problem for the Pythagoreans was that there is no way to determine this interval arithmetically as an integer ratio. Without an expression for the square root of 2, the Pythagoreans could not "rationally" determine the arithmetical position or value of the tritone relative to the tonic. And so, confined as they were to the integer series, the Pythagoreans called the tritone *alogos* or "irrational."

Defined by strict Pythagorean arithmetic, the flatted fifth and augmented fourth are not identical notes in the scale. The augmented fourth corresponds to the ratio 45:32, and the diminished fifth corresponds to the ratio 64:45—both highly dissonant—with the (imperceptible) interval between the two (a Pythagorean comma) an order of magnitude more so. Theoretically, as a formal bisection of the octave, the tritone is precisely in the middle of this imperceptible gap. In Pythagorean tuning theory the tritone is dissonant beyond quantification. Thus, in effect, the tritone was demonized for bedeviling the theory, for exposing the limitations of the Pythagorean attempt to comprehend the cosmic order. And yet, despite the irrationality of its arithmetic, the tritone is among the strongest, most colorful, and, as explained earlier, most powerful intervals in music. And it exhibits certain very interesting and attractive formal features, even if these cannot be captured in the form of an integer ratio. The tritone is, after all, derivable by means of a form of bisection, and it is thus fully commensurate within the octave, requiring no deformation or tempering to preserve its identity throughout the octave series. And unlike any other musical interval besides the octave, it is indifferent to ascending or descending melodic orientation. Going up or down from the tonic, the interval is the same, and the two tritones thus produced are exactly an octave apart. In terms of formal characteristics, then, I submit that the tritone is no more "diabolical" than any other musical interval. Indeed, it is arguably second only to the octave in formal appeal, despite its elusive arithmetic, and the story of its demonization reads more and more to me like a case of the impulse to rational command and control run amok. It was called "irrational" by the Pythagoreans, meaning simply that they could find no way to calculate it using integer ratios. The "diabolical" designation comes later, in Latin, a clue to its apparent origin in the Catholic church.[49]

"Formalism" and Its Limitations

Let us return to the question with which we began this chapter, the question of theorizing our subject matter. From within the framework of Plato's moral psychology, we may understand the theoretical impulse as the felt imperative of the rational element of the soul, which delights in number and seeks to find or formulate a pattern in and around whatever is presented in experience. "Formalism," then, is the general name that has been given to theories that attempt to explain or illuminate phenomena on the basis of abstract formal relationships such as the numerical ratios of Pythagorean harmonics. But reason cannot be fully satisfied with formal structure or pattern alone. That is, to know that music has formal mathematical properties in it is not by itself enough to *explain* the emotional power of music. Even if someone were to establish a minutely detailed set of correlations between emotional states and musical intervals, which of course no one has yet done, we would still be a long way from a fully satisfactory formalist account of the emotional power of music. Without a plausible and in principle verifiable explanatory theory to account for *how* tonal relationships move emotional energy, at best all we would have is a set of correlations.

Lo and behold, we have returned to the problem of explaining music's emotional power. Thus, Pythagorean harmonic theory, even coupled with Plato's moral psychology, has proven to be rationally quite a bit more tantalizing than satisfying. Let us review. Equipped with nothing but the integer series, Pythagorean tuning theory makes immediately dazzling progress, but after only a few giant steps it stumbles over "the irrational." To ensure cyclical identity throughout the octave series, the rest of the intervals (with the exception of the elusive tritone) must be deformed by increments that not only violate but exceed the quantifying capabilities of the theory. And tuning an actual instrument like a piano becomes a matter of such delicacy and subtlety as to qualify it as an "art." Incidentally, I should point out at this juncture that Plato was arguably well aware of these wrinkles, which can be seen to project rather elegantly through his moral psychology. Keeping the soul in tune, we may be sure, is likewise a matter of delicate subtlety.

Aside from this thorny problem of incommensurability within the octave series, Pythagorean tuning theory, although it retains its inherent appeal to reason as a paradigmatically formal system, is also by the same token cut off from the realm of sensory experience, as Plato famously points out. The forms, the numerical ratios themselves, are available to rational contemplation but cannot be heard. Audible harmony at best only approximates the formal relationships through which we comprehend it intellectually. Accordingly, just as carpentry inevitably strays from the geometry that informs it, strict Pythagorean tuning theory runs into additional frustration in actual practice. The theory says, for example, that, all other things being equal, halving the string length doubles the frequency of vibration and raises the tone by one octave. But with our blunt fingers and imperfect ears we can never ensure the accuracy of our intonation on an actual instrument. So even halving the string length exceeds our meager abilities, and we must cover our imperfections with vibrato and other distracting effects. Not only are the halves never equal, but all other things are never equal either. As our knowledge of the physics of sound and the neurophysiology of the perception of sound has grown, so has our appreciation of the multiplicity of variables affecting tonality, and perceived tonality, which are not always identical.

Another fundamental problem for formalist approaches to an understanding of the emotional power of music has to do with the complexity and context-sensitive integration of all discernible musical elements. As a formal system of pitch relationships, Pythagorean harmonics can at best account only for the melodic and harmonic dimensions of a piece of music. But a melody also has rhythm, and a song a lyrical text, each of which contributes to the meaning and emotional impact of the whole. And if the song is part of a larger work, a musical or an opera or a cinematic narrative, there will also be a plot and visual imagery and who knows what all else involved. In Leonard Bernstein's "Maria," for example, the use of the tritone in the melody imparts an unmistakable musical tension, whose precise emotional signature depends also on knowing that Tony is singing the name of his beloved. It depends also on his beloved's name being Maria (and not, say, Brunhilde). Thus, a formal harmonic analysis of Bernstein's use of the tritone leaves out of account much of what it takes to appreciate its *musical* contribution to the emotional impact he achieves with it. What the melodic contour of the composition means and does emotionally depend also on the textual elements of the composition. Imagine the size and complexity of the formal system that would be required in order to handle such context-sensitive compositional complexity, involving not just pitch intervals but also rhythm, poetics, and all other meaningful dimensions of complex works. Thus formalist theories have tended to suffer from the sort of clumsiness that derives from the need to isolate whatever the theory is equipped to handle. Harmonics can't do it all—not all by itself. The harmonic and melodic contours of the music have their effects in their rhythmic and lyrical context. A song is an integrated whole, "a poem that can walk by itself," as Bob Dylan put it. And a theory will not shed much useful light even on the harmonic and melodic contributions to the music's emotional power if it requires us to dismember the song.

Perhaps this is one reason why Bloom says nothing about harmony in his moral critique of rock music. He knows that you cannot distinguish between spiritually healthy and spiritually harmful music in strictly formal harmonic terms alone. Rhythm, about which we've said next to nothing yet, would seem to be just as amenable to formal mathematical analysis as are harmony and melody. But a fully elaborated and integrated formal apparatus capable of yielding a satisfying grasp in strictly formal terms of music's emotional power remains chimerical.

Intuitively we know *that* music arouses emotional energy, we just don't know *how.* Among the first fully mathematized areas of human activity, music's formal properties have been recognized for thousands of years. Music plays, arousing emotional energy. Reason sees numbers and envisions a science. But no theory has yet succeeded in linking music's rationally intelligible properties with its intuitively apparent emotional power in a satisfying explanatory account. This has led to a vast, contentious, and inconclusive literature in several distinct but overlapping disciplines, including psychology, neuropsychology, neurophysiology, musicology, philosophical aesthetics, and so on.[50]

And reason refuses to quit. Of course, mathematics has advanced considerably in three millennia. Perhaps now, in the age of chaos theory and fractals, *everything* in music—from arithmetically challenging intervals like the tritone to subtle nuances of timbre—may yet be reduced to mathematical formulae or just sampled and subjected to formal analysis in the digital domain. There is a company now offering a consulting service to the music industry based on something it calls "Spectral Deconvolution Software," claiming that this software program can be used to shorten the odds of picking hit songs by highlighting certain combinations of formal musical properties. Here is Malcolm Gladwell's account of a demonstration of the program.

> On his computer screen was a cluster of thousands of white dots, resembling a cloud. This was a "map" of the songs his group had run through its software: each dot represented a single song, and each song was positioned in the cloud according to its particular mathematical signature. [CEO Mike] McCready then hit a button on his computer, which had the effect of eliminating all the songs that had not made the Billboard Top 30 in the past five years. The screen went from an undifferentiated cloud to sixty discreet clusters.[51]

McCready says his system beats industry focus group research, but what is it really but a kind of mechanized, accelerated, and aggregated "focus group feedback loop"? It may yield predictive results in a good many instances, but it functions essentially as a system that can "learn" a history of responses of a large population and tell you when you're imitating more or less closely the musical behavior of the most popular artists of the past. This may have some advantageous commercial applications in an industry that depends on predicting consumer behavior, but from the point of view of culture it merely represents an acceleration of the homogenizing and deadening effects of marketing on a large scale. Is it any wonder that pop culture strikes those who are not caught up in it as narcissistic? And what does it *explain* about the audience responses it quantifies?

One can imagine similar research models applied to the question of music's emotional power. Listeners are hooked up to electrodes and exposed to a range of musical selections. Their brain states are monitored, measured, and recorded. They are interviewed about their emotional responses. Graphs and charts are generated. This is your brain on Bach. This is your brain on Coltrane. Eventually the results may be displayed as dots on a computer screen. Emotional response clouds are correlated with musical signature clouds. More correlations. But how much better do we understand the emotional power of the music? No doubt one of the most important reasons why formalism is still frustrated in its attempt to grasp the emotional power of music is our limited understanding of emotion.[52] But still reason refuses to quit.

Interesting programs of scientific research are being pursued in the intersection of medicine, biology, and physics.[53] I do not mean to denigrate this research, and indeed I will return to it in chapter 8. My point is simply this. Cutting-edge neurobiology and neuropsychology have thus far proven themselves to be more effective in opening up new and fascinating areas of *inquiry* than they have been in settling any of the long-standing questions about music and the health care of the soul. Citing the eliminative materialist philosopher Paul Churchland, Daniel J. Levitin catalogs the impressive fruits of scientific inquiry over the last two hundred years, underscoring the promise of neuroscience as an area and method of inquiry, but notes:

> One mystery has not been solved: the mystery of the human brain and how it gives rise to thoughts and feelings, hopes and desires, love, and the experience of beauty, not to mention dance, visual art, literature, and music.[54]

In other words, as promising as the research agenda may be, brain science remains an unfinished project whose results, even if we knew them, would not settle the metaphysical, moral, and spiritual (i.e., philosophical) questions in play. Again we are reminded of the importance of a high tolerance for unanswered questions.

There's something approaching the paradoxical in all of this striving and frustration. I like the way Douglas Hofstadter, a formalist if ever there was one, put it, when he said:

> I am a relentless quester after the chief patterns of the universe—central organizing principles, clean and powerful ways to categorize what is "out there." Because of this, I have always been pulled to mathematics. . . . The reason is that I still feel that mathematics, more than any other discipline, studies the fundamental pervasive patterns of the universe. However, as I have gotten older, I have come to see that there are inner mental patterns underlying our ability to conceive of mathematical ideas, universal patterns in human minds that make them receptive not only to the patterns of mathematics but also to abstract regularities of all sorts in the world. . . . To me, the deepest and most mysterious of all patterns is music, a product of the mind that the mind has not come close to fathoming yet. . . . However, I don't believe that these mysteries will ever be truly cleared up, nor do I wish them to be. I would like to understand things better, but I don't want to understand them perfectly. I don't wish the fruits of my research to include a mathematical formula for Bach's or Chopin's music. Not that I think it possible. In fact, I think the very idea is nonsense. But even though I find the prospect repugnant, I am greatly attracted by the effort to do as much as possible in that direction. Indeed, how could anyone hope to approach the concept of beauty without deeply studying the nature of formal patterns and their organizations and relationships to Mind?[55]

CHAPTER 5

Bio-Rhythms
(From Formalism to Somaesthetics)

It's got a back beat, you can't lose it.
—CHUCK BERRY

I don't think onstage. I feel. —KEITH RICHARDS

Melody for the mind, rhythm for the body.
—BONO

In chapter 4 the term *formalism* was introduced as the general name for theories that try to explain things on the basis of abstract formal structures or relationships. Plato is the primary source of formalist thinking throughout all of Western philosophy across all of its topical areas. Plato's famous Theory of Forms, according to which pure permanent, unchanging, abstract formal entities, available only to intellectual contemplation, are more real than the constantly changing material world, to which we gain access through our not very reliable five sensory modalities, has sent its ripple effects through every branch of philosophy.

Musical Platonism

In philosophical aesthetics (philosophy as applied to the arts) philosophers have often wondered, for example, about how best to anchor the notion of the identity of a given work of art. Similarly in philosophy of music, philosophers wonder about how best to anchor the notion of the identity of a given work of music. Although some cases are intuitively unproblematic—as in painting, where the canvas as the artist completed it is the work of art—in other areas (literature, the performing arts) things are not so straightforward or easy. For example, since there can be many distinct performances of a given work of music, each sounding markedly different from the others, what shall we say is the governing "work of music"? In response to this question, formalists posit an abstract entity, the composition, as the work. This abstract entity, as a formal structure or collection of formal relationships, is distinct from any of its material manifestations, including all performances, arrangements, recordings, the score and other notational renderings whether printed or written by the composer's own hand, digital sound files, and the like. This abstract formal entity, although no one can actually *hear* it, can nevertheless be used to explain how performances and recordings are identified, authenticated, and evaluated as renditions of a particular piece of music, how it is that we can identify "wrong notes" and other flaws and weaknesses in a given performance, and so on. Because this notion of an abstract entity standing behind, or floating above, the whole collection of instances of a work of music is so clearly derived from Plato's metaphysical Theory of Forms, this kind of theory is often referred to as musical Platonism.[1]

Plato and Music Censorship

Returning to the questions of music's emotional power and its effects on the condition of the soul, we find among the most widely familiar and frequently cited Platonic texts several passages in *Republic* Book III, where the education of the guardians of the model city is being discussed. The prescribed curriculum, consisting of sung epic narratives about gods and heroes, must be constructed so as to produce a warrior class with the delicately balanced capacity to manifest savage hostility toward enemies of the city while remaining loyal to and gentle with each other and their fellow citizens.[2] After the content of these stories and their mode of presentation (the use of mimetic narrative) have been determined, Socrates turns his attention to music, saying, "The harmonic mode and the rhythm must follow the speech."[3] In other words, the text and its message are of primary importance, and the music must provide "suitable accompaniment." Socrates' point that the harmony and rhythm must follow the speech is repeated with additional emphasis prohibiting the converse.

> We'll compel the foot and the tune to follow the speech . . . rather than the speech following the foot and the tune.[4]

And yet again:

[G]race and gracelessness accompany rhythm and lack of it. Further, rhythm and lack of it follow the style, the one likening itself to a fine style, the other to its opposite; and it's the same with harmony and lack of it, provided, that is, rhythm and harmonic mode follow speech, as we were just saying, and not speech them.[5]

And then, because there is "no further need for wailing and lamentation in speeches," several harmonic modes identified as suitable for wailing and lamentation—as well as drunkenness, softness, and idleness—are dispensed with, leaving only those few (unidentified) harmonic modes that fit and foster the bearing of a courageous and unflappable military leader.[6] With the musical palette thus restricted, a whole class of "pan-harmonic" instruments (instruments with the flexibility to play in many modes) and instrument makers are also dismissed from the city.[7]

There follows a brief discussion of rhythm focused entirely on poetic meter and expressed in terms of prosody, a metric system codifying rhythm in speech, especially poetry.[8] In prosody the basic rhythmic patterns, or "feet," include the "iamb" (a 2-syllable pattern pronounced "I *am!*" and accented "ka-BOOM"), the "anapest" (a 3-syllable pattern accented "bada-BING"), the "trochee" (another 2-syllable pattern, which rhymes with "trophy" and is accented the same way), the "dactyl" (another 3-syllable pattern accented on the first syllable, like in the word "*heav*enly"), the "amphibrach" (another 3-syllable pattern with the accent in the middle, like "Ma-*ri*-a"), and so on. Prosody uses a simple notation consisting of ($\cup$) for short or unaccented syllables and ($\_$) for long or accented syllables. Thus the iamb is ($\cup\_$), the anapest is ($\cup\cup\_$), the trochee is ($\_\cup$), the dactyl is ($\_\cup\cup$), and the amphibrach is ($\cup\_\cup$).[9] Again Socrates gets Glaucon to agree to seek out "the rhythms of an orderly and courageous life" and to "compel the foot and the tune to follow the speech of such a man."[10]

There is a general consensus in the philosophy of music and Platonic scholarship, based largely on these passages, that Plato held to a kind of unified emotional arousal theory of music according to which harmonic modes and rhythmo-poetic feet each had a distinctive "emotional signature," with a corresponding tendency to arouse sympathetic emotion in listeners, due to mimetic resemblances to emotionally expressive speech.[11] As regards the rhythms, Socrates defers to Damon, with the harmonic and melodic emotional correlations based on formal relationships codified by the Pythagoreans. If harmony and rhythm do influence the emotional life of the human soul, with possibly far-reaching and long-lasting effects, it is a short step to the notion of both spiritually healthy and spiritually harmful music. And so Allan Bloom is far from alone in reading Plato as a moralistic censor of music. Taken at face value, the passages just cited suggest to quite a few commentators that Plato is one of Western civilization's earliest and most important proponents of music censorship for the sake of the soul and its health.[12]

I should say at this point that I am deeply skeptical of this "conventional" reading of Plato as a serious proponent of music censorship. In my view, those who read Plato in this way are missing a rather loud note of irony in the text, which Plato calls attention to when he has Socrates point out (to Glaucon especially):

> "And, by the dog," I said, "unawares we've again purged the city that a while ago we said was luxurious."[13]

From Harmony to Rhythm

It is tempting to speculate how Plato might have elaborated his musicalized moral psychology and these apparently censorious passages on the use of music in education had the Greeks developed percussion to a level of sophistication comparable to Pythagorean harmonics or been exposed to the musical traditions of Africa and the African diaspora. Might Plato have characterized the soul of the just individual as not only well tuned and internally harmonious but "solidly in the groove"? Or would Plato have banished the drummers (along with the mimetic artists) from the model city?

> "But see here, Glaucon, won't our guardians need to be shielded and protected from exposure to seductive and subversive dance rhythms, just as from the dangerously slothful harmonic modes?"
>
> "Absolutely, Socrates. Neither wailing modes nor funky beats shall they hear!"

I'll return in chapter 7 to this question of irony. For present purposes let us simply note that on its face rhythm is every bit as congenial to mathematical (i.e., formal) analysis as are harmony and melody. Given this rather obvious fact, we might hope and expect to learn a great deal about rhythm in the leading literature of formalist music criticism and aesthetics.

Fear of Repetition

When it comes to music, formalists have generally given the most attention to what is variously described as "significant form" (Bell), "commanding form" (Langer), and "large-scale form" (Levinson)—meaning the network of inner and overarching structural relationships that make up a piece of composed music—in a word, the "composition." That is, formalism in music theory has generally started out with musical Platonism as a platform. This has, with few exceptions, left formalist treatments of rhythm oddly truncated and some important aspects of rhythm largely unappreciated. In the formalist literature rhythm is typically relegated to a relatively insignificant status—if it is mentioned at all. Instead, it is the *vertical* placement of the notes on the staff and the resulting contours of melodic line that seem to matter most to formalist analysis. Is this because of the "higher frequencies" of vibration involved? Is it because rhythm seems somehow more "bodily" than "mental"?

The great twentieth-century music theorist Leonard Meyer's discussion of rhythm is typical in this regard. In his reflections on the apprehension and appreciation of music as pattern Meyer posits what he calls the Law of Good Continuation. As a piece of music unfolds in time a trajectory or set of trajectories is established that are either continued or disturbed and set off in some new direction. Meyer goes on to discuss harmonic and melodic progression and development in Chopin, Wagner, Beethoven, Schumann, Haydn, and so on. Noting that disturbances in processes of musical continuation "play an important part in creating the affective quality" of passages of music, Meyer is interested in discovering the principles according to which such continuations and disturbances are well or ill formed.[14] He is careful to distinguish continuation from "mere repetition."

> Continuation always implies change within a continuous process, not mere repetition. And while continuation appears to be a normal mode of operation, repetition is [normal] only up to the point at which saturation sets in.[15]

Saturation, a music-theoretical term of art, is perhaps best understood as a vague threshold at which repetition begins to bore the audience, by which point the composer had better do something disturbing. Speaking as though of all music, and for all listeners, Meyer thus posits a normative standard.

> Since the meaning of a sound term is a function of its relationships to other consequent terms which it indicates, our normal expectation is of change and growth. A figure which is repeated over and over again arouses a strong expectation of change both because continuation is inhibited and because the figure is not allowed to reach completion. Our

expectation of change and our concomitant willingness to go along with the composer in this apparently meaningless repetition are also products of our beliefs in the purposefulness of art and the serious intentions, the integrity, of the composer. We believe that he will bring about a change.[16]

Formalists like to listen to the composition so as to appreciate the work of the composer. In this way formalists have taken up and appreciated the values that informed European classical music of especially the seventeenth, eighteenth, nineteenth, and twentieth centuries. Meyer, like Kivy and most other formalist music theorists and critics, clearly has European classical traditions of music in mind. But if the audience expectations he spells out are indeed appropriate for this kind of music, just imagine the frustration of someone approaching the blues or funk— or any other kind of music with a solid rhythmic groove—handicapped by rigid confinement within this set of listening expectations. Listen to what Bootsy and Catfish Collins are playing on James Brown's "Get Up (I Feel Like Being a) Sex Machine."[17] Talk about figures repeated over and over again!

Turning his attention eventually to rhythm, Meyer confesses:

> Thus far continuity has been discussed largely in terms of spatio-melodic and harmonic processes. The vital and ever present factor of temporal organization has received little attention. In view of the numerous and well-known difficulties involved and the incomplete state of our knowledge of the subject, it would indeed be pleasant to ignore the factor of temporal organization altogether.[18]

As Meyer reluctantly presses on, he follows Plato in conceiving of rhythms essentially in terms of prosody.[19] However, if we want to understand and appreciate music in which a rhythmic groove plays a central role, we cannot expect to get much help from a theoretical discussion so shot through with fear and loathing of repetition. A groove requires and *demands* repetition. Listen again to what Bootsy and Catfish Collins are playing on James Brown's "Get Up (I Feel Like Being a) Sex Machine." In funk, such interlocking rhythmic figures, played over and over again, arouse a strong expectation that the resultant interplay will *continue,* with as little variation in tempo and overall feel as the musicians can manage, more or less indefinitely. Our concomitant willingness to go along as listeners and stay "in the groove" with the musicians indefinitely is a function of our recognition of how interesting, "infectious," danceable, and *fun* the groove is.

Formalism Gets Hip

A more rhythmically aware and sensitive approach still within the formalist tradition of music theory and criticism is taken by Wynton Marsalis. Marsalis is a formalist, but his formalism begins with the recognition of rhythm as "the most fundamental element of music."[20]

> Now you may think the melody is the most basic component of music because that's what we recognize and remember most easily. . . . We may recognize the melody of Brahms' lullaby as a particular sequence of tones, but that sequence is organized in time by rhythm. Melody is dependent on rhythm. Without rhythm to move a melody along, we would never get past the first note. No motion, no rhythm. No rhythm, no music.[21]

One way to approach rhythm philosophically as a formal dimension of music would be to start with a pitched tone—something vibrating at a constant frequency. Now gradually reduce the frequency of vibration. As the frequency is reduced, the pitch gets lower and lower until it eventually reaches a threshold where it disintegrates as a pitched tone and becomes instead a (rapid) ongoing series of beats—what Meyer calls a "pulse."[22] Continue to reduce the frequency, or "tempo," of the pulse. The pulse, at whatever tempo, that is, however rapid or slow its frequency, is not yet perceived as musical as long as the beats remain uniformly undifferentiated from each other. Reason wants to count, and so it will either find or imaginatively superimpose a distinction, an "accent," at some regular frequency or interval, let us say every three beats or every four beats.[23] This creates a "meter," a way of measuring or keeping track of what is going on. The meter provides an orderly matrix within which beats can now be further grouped and accentuated in interesting ways, creating "rhythms."[24] Meyer and Marsalis are in conformity with each other in their accounts of accent, rests, meter, tempo—the basic theoretical formal apparatus of rhythm—but notice how Marsalis gets at the fun element.

> [I]f I ask you how far from home to school, you might say 5 blocks, but you wouldn't say 6,737 steps. Or you might say 10 minutes, not 600 seconds. You divide the distance or organize the time into convenient units. In music we organize the beats, accents and rests into something called *meter*. And meter is counted just like numbers. . . . But what do musicians like to do most with rhythms? Well, we like to do what everybody likes to do. We like to play. That's right. In basketball, when we

first learned how to dribble, it was an achievement just to bounce the ball in a steady motion. . . . It might take two weeks to learn how to do that comfortably. . . . But in order to have fun playing, we have to vary the bounces with accents and rests.[25]

Marsalis makes the point that the fun comes not so much with the simple regularity of repetition as with the variations. But Marsalis is neither contemptuous of nor impatient with repetition. And that is a good thing because variation *presupposes* repetition. No repetition, no variation.[26]

The crucial importance of repetition in music is not limited to the establishment of meter or of the ground rhythm in a movement or passage of music. Besides being essential to a rhythmic groove, repetition also plays a fundamental structural role in compositional form. Standard 32-bar song form generally follows an AABA format, with an 8-bar verse repeated then followed by a bridge (what John Lennon called the "middle eight") followed by a third verse. Standard chorus format in jazz consists of some fixed or flexible and indefinite number of repetitions of a given song form (read: play the same changes or chord progression over and over) with lead and accompaniment assignments in the ensemble shifting from chorus to chorus. Sonata form closes with a "recapitulation." Repetition is nearly everywhere you look in music. As Peter Kivy eventually comes to observe:

> Indeed, because quite frequently the repetition is literally *literal,* there is no need for the notes to be written down or printed a second time. So musicians have devised instructions, such as double dots in front of a double bar, or *da capo,* or *dal segno,* all of which tell the performer to go back to some designated place in the score or part and simply play the thing over again.[27]

As Kivy goes on to explain, this rather obvious fact constitutes an embarrassment to formalist theories of music, which have historically by and large tried to ignore it or sweep it under the rug. This happens because the theorists are trying their best to account for what lovers of European classical music value most highly in the music they love and the theoretical models that seem most promising (the model of literary development and the model of organic growth) can't make much sense of repetition. On Kivy's reading of the relevant theoretical literature (as thorough a reading as you're going to find), the only extant theory capable of accounting for the central role of repetition in music is to be found in Immanuel Kant's *Critique of Judgment* where music, treated as "pure, empty decoration," is accordingly demoted from the status of high art and assimilated into the rank of wallpaper.[28] Kivy thus finds himself in the somewhat awkward position of having to rehabilitate wallpaper by installing it on the floor. (He finds an example of pure decorative and repetitive patterning—analogous to wallpaper, but worthy and rewarding of deep aesthetic contemplation—in his Persian carpet.)[29]

Organic Repetition

The deepest vein of insight into rhythm I have been able to find in the literature of formalist musical aesthetics is in Susanne K. Langer's *Feeling and Form.* There, following the pragmatist philosopher John Dewey, she makes the subtle but startling observation that although repetition is *essential to* rhythm it is not *the essence of* rhythm. A machine can do repetition, but rhythm is organic. Although rhythm *is* essentially repetitive, it is not mechanical. It is alive.

> There have been countless studies of rhythm, based on the notion of periodicity, or regular recurrence of events. It is true that the elementary rhythmic functions of life have regularly recurrent phases: heartbeat, breath, and the simpler metabolisms. But the obviousness of these repetitions has caused people to regard them as the essence of rhythm, which they are not.[30]

The central insight of both Dewey and Langer is in understanding rhythm primarily in biological rather than mathematical terms. All of life is rhythmic. In biology rhythm is the difference between life and death. Rhythm is better understood thus in terms of the dynamic interplay of oscillating tensions or, to put it another way, in terms of energy exchange rather than in terms of equal divisions of time. In breathing for example, as we inhale the body builds up a need to exhaust carbon dioxide. We resolve this tension by exhaling while the body is building up a new tension in the need for oxygen, leading us to inhale. Throughout life the resolution of one set of tensions gives rise to a new set of tensions.

> The heartbeat illustrates the same functional continuity: the diastole prepares the systole, and vice versa. The whole self-repair of living bodies rests on the fact that the exhaustion of a vital process always stimulates a corrective action, which in turn exhausts itself in creating conditions that demand new spending.[31]

This approach illuminates a number of important aspects of rhythm in music. For example, it enables Langer to explain how harmonic and melodic progression can and do function as rhythmic elements in a composition.

> The concept of rhythm as a relation between tensions rather than as a matter of equal divisions of time (i.e. meter) makes it quite comprehensible that harmonic progressions, resolutions of dissonances, directions of "running" passages, and "tendency tones" in melody all serve as rhythmic agents.[32]

Here is another corollary insight. Biological rhythms, although they are essentially repetitive, are also essentially characterized by endless subtle variation. Thus, as Langer notes:

> The ticking of a clock is repetitious and regular, but not in itself rhythmic.[33]

And further:

> A person who moves rhythmically need not repeat a single motion exactly.[34]

Thus, as Marsalis brings out in the passage quoted earlier, the fun element in the groove arises out of its vitality, the variety *in* the repetition. This point also illuminates the crucial differences between a metronome (or click track) and a live drummer. The mechanical timekeeper, the metronome, click track, or drum machine is inflexible and unresponsive. As drum machine technology has evolved, a "humanize" function was incorporated to introduce subtle variation or "feel" into computer-generated grooves. But the difference between even a "humanized" drum machine track and a live drummer is that the live drummer is responsive. A live drummer brings elasticity into the ensemble or the mix. Live musicians hear and respond to what the other musicians are doing. There is an exchange of energy. The drum machine isn't listening and remains therefore essentially inflexible, even in the subtlest of its fluctuations and departures from strict meter, whether these are generated algorithmically or at random.

Langer's treatment of rhythm as organic repetition is quite *un*-Platonic, a striking innovation in the history of formalist thinking about the arts. That it embraces variation is one obvious departure from the Platonic Theory of Forms, according to which pure form is absolutely invariant. Langer's interest in vital processes as revelatory of rhythm's essential nature indicates another departure from Plato and the formalist tradition he started. As an essentially biological phenomenon, rhythm is apprehended, indeed known, not exclusively or even primarily by means of the intellect but rather bodily. This is in stark contrast to the Platonic account of formal apprehension as strictly and exclusively intellectual.

Moreover, by "bodily" I mean not just the ears. Rhythm is apprehended not just aurally, through the sensory modality of hearing, but somatically. If the physics of sound and the physiology of sense perception jointly determine that the bodily organ most sensitive to differences of air pressure created by sound waves is the ear, nevertheless the awareness of rhythm is widely distributed throughout the body, from the extremities to the core. Toe tapping, finger snapping, hand clapping, pogo dancing, arm waving, head banging—rhythm is not just heard but *felt*.[35]

Somaesthetics

Langer's treatment of rhythm is reminiscent of certain general and fundamental observations offered a generation earlier by John Dewey in his William James Lectures on the philosophy of art and the book that grew out of them, *Art as Experience*. There Dewey begins his search for the roots of art, of beauty, and of aesthetic experience generally by exploring something we humans, as living organisms, have in common with all other life forms: the constant rhythmic oscillation between equilibrium and disequilibrium in relation to our environment. This condition of ongoing struggle to restore fleeting and dynamic conditions of equilibrium between an organism and its environment, manifested at all times throughout the body of "the live creature," is where Dewey finds the roots of the human impulse to art.[36] Indeed, Dewey founds the very notion of form in the arts upon natural rhythm. For Dewey, rhythm in nature is more basic than form.[37] The contemporary pragmatist philosopher Richard Shusterman describes this as Dewey's "somatic naturalism."[38]

Following in this tradition, Shusterman proposes the development of a body-centered discipline he calls "somaesthetics" to explore the body's crucial and complex role in aesthetic experience. Central to his proposal is a plea for a renewed appreciation of the body as an intelligent site and instrument of meaningful and valuable aesthetic perception, perceptual discrimination, sensory experience, and knowledge.[39] What is meant by "*renewed* appreciation" is that the role of the body as an intelligent instrument of perceptual discrimination, sensory experience, and knowledge is recognized and appreciated in Stoicism, Yoga, Tai Chi, and others among the world's ancient wisdom systems as essential to the art of living well. In effect, Shusterman is attempting to overturn a history of neglect and denigration of the body in Western philosophical aesthetics stretching back 250 years and more to its eighteenth-century origins as a branch of modern philosophy.

The term *aesthetics* was first introduced into Western philosophical discourse by Alexander Baumgarten, in works published between 1735 and 1758, to found a "science of sensory cognition"—a formal philosophical discipline aimed at the refinement, and ultimately the perfection, of sensory cognition.

> "The end of aesthetics," writes Baumgarten, "is the perfection of sensory cognition as such, this implying beauty."[40]

And yet, as Shusterman notes with astonishment, Baumgarten excludes from his proposed discipline and its program of exercises something obviously and necessarily required for the refinement and improvement of perceptual acuity and reliability: the cultivation of the body. Shusterman attributes this exclusion in part to Baumgarten's rationalist philosophical lineage from Descartes through Leibniz to Baumgarten's own mentor, Christian Wolff, where the essential imperfectibility of the senses is presupposed, and to the pervasive theological orthodoxy of the early Enlightenment, with its hostility to the body. Shusterman remarks that the somaesthetic art form par excellence is dance. In dance music, music composed for dance (or for dancing), the somaesthetic element par excellence is, of course, rhythm.[41]

The Promise of Somaesthetics

Let us pause for a moment to reflect on the major themes of our inquiry, beginning with the observation that dividing music into the categories of the divine and the demonic seemed to presuppose that music has the power to affect the condition of the soul in both positive and negative ways. In chapter 3 the question arose: what, after all, *is* the relation between the flesh and the spirit, between body and soul? We saw then the importance of what theologian James H. Cone referred to as "the essential *spiritual* function of the human body" in the historically situated spiritual strivings of the African American people as expressed especially in music, primarily through rhythm.[42] How do music and the soul interact? What is it in the soul that is so profoundly affected by music? And what is it in the music that accounts for these effects? A somaesthetics of rhythm is a plausible and promising source of illumination here, and, as noted above, it would dovetail quite nicely with emerging theories of the emotions.[43]

So consider where we left the unfinished business of explaining music's capacity to arouse and direct emotional energy in chapter 4. Philosophy of music had by and large abandoned the effort to explain music's emotional power in favor of an effort to account for music's emotional "expressiveness." And we briefly examined a representative theory of musical expressiveness offered by a preeminent philosopher of music, Peter Kivy, according to which music has objectively verifiable emotionally expressive properties not because it arouses sadness or joy or anger in us as listeners but because it sounds the way sad or joyful or angry people look and behave. In order to explain this Kivy develops what he calls a "physiognomy" of musical expression, a more or less systematic set of correlations linking formal musical relationships (such as melodic contours—the rising and falling of pitch in melody and so on) to characteristic embodied or behavioral expressions of emotion. In this connection, Kivy makes the following observation about rhythm.

> The most obvious analogue to bodily movement is, of course, rhythm. And it is an embarrassing commonplace, but nonetheless true, that in all sorts of ways, the rhythmic movement of the human body in all kinds of emotive expressions is mirrored by and recognized in music. To state the most common of the commonplaces: *of course* funeral marches are slow and measured, as sadness slows and measures our expression of it.[44]

The most puzzling thing about this observation is why such a commonplace truth should be "embarrassing." Embarrassing to whom or to what and why? From the point of view of somaesthetics, to say that the slow and measured rhythm of a funeral march mirrors the way sadness slows and measures our expressions of it is as good as to say that rhythm in music *feels* like emotions feel.

This is of course a simile and inexact to be sure. Emotions *seem* to emanate from within while rhythm in music *seems* to impact and penetrate from without and so on. And so the machinery of rhythmic emotional arousal still remains to be explained at some level. But a somaesthetics of rhythm invites us to consider that such explanations will come easier and make more sense if they attend to the whole body (not just the brain), that is, if they take into consideration such processes as muscular contraction and relaxation, the accumulation of somatic stress and its release, and so on.

Rhythmic "Feel"

Consider, for example, one of the most distinctive applications of music in American culture, the New Orleans jazz funeral service, wherein the body of the deceased is escorted to the grave site by mourners and a marching band. To appreciate how the music functions to support and enhance the grieving process the best place to start is by simply *feeling* the rhythms. On the way to the grave site, the band plays a dirge or funeral march. Returning from the grave site, the band plays the "second line." The rhythms are emotionally appropriate *and effective.* As the deceased is escorted to his or her final resting place, the dirge reinforces the communal expression of grief. As the funeral party returns from the grave site, the second-line dance rhythm pulls the mourners back up into ongoing life.[45]

In modern musical notation indications to specify tempo (the speed or pace at which the music is to be performed) are given above the staff near the time signature using a vocabulary that originated in seventeenth-century Italy. "Tempo" (Italian for "time") is itself a part of this vocabulary. The basic "tempi" (in order of increasing speed, *Largo, Lento, Adagio, Andante, Moderato, Allegro, Presto*) have become conventionally standardized within ranges in clock time as beats per minute ("♪ = 120 bpm" indicates a metronome setting of 120 beats per minute for eighth notes); for example, *Adagio* is 66–76 bpm for quarter notes. But the vocabulary itself, and thus the traditional understanding of it, particularly in its fuller elaborations, is full of expressive references to bodily movement. *Andante* means "walking pace." *Adagio* means "slow and stately" (literally "at ease"). *Allegro con brio* means "fast and bright with vigor or spirit." As these notational conventions have been adapted to popular music the vocabulary has grown to incorporate words for what musicians refer to as "rhythmic feel." Some of this vocabulary is based on dances (e.g., samba, rumba, polka). But some words are derived from other activities.

A paradigm example is "swing." *Swing* denotes not only a style of music but at a more fundamental level the rhythmic feel characteristic and indeed definitive of the style. Typical definitions of *swing* in terms of conventional notation refer to eighth-note triplets, of which the second one is either tied to the first or omitted. But such definitions are notoriously wooden and inept at conveying the *feel*—the distinctive rhythmic "lilt"—of swing: as one jazz glossary puts it, "an irresistible gravitational buoyancy that defies mere verbal description."[46] A better place to start is with the familiar childhood experience of the playground apparatus for which the rhythmic feel is named, bearing in mind Langer's approach to rhythm as the dynamic interplay of oscillating tensions. In full swing, gravity accelerates us through the arc to a moment of weightlessness at the apex and then back through the arc to another moment of weight-lessness, and so on. There's really no better way to describe the rhythmic feel of swing than this.

A related paradigm is the "shuffle," prevalent in blues to the point of being almost definitive. Like swing, shuffles are rendered in conven-tional notation in terms of eighth-note triplets with the second either tied to the first or omitted. But unlike swing, with its characteristic "lift," shuffles "drag." The term *shuffle* comes from the name for a way of mov-ing, literally "to drag (the feet) along the floor or ground while walking or dancing." As with swing, conventional staff notation fails to capture or communicate this essential ingredient of the shuffle feel. In conven-tional staff notation a Jimmy Reed shuffle is indistinguishable from a Count Basie swing and for that matter from John Philip Sousa's "Liberty Bell" march (notorious in recent memory as the Monty Python theme song). The "Liberty Bell" is composed in 6/8 meter, and is played with strict metric precision, appropriate to its function as a piece of ceremo-nial military music for marching band. By contrast, the distinctive shuffle feel is created by accenting the third of each set of eighth-note triplets and by playing it late or "behind the beat." This stretch or deformation of strict meter creates the musical tension that characterizes the shuffle feel and explains why inexperienced players, especially drummers, often find it hard to maintain tempo in a shuffle.

Syncopation and the Back Beat

Recorded in concert in Germany by Radio Bremen in 1993, Taj Mahal kicks off the fourth song in the set, Walter Jacobs's "Blues With a Feel-ing." The audience, warming to his music, begins to clap along. Taj stops. "Wait, wait, wait. . . . This is schwarz musik!" he instructs his audience. "Zwie, vier! One **TWO** three **FOUR!**"[47] In the history of American popu-lar music there is probably no single development that has attracted more inflamed and inflammatory attention than "the back beat"—which consists of heavily accenting the second and fourth beats in each mea-sure of 4/4 meter. This is the rhythmic feel that initially defined rock & roll, the beat that so excited the teenagers on *American Bandstand* in the 1950s ("I give it an 8, Dick, because it has a good beat and you can dance to it"), the "beat" that reactionary cultural commentators like Allan

Bloom have complained about so bitterly from the dawn of rock & roll more than fifty years ago.

If there remains any uncertainty as to the cultural history of this particular musical development it is in any case clear that the back beat has an African lineage and that it broke through massively to an audience of white teenagers, and thereby into the mainstream of popular culture in America, in the early 1950s with what eventually became known around the world as rock & roll music. Following musicologist Rene Lopez, Robert Palmer traces the roots of the back beat through Louisiana and Cuba to Haiti and from there to the Yoruba and Fon tribes.[48] The earliest recordings featuring the back beat as the basic ground rhythm for the entire song began coming out of New Orleans in 1949, according to celebrated New Orleans session drummer Earl Palmer, who used it on Fats Domino's "The Fat Man" in that year, and on subsequent recordings by Lloyd Price, Larry Williams, and Little Richard.[49] Earlier examples of the back beat do occur in some arrangements for swing band in the 1940s (typically in the final or "out" chorus) and are audible in hand-clapping percussion accompaniment on some boogie-woogie piano recordings dating from the 1930s. In gospel music, of course, emphasis on the back beat, using hand claps and tambourines, goes all the way back—to Africa.

Western musicology has been given to theorizing the back beat as a "displacement" of accent from presumed normal expectations (emphasis on the one of any measure and on the one and three of any measure of 4/4 meter), and thus as an instance of "syncopation," which is in turn understood to be basically a matter of upsetting rhythmic expectations—of doing something rhythmically surprising—or, in Leonard Meyer's terminology, defying the Law of Good Rhythmic Continuation.[50]

From the point of view of somaesthetics, it is worth noting the etymological connection between the musical term *syncopation* and the clinical term *syncope*, defined in medicine as "a partial or complete temporary suspension of respiration, circulation, or consciousness due to cerebral ischaemia (oxygen deprivation), a fainting spell or swoon." Links between this sort of somatic disturbance and emotion (especially the thrill or rush of overwhelming emotion) abound in the lyrics of popular music ("My heart skipped a beat," "You take my breath away"). Syncopation might thus be explained somaesthetically as a musical device that adds excitement akin to an emotional thrill by temporarily suspending or interrupting rhythmic continuity, especially of a groove.

Regarding displacement, however, the presumption as to which expectations are "normal" is objectionable from the point of view of ethnomusicology for what should by now be obvious reasons. I have a vivid recollection of my early experience of hearing rock & roll in the 1950s, by which time I was already receiving musical training in the European classical tradition. I do not remember being particularly "surprised" by the rhythmic feel of the back beat as a "departure from established rhythmic expectations," although I don't suppose that at age seven or eight my sense of musical order could have been very firmly established. What I do remember is finding the rhythmic feel of rock & roll irresistibly exciting, compelling to movement; I loved the way it *felt*. To this day I still love the rhythmic feel of rock & roll, although I am by now thoroughly accustomed to the back beat and don't find it surprising at all.

But let us consider the question of "normal rhythmic expectations" more closely and carefully. We may assume that any system of rhythmic organization in music or dance will incorporate "reference beats" for the purpose of coordination within the group of musicians and/or dancers. Whatever the pattern is, the musicians and dancers will need to be able to count, and it surely makes sense to start counting on the one. But as Gerhard Kubik points out, unlike European and European-derived musical traditions, African-derived rhythmic organization does not always *accent* the reference beat (the one). Indeed, the one need not even be enunciated—it can be "implied."

> *Beat 1* of a metrical scheme can be so unobtrusive acoustically that it functions like a black hole (with a powerful gravity, but virtual invisibility). Not pre-accented, accents can then be set on-beat or off-beat according to the melodic-rhythmic structures to be developed.[51]

The back beat is also rooted in the African musical practice of call-and-response, where because the call issues from an individual and the response from the group, the response is typically "bigger," more "voluminous." Thus, in other words, it would be a misleading and objectionable presumption to theorize the back beat as essentially or necessarily a "*displacement* of accent" or a "*departure* from normal rhythmic expectations."

Social and Political Philosophy of Music

Some scholars have attempted to explain African and African American musical practices, including the back beat, in sociopolitical terms. It is not always clear whether these are intended primarily as illuminating metaphors or as somehow more directly related to the principles of social organization and distribution of power that inform the actual music-making practices. In his discussion of rhythm in rock music Theodore Gracyk adopts jazz historian Gunther Schuller's term *democratization of the beat* to describe the leveling effect of ignoring the "traditional" downbeat and allowing "weak" beats (weak under traditional Western assumptions) to be emphasized on a par with or even above the so-called strong beat.[52] Although I think there are important insights contained and hinted at here, their proper appreciation depends upon clearing up certain confusions. So first the criticisms.

Schuller's own explanation of this coinage is itself confused and confusing, an earnest but troubled attempt to bring conceptual order and clarity to several distinct phenomena. In his glossary he defines *democratization* as "the rhythmic and dynamic equalization of the smallest units within a rhythmic pattern or phrase."[53] Here he appears to have in mind a leveling of all *beats* in accordance with an egalitarian ideal so as to open the widest possible array of rhythmic options for lead improvisational phrasing. And he develops this notion in terms of jazz instrumental technique on wind instruments, stressing the maintenance of "*equality of dynamics* among 'weak' and 'strong' elements" and the preservation of "full sonority of notes" wherever they may fall in the meter.[54] This notion of "equality before the law of meter" is then complicated by a discussion of polyrhythmic and polymetric organization in African music.[55] Here he is referring to the simultaneous use of multiple distinct patterns of rhythmic organization, whose reference beats may never line up with each other. This distinctive African musical practice, also manifested melodically in polyphonic heterophony (the simultaneous interplay of multiple melodic lines crisscrossing each other in overlapping phrases, as in early New Orleans jazz) has often been described as remarkably "democratic" but for reasons having more to do with individual autonomy merging into cohesive community than with equality. For example, Alan Lomax describes a music

> composed of many intertwined parts improvised by the singers joining and leaving the chorus as they pleased, stroking in tones, part phrases, and harmonies just where they were needed to round out the blend. . . . This intertwined, unified, overlapping style is peculiar to black Africa and African America. It is one manifestation of a group-involving approach to communication that allows everyone present to have an input in everything that is happening. Dance, ritual, work, even conversation, are all performed in this overlapping, participatory way.[56]

In this connection, it is primarily the *players,* individually and collectively, and the *process* that seem to be "functioning democratically" in that each player enjoys full autonomy as a participant in the conversation, which thus takes on the striking and zany complexity of an emergency town meeting. E pluribus unum.

But all of this (the egalitarian leveling of all beats, wind instrumental technique, polyrhythm) seems to me to be essentially tangential to what rock & roll *drummers* are typically doing with the back beat, which is to smack it harder than anything else. If rhythm is "democratized" in jazz, in rock & roll the back beat occupies a distinctly privileged position, as indeed Schuller and Gracyk both notice.[57] In rock & roll not all beats are equal. The one is eclipsed by the back beat to such a degree that James Brown was able to create a whole new revolution in rhythmic feel (funk) by *simply reasserting it* (the one).[58] Nor is rock & roll especially polyrhythmic, and it is certainly not polymetric. The bass player may be playing a walking bass line in quarter notes while the guitar player plays the Chuck Berry eighth notes and the piano player beats out eighth-note triplets in the upper register. But it all converges on the back beat in straight-ahead 4/4 time.

Reflecting on the rise and reign of Motown in its heyday, jazz and pop music critic Gene Santoro recalls:

> It was rumored that there were 2 by 4s stomping through "Baby Love" to make sure white Americans could learn to feel the backbeat—a cultural twist I remembered years later in Perugia, when I watched a church full of enthusiastic Italians at a gospel music concert by African American groups clap resoundingly on the one and three.[59]

As far as rhythmic feel is concerned, in rock & roll the back beat is much more important than the one or the three. If you have a mind to join in, it is not a matter of indifference whether you clap along with the back beat or on the one and the three. An audience that enters into the energy exchange by clapping along on the one and the three not only demonstrates its ignorance of the operative rhythmic conventions, it *undermines the groove!* Somaesthetically speaking, it *feels,* and therefore *is,* wrong.

We ought not to confuse the back beat with "off-beat accentuation" as such—in effect distinguishing only two sorts of rhythmic emphasis: "on beat" (emphasis on the one, or the one and the three) and "off beat" (everything else lumped indiscriminately together). This would arguably be just another case of the natural tendency to interpret sound events in culturally familiar terms, a point I won't belabor further here.[60] Nevertheless, there may well be something socially and politically significant, something closely akin to "democratization," characterizing off-beat accentuation *as such,* something the back beat therefore shares with other varieties of off-beat accentuation, particularly as a response or reaction to on-beat accentuation. One thing on-beat accentuation is particular good for is supporting and reinforcing regimentation, which is why military music (marching music) in particular is always informed by it. Thus, in one important respect, to the extent that the established social order in America in the 1950s involved regimentation or was sustained and reinforced by it, the alarmed and horrified reaction to the back beat on the part of so many of the guardians of social order makes a certain kind of sense. When America's teenagers began to shake their bodies and dance with abandon to the big beat of rock & roll, everyone could feel the subversive energy of the back beat.[61] Off-beat accentuation, whether on the back beat or on other off beats or ahead of the beat or behind the beat, subverts regimentation and is thus "liberated," and "liberating."[62]

CHAPTER 6

Fake It Till You Feel It
(Race, Ethnicity, Authenticity in Performance)

The idea of a white blues singer seems an even more violent contradiction of terms than the idea of a middle class blues singer.

—AMIRI BARAKA (LEROI JONES)

Eddie "Cleanhead" Vinson used to say that white performers, and particularly the singers, had the blues "Bassackwards." [Not] that the world perceives or understands the qualitative difference. This goes for the so-called experts and critics as well.

—JOHNNY OTIS

No, you don't have to go pick cotton or any o' that to play the blues, . . . but it helps.

—B. B. KING

Music is your own experience, your own thoughts, your own wisdom. If you don't live it, it won't come out of your horn. They teach you there's a boundary line to music. But, man, there's no boundary line to art.

—CHARLIE "YARDBIRD" PARKER

Shut up!

—LITTLE RICHARD

I first got interested in the issue of the "authenticity" of white blues in the late 1960s. At the time, I was majoring in philosophy at the University of California. But, as committed as I was to my studies, what I *really cared about* was the popular culture of the moment—especially the music. Slogging through Kant's *Critique of Pure Reason* and Edmund Husserl's *Cartesian Meditations* was, let's face it, a long and lonely regimen with few consolations compared to the extracurricular dimensions of college life at the time, which were overflowing with excitement and interest. They were also, as my generation would come to recognize and appreciate more and more deeply over time, pregnant with political significance. The times, as Dylan put it, they were "a-changing." In California particularly—though with equal force and vivacity in New York, Boston, Chicago, Detroit, Memphis, London, Paris, and other major theaters of culture—colorful outbursts, uprisings, teach-ins, human be-ins, both on and off campus, were going off in a seemingly spontaneous crescendo like some kind of global fireworks display. What a great time to be a student!

Can White People Play the Blues?

As a college freshman in 1965 I was *completely blown away* by the Paul Butterfield Blues Band's first (eponymous) album on the Elektra Records label. Elektra was then primarily a "folk music" label. I had not heard very much in the way of blues music up until this time. I was still living at home with my parents and attending the local community college (where I now teach). My parents' music collection included mostly classical music, but they also listened to quite a bit of socially and politically conscious "folk music" along the lines of Pete Seeger and the Weavers. So what blues I had been exposed to was either presented as recorded "folk music" (Odetta, Leadbelly, Sonny Terry and Brownie McGee) or broadcast as part of the broader mix of "rhythm & blues" on Oakland's KDIA, whose playlist included B. B. King, Jimmy Reed, and Bobby "Blue" Bland.

Of course, I had also been listening to rock & roll for at least ten years. This included Bo Diddley's "novelty" hits, as well as Fats Domino, Little Richard, Chuck Berry, and Ray Charles. Still, I had no real awareness of the blues as such or as the source of what I *was* listening to. I hadn't heard any Chicago blues or delta blues yet. I didn't yet know about Muddy Waters or Elmore James or Junior Wells or James Cotton or John Lee Hooker or Robert Johnson.

In its time, the Butterfield Blues Band opened a very important door for a whole lot of people. There was nothing remotely like it on the radio. On the album cover, a portrait of the band: five young guys leaning up against the funkiest urban apothecary storefront you ever saw offering "Incense, Herbs, Oils." From left to right, lead guitar player Michael Bloomfield, bandleader and harmonica player Paul Butterfield, drummer Sam Lay, rhythm guitarist Elvin Bishop, and bass player Jerome Arnold. On the back of the cover was a notice: "We suggest that you play this record at the highest possible volume in order to fully appreciate the sound of the Paul Butterfield Blues Band." No kidding! We broke stereos listening to this record. "What is THIS?! What *IS this?!*" Well, it was the first electric "blues band" anyone of us white rock & roll teenagers had ever heard. (For African Americans it was the first "electric *white* blues band.") It was at the same time strangely familiar—it had the spirit, the passion, the excitement and abandon of early rock & roll. Suddenly we (white college kids weaned on rock & roll) were all forming "blues bands."

Of the individual "voices" in the Butterfield band, Bloomfield's probably had the greatest impact. One of the definitive marks of the transition from rock & roll to rock is the emergence of the electric guitar as a solo lead voice in the ensemble. Bloomfield was as much responsible for this development as anyone.[1] On his instrument he was a (very reluctant) deity—one of, perhaps *the,* first of the guitar heroes (or "guitar gods") of the rock era. Eric Clapton was emerging at about the same time in Great Britain, with Jimi Hendrix to come very shortly after. For several succeeding generations electric guitarists have continued to trace their original inspiration to Bloomfield. Robben Ford, one of the most advanced and versatile of the current generation, has said:

> After I heard [Bloomfield] with the Paul Butterfield Blues Band, I just went nuts for the electric blues guitar and I got very serious about it.[2]

Carlos Santana put it this way.

> The first time I saw Michael Bloomfield play guitar was when the Butterfield Blues Band came to San Francisco. I was still in Mission High School. And it literally changed my life enough for me to say, "This is what I want to do and want to be for the rest of my life."[3]

Even though I was a piano player, not a guitarist, Bloomfield was a hero for me, too. For one thing, he was Jewish! And he was scholarly in his approach to his music. All stuff I could relate to very directly. And what he was doing was *WAY TOO COOL FOR SCHOOL* (if you know what I mean).

Fast-forward three years to 1968. Free-form FM radio, dance concerts at Bill Graham's Fillmore Auditorium and the Avalon Ballroom (run by the more organic collective the Family Dog), free impromptu performances in Golden Gate Park by local rock bands the Grateful Dead, Quicksilver Messenger Service, Jefferson Airplane. San Francisco had just celebrated 1967's Summer of Love, and was now a major magnetic global cultural epicenter. Bloomfield had left the Butterfield band and relocated to San Francisco to form the Electric Flag. The Flag (as we liked to call it) was a large band with a horn section like the more commercially successful Blood Sweat & Tears and Chicago. Like the Butterfield Blues Band, the Flag was racially mixed and played what Bloomfield, like Ellington before him, would characterize only as "American Music." I was in my senior year at the Santa Barbara campus of the University of California—still majoring in philosophy, trying to come to grips with Wittgenstein. As an extracurricular activity I was involved in concert production through the Concerts Committee of the Associated Students organization. In that year we brought the Flag plus Cream (Eric Clapton in the world's first power trio) on a double bill to campus. Also Jimi Hendrix, the Doors, and Carlos Santana, who played a free concert in the Student Union—all in one school year!

And of course I was in a college "blues band." Naturally I read all the press about all of this stuff. I was brought up short by some commentary published in fledgling *Rolling Stone* magazine by a founding and contributing editor named Ralph J. Gleason. Gleason was ragging on the Flag.

> When I first heard Paul Butterfield's band I was disappointed. Here, I thought, were white musicians trying to sound black . . . kids trying to sound like Muddy Waters. . . . Now they're trying to sound like Wilson Pickett and Otis Redding. . . . Bloomfield is a fine musician. But he will always be a Jewish boy from Chicago and not a black man from the Delta. Originality is the key. If this nonsense continues, Bloomfield will end up being the Stan Getz or Chet Baker of rock.[4]

I suppose I took this rather personally. Who was this Ralph J. Gleason and what did *he* know?! As it turned out, Gleason was one of the more important and influential music critics of his day. Based in San Francisco, Gleason wrote regularly for the *San Francisco Chronicle* primarily about jazz. His criticism also appeared in *Down Beat* and other important music journals. He was cofounder of the Monterey Jazz Festival. As the host of the first nationally televised jazz program, *Jazz Casual* on National Educational Television (now PBS), he had significantly expanded the audience for jazz music. And in 1967, with Jann Wenner, he cofounded *Rolling Stone*. Gleason had not only been around; he had been *involved.* And gradually, on reflection, I began to see Gleason's reaction to Bloomfield's Electric Flag and the Butterfield Blues Band as part of a larger, deeper, and more intricate set of problems. There were arguments to consider.

The following year, entering upon graduate school, I went in search of faculty supervision for a research project on the subject. No one would take me on. I was told the topic was unsuitable for graduate-level research in philosophy. A philosophy PhD dissertation on *what?* What would I be reading? What sources were there for me to consult or cite in my bibliography? Where would I get any footnotes?

In 1969 there was, of course, *nothing* on the subject in the philosophical literature. And why *would* there be? What was written on the subject was appearing in journals of folk music scholarship, jazz criticism, and the new rock journalism, and if none of these discourses was then considered worthy of philosophical attention, that meant simply that academic philosophy had not begun to take an interest in "popular culture." And in a way I suppose that was fair enough. Popular culture was not particularly interested in academic philosophy either.

It would take twenty-five years for the discussion of this nest of issues and arguments to find its way into the professional literature of academic philosophy. In 1994 I published what I'm pretty sure was the first paper on the topic in a refereed academic journal of philosophy.[5] In the intervening years, aside from scholarly citations, that paper has been anthologized several times and still turns up on assigned reading lists in college courses around the country and overseas in disciplines ranging from anthropology and art history to cultural studies and musicology, as well as philosophy. But I have come to think the positions I took in that paper were insufficiently deep and the arguments I made for them inadequate. And so I now revisit the topic and shall try to do a little better.

Race versus Ethnicity

In the original paper I used a standard philosophical approach, trying first to "disentangle" several distinct arguments for the relative *in*authenticity of white blues and then to "neutralize" the strongest versions and best expressions of them I could find. Besides Gleason, I found these arguments in the writings of white British blues historian Paul Oliver; white American blues historian and former editor at *Living Blues* magazine Paul Garon; and, most important, African American critic and playwright Amiri Baraka (LeRoi Jones).

I was of course antecedently committed to defending the authenticity of white blues. Even so, there is nothing wrong methodologically with this approach—provided one really understands the arguments. I did understand that the arguments had more to do with politics, morality, and race than with aesthetics or music as such, but at the time I thought I could "finesse" the crucial problem of race and racism and as a result failed to appreciate some of the deeper arguments.

I went about my argumentative agenda by first introducing a distinction between race and ethnicity as a means of "rescuing" the negative position (that white blues is *in*authentic) from automatically damning classification as simply an instance of racism (in reverse). I took it as too obviously facile to fall for some clumsy "mirror-image gotcha" argument like the ones that were being used to dismantle affirmative action as "reverse discrimination." So I recast the arguments for the negative position in terms of ethnicity. I considered two interrelated arguments—one having to do with proprietary claims to "ownership" as applied to culture and the arts and the second with experience, understanding, and levels of meaning. Even though these two arguments, as I initially understood them, don't go deep enough for me now, they remain historically important, and they continue to appeal to many people as soon as the subject is broached. And so they continue to occupy a position at the top of the agenda of discussion.

The Great Music Robbery

Writing in *Jazz and Pop* magazine in 1968, Ralph Gleason said:

> [T]he blues is black man's music, and whites diminish it at best or steal it at worst. In any case they have no moral right to use it.[6]

On its face, this speaks to questions of "ownership," although one ought to notice right away that the proprietary interests and concerns Gleason invokes here extend well beyond "property" and quickly merge into more general considerations of propriety. Who has legitimate authority to use the blues as an expressive idiom, as a performance style, to interpret it, to draw from it and to contribute to it as a fund of artistic and cultural wealth—and of course to profit from it? The argument proceeds from the understanding that the originators and the major innovators of the blues were African Americans—Ma Rainey, Bessie Smith, Charlie Patton, Robert Johnson, Muddy Waters, Howlin' Wolf, John Lee Hooker, T-Bone Walker, Professor Longhair, and so on. To whom does this cultural and artistic heritage belong? Who are Robert Johnson's legitimate cultural and artistic heirs and conservators?

The ownership argument says in effect that the blues as genre and style belongs to the African American community and that white people who undertake to perform the blues misappropriate the cultural heritage and intellectual property of African Americans and the African American community. Amiri Baraka refers to this as "the Great Music Robbery"—a systematic and pervasive pattern of cultural and artistic cooptation and misappropriation running throughout the history of black people in America. According to Baraka, the blues, as well as every other

major black artistic innovation, after surviving an initial period of condemnation and rejection as culturally inferior, eventually wins recognition for superior artistic significance and merit, only to be immediately
appropriated by white imitators whose imitations are profitably mass
produced and accepted in the cultural mainstream as definitive, generally without due credit to the source. Calling the blues "the basic national voice of the African-American people,"[7] Baraka traces the pattern
through the evolution of jazz.

> [A]fter each new wave of black innovation, i.e., New Orleans, big band,
> bebop, rhythm and blues, hard bop, new music, there was a commercial
> cooptation of the original music and an attempt to replace it with cor-
> porate dilution which mainly featured white players and was mainly in-
> tended for a white middle-class audience.[8]

According to Baraka this is part and parcel of a sometimes subtle and at
other times more blatant form of institutionalized racism—effectively
maintaining and exploiting racist socioeconomic class structures.

> The problem for the Creators of Black Music, the African-American
> people, is that because they lack Self-Determination, i.e., political
> power and economic self-sufficiency, various peoples' borrowings and
> cooptation of the music can be disguised and the beneficiaries of such
> acts pretend they are creating out of the air.[9]

Rock & roll, for example.

In my original reflections on this argument I did not challenge the
claims that deceptive and predatory exploitation of African American
creativity was prevalent and pervasive in the music industry. Instead I
took the collective "ownership" claim on behalf of the African American
people as the crucial premise and wondered at considerable length how
such a claim might be coherently articulated in terms of intellectual
property. Could the ownership claim overcome the obstacles posed by
the vagueness of both the claimant's collective identity as an evolving
community and the property's elusive and ephemeral nature as musical
style? Could a people coherently claim to "own" a rhythmic feel, a 12-bar
song form, a rhyme scheme, or a harmonic mode? If not, then the ownership argument would not by itself uphold the negative position. However, eventually I arrived at the conclusion that the whole discussion of
collective intellectual proprietary interests in a musical genre consti-
tuted an "elaborate red herring" because the traditions and concepts of
"intellectual property" were so alien to the cultural practices that at-

tended and animated the blues in its community of origin. And with that I turned my attention to the second argument.

"Authenticity": a Provisional Definition

What makes one blues performance more or less "authentic" than another? Suppose we start with this: authenticity is a value—a species of the genus credibility. It's the kind of credibility that comes from having the appropriate relationship to an original source. Thus authenticity's most precise, formal, and fully institutionalized application in the art world is to distinguish a work "by the author's own hand" from the forgery. When we authenticate a work in this sense, what we want to know is whether or not the putative author is who he or she is represented to be. In this application the distinction between authenticity and inauthenticity is a strict dichotomy, the alternatives both mutually exclusive and exhaustive, and the appropriate relationship is one of identity. Similarly, if less precisely, "authenticity" is applied to the artifacts and rituals that constitute a culture's "currency," conferring value on those "acceptably derived" from original sources. So, for example, an authentic restoration of a nineteenth-century Victorian mansion might be one reconstructed according to original plans and specifications and perhaps using only the tools, techniques, and building materials of the period. An authentic Tuscan recipe might be one traceable to a source within the indigenous culture of Tuscany using ingredients traditionally available within the region. In such applications authenticity admits of degrees. A given piece of work may be more or less authentic than another. And the standards or criteria of authenticity admit of some flexibility of interpretation relative to purpose.

In the literature of musical aesthetics the authenticity question has been focused largely on the relation between performances and "the work" and, because the work is conceived of as a composition, between performances and what the composer intended. And so the criteria for authenticity have been understood in terms of accuracy or conformity with performance specifications that constitute the work. As applied to blues performances the authenticity question must be focused rather differently for, although we may speak of blues "compositions," what we thereby refer to consist of a simple chord progression shared by many other blues songs, with no particular key signature or prescribed instrumentation, and a lyrical text that itself is open to ad-lib interruption, interpretation, and elaboration in performance. As a musical genre, the blues is characterized by what we might call "compositional minimalism" and a complementary emphasis on expressive elements. The question of the authenticity of a given blues performance is thus one of stylistic and expressive authenticity, and our question becomes "Is white blues 'acceptably enough derived' from the original sources of the blues to be stylistically authentic and authentically expressive within the style?"

Acting Like You Know

The negative position can now be understood as follows. White musicians cannot play the blues in an authentic way because they do not have the requisite relation or proximity to the original sources of the blues. Where the proprietary argument addressed the question of ownership, this second argument addresses questions of meaning and understanding as these bear centrally on issues of culture, its identity, evolution, and transmission. What is the significance of the blues? Who can legitimately claim to understand the blues? Who may speak with authority about the blues and its interpretation? Who can legitimately claim fluency in the blues as a musical idiolect? Who has authority to pass it on to the next generation? Who are the real bearers of the blues tradition? Thus comes the argument that one cannot really understand the blues or authentically express oneself in the musical idiolect of the blues unless one really knows what it's like to be a black person in America, and one cannot really know what this is like without *being* one. I called this the "experiential access argument." And I tried to understand and explain it as follows.

Jazz players have an expression, a motto of sorts: "Fake it till you feel it." The premise is that authentic expression comes from genuinely felt emotion and lived experience. It is "testimony." The experiential access argument in effect posits the experience of living as a black person in America as a precondition of the felt emotion essential to authentic expression in the idiom of the blues. The appeal to experience functions to either establish or challenge authority based on some such principle as this: other things being equal, the more directly one's knowledge claims are grounded in firsthand experience, the more unassailable one's authority. In the liner notes to his brother Branford's 1992 release *I Heard You Twice the First Time*, trombonist Delfeayo Marsalis writes:

> Yes, one must pay serious dues in order to accurately translate the sorrow and heartache of the blues experience into musical terms. The great blues musician Charlie Parker once said, "If you don't live it, it won't come out of your horn."[10]

It's worth noting that the quotation from Charlie Parker, when read in its full context,[11] balances Marsalis's point about the necessity of "paying one's dues" in at least two ways. Parker seems to be talking less about prerequisite suffering than about *really meaning* what you play (by living in a manner consistent with its deepest implications). And he explicitly repudiates "limitations" as applied to music and the rest of art, presumably including barriers based on race and ethnicity. Nevertheless, Parker continues to be widely quoted in support of what I'm calling the "experiential access argument." And in *Blues People,* Baraka writes:

> Blues as an autonomous music had been in a sense inviolable. There was no clear way into it, i.e., its production, not its appreciation, except as concomitant with what seems to me to be the peculiar social, cultural, economic, and emotional experience of a black man in America. The idea of a white blues singer seems an even more violent contradiction of terms than the idea of a middle-class blues singer. The materials of blues were not available to the white American, even though some strange circumstance might prompt him to look for them. It was as if these materials were secret and obscure, and blues a kind of ethno-historic rite as basic as blood.[12]

Although the appeal to direct experience as a test of the legitimacy of one's authority is plausible within a range of applications, I argued and still hold that it also invites plausible objections. It could be argued, for example, that the experiential access that contemporary African Americans have to the experience of slavery or early-twentieth-century sharecropping in the Mississippi Delta is practically as remote, mediated, and indirect as that of any white would-be blues musician. Nor can you argue convincingly in any straightforward way for a "Myth of Racial or Ethnic Memory" whereby mere membership in a "racial" or ethnic group confers special access to the lived experience of ancestors and other former members. I do not hold, for example, as a Jewish American baby boomer that only Jews can adequately comprehend the experience of the holocaust. I have to admit that my own comprehension of the holocaust is limited by my situation. I am not a holocaust survivor. My access to the experience is remote, mediated, and indirect. I have to use my imagination. And yet, on the other hand, distant relatives of mine perished in the camps. And so I find it easier to "identify" with this heritage than others might who are not Jewish. Thus the argument from direct experience as a precondition of authenticity seems to me to morph into something more complex, reaching more deeply into questions of "identity," and will need to be refocused more clearly in those terms.

A Hit Up Side the Head

But before wandering any farther into this labyrinth I want to share a mind-opening experience I had a few years ago. As a result of having published a philosophy paper on the subject of blues and authenticity, I got several invitations to contribute as a panelist or commentator at academic conferences and colloquiums on topics such as authenticity and the ethics of intercultural appropriation. On one such occasion we were at the lovely Asilomar conference facility in Pacific Grove, California, where I was to comment on a paper about Afrocentrism in the postmodern critical theory of jazz.[13] At one stage we were discussing what we were calling the "Marsalis Problem": where to situate Wynton Marsalis vis-à-vis the contested boundaries of jazz and black culture. Did Wynton Marsalis's work, especially at the Lincoln Center, represent the academic canonization and Europeanization of jazz as "America's classical music," and to the extent that it did, could his work be considered faithful to the authentic history of jazz? And we were agreeing that this would be an embarrassing problem for a critical and self-consciously "theoretical" position committed to an Afrocentric and anticolonial account of the history of jazz.[14] I said that I thought the Marsalis Problem was "symptomatic"—the kind of thing you get when people are not really talking about what they're really talking about (if you see what I mean). So, if it wasn't "jazz theory" that we were *really* talking about, what *were* we really talking about? The immediately obvious answer (the answer I would have expected the critical theory of jazz to propose) is "race." At this point I had to confess to a level of discomfort and embarrassment about my own situation. It occurred to me that someone might argue that, as a white American baby boomer and the occupant of a comfortable and privileged academic position as a philosophy teacher, I had no business holding forth in public about how well Wynton Marsalis "represents" his people and their music, and further that all such "academic" gatherings and discussions, such as the one I was addressing, were, to put it politely, impertinent. As ugly as this argument might have looked, I couldn't deny the truth in it—an ugly truth, I suppose, one that made me uncomfortable and eager to change the subject. But it was already far too late for that. The truth was that I hadn't yet considered the problems of race and racism deeply enough to have disposed of them by substituting "ethnicity" for "race."

Coming to Terms with Racism

I have on occasion used the following as a classroom demonstration. First I ask the students in the class to raise their hands if in their opinion the society in which they are situated is a "racist society." In my admittedly limited experience, an overwhelming majority, often unanimous, of the hands invariably goes up. Then I challenge the class, "OK. Now raise your hand if you're a racist." Typically, as one would expect, only a tiny minority of students will identify themselves as racists. As an opening to a discussion this has the effect of establishing a couple of benchmarks. First, that "racism" is already in the working vocabulary of all those present. No one needs to go look up the word in order to understand the question. However, as the discussion progresses it will invariably emerge that there are multiple and often conflicting understandings of what racism precisely and essentially is. Thus, although the question may be generally "understood" by all those present, it may yet fail to be understood by all those present *in the same way*. But most important, it exposes a tendency to "alienate racism." As the discussion progresses it will again invariably emerge that *however* racism is defined it is understood to be worthy of condemnation, and so however we understand racism we are generally and understandably loath to find it in ourselves. This widespread self-perception or self-image as a nonracist situated in a racist society can, indeed should, give rise to some form of cognitive or, more to the point, "*moral*" dissonance. The philosopher Kwame Anthony Appiah describes the conundrum.

> [V]isitors from Mars—or from Malawi—unfamiliar with the Western concept of racism could be excused if they had some difficulty in identifying what exactly racism was. We see it everywhere, but rarely does anyone stop to say what it is, or to explain what is wrong with it. Our visitors from Mars would soon grasp that it had become at least conventional in recent years to express abhorrence for racism. They might even notice that those most often accused of it—members of the South African Nationalist Party, for example—may officially abhor it also. But if they sought in the popular media of our day . . . for an explicit definition of this thing "we" all abhor, they would very likely be disappointed. Now, of course, this would be true of many of our most familiar concepts. *Sister, chair, tomato*—none of these gets defined in the course of our daily business. But the concept of racism is in worse shape than these. For much of what we say about it is, on the face of it, inconsistent.[15]

Appiah goes on, despite the striking irrationality of so many of the racist practices and policies abroad both historically and currently in society, to carefully disentangle racist claims and propositions from racist attitudes and dispositions, and further between several distinct yet more or less coherent racist doctrines so as to subject these to rational critique. His analytical philosophical approach to racism seeks, in other words, to make sense of racism as the practice of reasoning human beings.[16]

He takes this tack, exhibiting some of the values that informed his Oxford training as an analytical philosopher, because:

> To the extent that a practice cannot be rationally reconstructed it ought, surely, to be given up by reasonable people. The right tactic with racism, if you really want to oppose it, is to object to it rationally in the form in which it stands the best chance of meeting objections. The doctrines I want to discuss . . . are worth articulating rationally in order that we can rationally say what we object to in them.[17]

Having also been trained in the traditions of analytical philosophy, I thought, and still do think, that Appiah's approach is fundamentally sound—the very same approach I had adopted in my attempt to defend the authenticity of white blues. And accordingly, I followed Appiah's analysis in my original attempt to finesse the problems of race and racism—by steering the discussion away from arguments expressed in terms of any assumptions or claims that would qualify as racist under Appiah's account and instead toward arguments expressed in terms of ethnicity and ethnocentrism. But an interesting objection can be raised to the effect that Appiah's analytical approach isn't "quick enough" to capture the reality of racism as a living social phenomenon—a set of relationships and practices that survives and evolves by adapting and mutating. The philosopher Paul C. Taylor raised this objection as part of his critique of my original defense of white blues authenticity. Taylor was unsatisfied with my disposition of the "experiential access argument" and with my notion that it presupposed or depended on a dubious Myth of Racial or Ethnic Memory.

> There is no need to posit a myth of racial memory; fairly pedestrian sociological commonplaces will suffice. So it is not the case that, as Rudinow contends, membership in the ethnic group confers special access to the lived experiences of ancestors and other former members; to the contrary, membership is *constituted,* at least in part, by such access—access forced upon contemporary blacks by the persistence of racial and racist conditions.[18]

In other words, in a society in which racism persists, contemporary African Americans are linked to their ancestors by continuity of experience in ways that white Americans do not share. Thus, for example, it can be argued that African American artists like Eric Bibb, who grew up in the midst of the Greenwich Village folk music scene (the son of folk musician Leon Bibb) and honed his chops for twenty years in Sweden, or Corey Harris, born in 1969 and raised in Colorado, with a Bates College degree in anthropology and a MacArthur Fellowship to his credit, remain closer culturally in some crucial respects to Robert Johnson and Muddy Waters than even a Charlie Musselwhite (who is white), despite the fact that Charlie was born in Kosciusko, Mississippi, came of age in Memphis and honed his chops in South Side Chicago blues clubs.

Taylor addressed his objections to my argument from a particular position in the blues audience, the position of an audience member for whom the blues is political discourse, and for whom therefore the racial identity of the performer remained a crucial factor in determining the credibility or authenticity of a blues performance. Here the thrust of Taylor's argument was that race indeed matters aesthetically because race still matters socially and politically.

> [T]he blues is a racial project, and moral deference is owed to black contributions to the project. . . Blues performances in which whites participate fail because the [politically sensitive listener] is unconvinced that the performer can properly bear witness to the racialized moral pain that the blues is about.[19]

What is a "racial project"? The sociologist Howard Winant explains this concept as a means of theorizing the dynamic political struggle over race still ongoing in our society. Interest groups of *all* sorts are to this day engaged in a struggle to interpret and reinterpret the meaning of race through what take shape and evolve as variously "racialized" discourses. Thus a "racial project" is an essentially political project of interpreting racial dynamics while at the same time articulating and advancing some agenda or other for their further development.[20] Racial projects take place and evolve in a wide variety of discursive contexts, including of course the arts, art criticism, and Philosophical aesthetics. The blues, as an art form rooted in America's historical and ongoing political struggle over race, can thus be understood as a racial project (as can the various arguments of Baraka, Gleason, Oliver, Rudinow, and Taylor). More specifically, the blues can be understood as advancing an evolving but consistent agenda for the reform of racial dynamics in America since Reconstruction, always in the direction of racial justice. Given this general interpretive hypothesis, Taylor's argument concludes that white blues is in effect the usurpation of the "voice" of black people. It is talking out of turn.

Now, I have to confess that I didn't get any of this at first. In my published rejoinder to Taylor, I'm embarrassed to say, I was too busy being defensive—of my published argument and, more significantly I now think, of the social position I wanted to assume for myself as a "hip and in the know" white person—to hear any of this clearly, and I took refuge in what Paul Garon derides as the "it's the music, stupid!" defense.[21] In his widely read essay "White Blues," Garon recounts how his own published defense of the editorial policies of *Living Blues* magazine, emphasizing the importance of African American blues artists to the almost complete exclusion of white artists, prompted some outraged readers to holler back, "It's the music, stupid!" and how one of the editors of a rival publication, *Blues Revue Quarterly*, seized on this phrase, made it into a poster, and enshrined it on his wall just to remind him of "what the blues is really about."[22] For Garon, all of this pious concentration on "the music" (meaning what: just the *sounds?*) is a liberal white conceit. Garon, who is white, a long-term blues enthusiast and historian, the author of several important books of blues history and appreciation, and a former editor and regular contributor to *Living Blues* magazine, is also a member of the editorial collective behind *Race Traitor*, a periodical journal whose editorial motto is "Treason to whiteness is loyalty to humanity." The motto stands for a racial project, the "abolition of the white race," where "the white race" refers to a "historically constructed social formation (like royalty)" based on nothing in nature or science but conveying special status and privilege to white people.[23]

This is a very interesting racial project and challenging to the understanding in several ways.[24] Is "treason to whiteness" just the deconstruction of *whiteness* as a racial essence while continuing to recognize and exalt the essence of blackness (remember: "soul")? Doesn't the racial project of repudiating and dismantling white privilege recognize people "of color" as disadvantaged by it? Would it not make more sense to undertake the deconstruction of *race* altogether? Thus a "radical antiracist" agenda might be committed to arguing that there is no objective basis in biology, genetics, or anywhere else in nature or science for *any* system of classification of human beings by "race" and hence no basis for any assignment of status or privilege by race. And yet, given the historical and social fact of racism past and present, the part one can play in *that* racial project seems to depend crucially and absolutely on what color you are. If you are part of the privileged status-beneficiary group, it entails being mindful of the degree to which the privileges you enjoy come to you as a result of your "race" and, to the extent that they do, repudiating those privileges as illegitimate. This is "treason to whiteness." It wouldn't make much sense for people "of color" to take this part in that project, although they might well be moved to applaud it. In my Asilomar epiphany this is what I was beginning to understand.

Which brings me back to the arguments of Baraka, Gleason, and Oliver, whose deeper dimensions I missed the first time around. I'll begin with Baraka. In an essay entitled "Class Struggle in Music," Baraka makes the following disclaimer.

> It is not that we are proselytizing for some "black purity" in the music. Cultural "purity" in anything sounds like backwards cultural nationalism of one sort or another."[25]

In that case, what sort of sense *can* we make of Baraka's insistence on a distinction between authenticity and inauthenticity applied to African American music and based in some way upon considerations of race and/or ethnicity? He says further:

> Just as we can distinguish between German music and French music, we can also distinguish between African-American music and white styles—in the main because they reflect a different aesthetic, reflective of a different *place* in society. . . . Any personal aesthetic is a reflection, in a general sense, of where one is in society.[26]

I take it that Baraka means something like this. In a society that has yet to transcend racism, white people and black people cannot but occupy fundamentally different racially identified social positions. And also the racial projects of both the artist and the intended audience will show up in all of the artistic discourses. Music made by black people for black people differs in significance—if not in discernible formal or sonic ways, though often in these ways, too—from music made by white people for white people. Music made by black people for black people also differs in sound and meaning from music made by black people for white people (compare James Brown to the Supremes). By the same token, when Ellington pointedly refers to his music as simply "American music" that means one thing. It necessarily means something different when Michael Bloomfield pointedly refers to his own music in precisely the same terms. They may each be intending to contribute to a postracist America. Nevertheless, their respective racial projects are not and cannot be identical. Even if they aim at the same end, they are coming from different positions.

Play That Funky Music, White Boy!

All of this points in the direction of an argument I failed to mention in my original defense of white blues authenticity, although it is right there in the early *Rolling Stone* column with which Ralph Gleason first got my attention.

> Here, I thought, were white musicians trying to sound black . . . kids try-ing to sound like Muddy Waters. . . . Now they're trying to sound like Otis Redding and Wilson Pickett. . . . Bloomfield is a fine musician. But he will always be a Jewish boy from Chicago and not a black man from the Delta. Originality is the key. If this nonsense continues, Bloomfield will end up being the Stan Getz or Chet Baker of rock."[27]

At this stage of his career, Mike Bloomfield was using Memphis (more than Clarksdale) as his model, striving in the Electric Flag for a West Coast psychedelic version of a Stax soul band. The Flag even shanghaied Wilson Pickett's drummer, Buddy Miles. So Gleason was correct in his observation that the Flag was imitative and derivative. But that by itself was not Gleason's rationale for dismissing the Flag as an *inauthentic* imi-tation. He goes on to say, "Originality is the key." What I believe he meant by "originality" is a kind of artistic "authenticity of voice." In this chapter up until now, *authenticity* has been used to refer to "the kind of credibil-ity that comes from being *appropriately related* to an original source." But here *authenticity* means something more like *being* original, something like "speaking as an artist in a voice distinctively your own," or to put it more simply, "being true to yourself."[28] This notion illuminates the ex-ception Gleason makes for Mose Allison in his essay "Can the White Man Sing the Blues?"

> Mose Allison, a white Mississippian . . . is acceptable to many jazz and blues people as a blues singer because he is not assuming an accent not his own.[29]

Mose Allison is not trying to sound like anyone other than Mose Allison. He is just being Mose Allison, expressing himself.

And yet Mose Allison has absorbed the influences of blues and jazz and integrated them into his music. Mose Allison could not be the Mose Allison we have come to know without the blues and jazz traditions he has entered into. And Mose Allison's music is bluesy and jazzy enough for Gleason, whose strong hint that Bloomfield should stick to klezmer music and bar mitzvah gigs calls to mind the example of black jazz clarinetist Don Byron. Byron is an eclectic musical omnivore who in addition to jazz has digested classical, klezmer, ragtime, and salsa music. As an undergraduate student at the New England Conservatory, Byron joined the Klezmer Conservatory Band, about which he says:

> I immediately responded to the mischief in the music, where the clarinet would play the most out thing he could think of . . . [and] as time went by, I developed my own voice in that language.[30]

So the question now seems to have become one of fashioning a personal and artistic identity and developing or finding one's own voice particularly in culturally unfamiliar idiolects and discourses.

Finding and developing one's own artistic voice is not easy even in familiar cultural spaces using one's native language and idiolect. Often one is confronted by the rigid orthodoxies of one's own tradition. Consider the experience of folk singer Rosalie Sorrells.

> I had accepted the idea that you should keep yourself out of the performance when you sang folk songs: "The song—not the singer." But at the [1966] Newport Festival . . . it became clear to me that you take it all in, turn it over and over until you find your own voice, and you take your place in the chain. The music does not need to be protected.[31]

As the interviewer David Whiteis explains, Sorrells was surprised at the resistance she and her colleagues often had to overcome in order to introduce new original material of their own composition. Sorrells again:

> Jean Ritchie wrote a whole lot of great songs about where she came from [in rural Kentucky], marvelous songs, and when she put them out she said they were written by an uncle of hers (because she got so much shit for writing her own songs)! I take it now, when I look back on it, as a control-freak thing. Purists are usually people who haven't touched life very much.[32]

Or consider the similar reaction of the folk music establishment to the journey of Bob Dylan, as described here by Greil Marcus.

> He first made himself known to more than a few in the early 1960s, in New York City, as the self-proclaimed heir to Dust Bowl balladeer Woody Guthrie. . . . As the familiar standards of the folk music revival faded from his repertoire, he became . . . the voice of the civil rights movement; then he became the voice of his times and the conscience of his generation. . . . All of this was suspended in the air—and, for thou-

sands who had followed Dylan's progress as a confirmation of their own, dashed to the ground—when in July 1965 the folk singer who once dressed only in fraying cotton appeared onstage at the Newport Folk Festival with an electric guitar in his hands and a high-style leather jacket on his back ("a sellout jacket"). . . . [T]he result was an uproar: a torrent of shouts, curses, refusal, damnation, and perhaps most of all confusion.[33]

In some cases a perceived "betrayal of the cultural cause" is denounced; in other cases defenses of cultural space are erected against trespass by inauthentic interlopers; in some cases a Platonic-seeming quest is undertaken for cultural essences whereby to mark off the "real thing" from the inauthentic imitation and/or dilution. What is essential to all such critical positions is concern with the delineation and defense of cultural boundaries or thresholds and only incidentally, if at all, with the artist's "authenticity of voice."

But always and inevitably the artist faces the profound challenges of self-knowledge and self-acceptance essential to the attainment of mature and responsible adulthood. All cultural transmission—literate, oral, whatever—involves imitation. So every new generation of culture in any tradition will be deeply imitative and derivative. It's worth noting that, although the Butterfield band is everybody's first and favorite example of a "white blues band," it was always racially mixed. The classification "white" flows from the fact that the bandleader, who sang lead vocal and played one of the lead solo instruments (harmonica), was a white man. But let us not forget that Paul Butterfield got to be bandleader in large part because he commanded respect as a player. You don't get Howlin' Wolf's rhythm section if you can't play. And Butterfield earned respect as a player in a way typical of oral musical traditions generally. He apprenticed, and got better and better, until his playing began to do credit to Junior Wells and Little Walter. Finding one's own authentic voice, then, is a rite of passage into maturity. Listen to how this is described by jazz pianist Ben Sidran (who sounds a lot like Mose Allison, by the way).

I was playing to find me—or to feel me. To feel whatever it was I felt . . . I had accidentally stumbled on the real meaning of music in my life . . . and for the first time I no longer wanted to sound like McCoy Tyner or Horace Silver or Sonny Clark. I just wanted to discover what I was feeling. As inconsequential as it may seem, I was listening. I went back to playing, but this time I accepted my limitations. . . . Each problem that came up was my own, something interesting to solve rather than an indictment of my lack. Owning my bad habits and being entertained by my lines, I was able to hear myself, perhaps for the first time, and to say what I wanted to say with authority. I didn't sound like anybody else. I sounded like me, for better or worse. The birth of a personal style, it seems, comes from this acceptance of who you are rather than who you dream of being.[34]

So in this way Gleason's critique of the Flag's debut at the Monterey Pop Festival amounted to "Grow up, Mike!" And a reconstruction of the scene culminating in that day's performance is helpful to see how much justice there was in Gleason's assessment.[35] For one thing, due mostly to Bloomfield's notoriety, the Flag was already being touted as a "super-group" although it had yet to record or perform in public. The entrepreneur Albert Grossman—who managed Bob Dylan and Janis Joplin and had glommed onto Bloomfield when he was recording in New York on Dylan's 1965 album *Highway 61 Revisited*—swooped in to control the band's recording and publishing interests and was orchestrating a bidding war between the Atlantic and Columbia record labels. Monterey Pop had attracted one of the largest audiences, some fifty thousand, ever assembled for a program of music at that time. The Flag was scheduled to close the eight-hour afternoon program on the second day, following Canned Heat, Janis Joplin with Big Brother and the Holding Company, Country Joe and the Fish, Al Kooper, the Butterfield Blues Band, Quicksilver Messenger Service, and the Steve Miller Band. The evening program to come would include Moby Grape, the Byrds, Jefferson Airplane, and Booker T and the MGs with the Mar-Keys and Otis Redding. And the Sunday program was to feature an afternoon raga by Ravi Shankar, followed in the evening by the Blues Project, Buffalo Springfield, the Who, the Grateful Dead, and Jimi Hendrix, who set fire to his guitar onstage. According to Barry Goldberg, the Flag's keyboard player:

> By the time we actually played, everyone was so anxious and nervous and freaked out that it probably wasn't our best set. . . . [T]hings were faster than they should have been, because Michael had a tendency, when he was nervous, to count things off at twice the speed.[36]

And here is Bloomfield's own assessment.

> I was jacked up on adrenaline. It was the end of a long afternoon, and we were the last act to play, and we were scared shitless. Everybody we saw were old friends of ours, and it was their greatest hour. Steve Miller did a set. No one could beat it. Moby Grape came after Miller, and between guitar breaks they were giving each other high fives, right when

they were doing their show. Then Butterfield came on. He had horns. He was better, he was just—we couldn't follow any of them. And then we came out, and we weren't very good. We really weren't. We were too nervous. First number, digging my pick in and getting it caught in the string—oh, it was just so terrible. But they loved us. What a lesson that was. . . . I have to disassociate myself from the hype. Monterey Pop was the perfect example of hype. . . . And this was the Electric Flag's first major gig. Probably the biggest gig we ever played. And we played rotten, man. I ain't jiving you. We really sounded lousy. And the people loved it. And I could see—oh my God, the hype, the image, the shuck, the vibes.[37]

Bloomfield, still in his midtwenties, had already distinguished himself as a guitar player with a unique and original voice on his instrument. So let us just say that Monterey Pop was another "learning experience" for him.

There are some musical genres where singing is like acting. Let us suppose that moving an audience emotionally depends on a performance in which real emotional energy is invested. But no one will expect you to have grown up in the court of a Japanese emperor in order to sing the role of Yum-Yum in Gilbert and Sullivan's *The Mikado*. No one expects a real Ethiopian princess in the role of *Aida*. Although lived experience and imaginative empathy may inform technique, the name of the game is credible simulation. The actor's job is to support the audience's willing suspension of disbelief. The blues, and also gospel, impose more stringent or at least different requirements. In these idioms, technique plays a more subservient role. In order to effectively arouse emotion in the audience it is essential to put your *self* into the performance. Whatever you are trying to say, you have to "really mean it." This, once again, is what I take to be the deeper point of Charlie Parker's widely quoted remark about "paying dues." I have sometimes wondered, for example, how to approach certain blues lyrics. How does a polite and reserved Englishman like Eric Clapton bring himself to sing a line like "I'm gonna beat my woman till I get satisfied"?[38]

To be authentic in the sense we are currently exploring—to be, in a word, "real"—you have above all else to be honest with yourself. Honest about who you are and where you come from and about what your situation is and what your intentions are. In the language of chapter 1, the locus of one's awareness and the agency of one's actions must become fully integrated—one's soul must manifest integrity. Only then, as Sidran observed, can you say what you have to say "with authority." Can white people play the blues with this kind of authenticity?

One of the passages that opened my mind to the need for a deeper reconsideration of my position on this question is the closing passage of philosopher Ted Cohen's book *Jokes*. Cohen's theory is that when we share a joke with someone we create a bond of intimacy. Cohen's book is, of course, full of jokes—including a lot of what are sometimes called "ethnic jokes." At the end of his book he ponders the questions of taste and morality that inevitably arise in connection with the telling of such jokes, and in this connection he tells the following story.

> The Secret Service has an opening in its ranks, needing to recruit some-one to join those who guard the President of the United States. They post a notice in bulletins for government workers, and soon they re-ceive three applications, one from an F.B.I. man, one from an agent from the Bureau of Alcohol, Tobacco, and Firearms, and a third from a Chicago city policeman. Each of the three is given a qualifying exami-nation, beginning with the F.B.I. man.
>
> The F.B.I. man is given a revolver and told to go into the adjacent room and shoot whomever he finds there. When he has been gone only a few minutes, the F.B.I. man returns, saying, "You must be out of your minds! That's my wife. I'm not shooting her."
>
> "Fine," say the examiners. "You must be a good family man, but you're not cut out for the Secret Service."
>
> Next the A.T.F. agent is sent in with the revolver, with the same in-structions to shoot whomever he finds in the next room. He too returns in minutes exclaiming, "That's the mother of my children, you lu-natics."
>
> "Good for you," say the examiners. "Enjoy your career in the bureau and continue looking after your wife; but we can't use you in the Secret Service."
>
> Finally, the Chicago policeman is given the same test. When he has been in the adjacent room for about ten minutes, sounds are heard, the sounds of struggle and muffled groaning. A few minutes later the cop reappears, looking somewhat mussed, and says, "Some moron put blanks in the gun; I had to strangle her."[39]

Cohen's philosophical point in relating this joke becomes clear when he reveals that he learned this joke from his wife, who worked as a court-room sketch artist for a Chicago television station and learned it from a Chicago policeman on her way to court.[40] The "moral" of the story for Cohen is that the dynamics and morality of joking, and even the very *meaning* of the joke, depend absolutely upon who tells the joke to whom and under what circumstances.[41] Whatever it may mean when shared among Chicago policemen, it would mean something else when told by a Chicago police*man* to a Chicago police*woman* or by a Chicago policeman to a civilian and so on. In much the same way, I have come to think, the significance of performances in African American (and other culturally identifiable) idioms may well have something to do with the racial and/or ethnic identities of both performers and audiences. But that *still* leaves open the question of whether white people can sing the blues with the kind of authenticity under consideration here. In principle, I'd say, yes. It's a matter of personal integrity. It's a matter of knowing who you are and who you're addressing and what you have to say and then saying it with integrity.

In 1998 and 1999, when I was in my fifties, I was hired and got to tour as the piano player in Elvin Bishop's band. Elvin is today one of the most enduring and intriguing in the long line of "white bluesmen" that began with the Paul Butterfield Blues Band, of which he was a founding member. Of the many memorable lessons I learned in that context, one that stands out to me now as especially relevant, was taught to me by Ed Earley, Elvin's trombone player. Ed, who had studied French horn at the University of Missouri and taught music in the Saint Louis public school system before hitting the road with Albert King in 1979, explained to me once that one of the worst things you can do in blues is to act like you *don't* know. What he was talking about was a tendency among white musicians with some training in music to feign musical illiteracy, hoping to sound more "authentic" in their imitations of the expressive achievements of those who were relatively untutored in music.[42] This does those you are imitating no credit. And it does YOU no credit, so what's the point? Be yourself. Bring everything you've got to the work.

This reminds me of a point philosopher Stanley Cavell made about the nature of appreciation in general: "A measure of the quality of a work is the quality of the work it arouses." I take this to mean that in responding to a work, and especially when we imitate, we should try to be "appreciative." We should try to produce work that does credit to the artist whose work we appreciate, and we should intend in our own work to inspire and call forth further appreciative responses in turn. That is the proper and respectful way to enter into and contribute to an artistic tradition.[43]

Call-and-Response: Soul on a National Scale

The central analogy in Plato's *Republic* is the one introduced in Book II between the polis (or city-state) and the individual human soul. It is one of Plato's most powerful and enduring comparisons, marvelous for the light it sheds in both directions. Much can be learned about the inner life of the individual human soul by studying the dynamics of the political and cultural life of a community. This is the way Socrates intends the analogy to function when he first introduces it. But the reverse is also true. It is often quite illuminating to frame questions about the political and cultural life of a community, a city or a nation or a people, as questions about the state of the community's collective soul. Expanding the questions in this way, I should point out, does not stretch or stress the minimalist definition of "the soul" I have been assuming since chapter 1. To the extent that a community can manifest states or conditions of collective consciousness or awareness and to the extent that a community can exercise voluntary agency as a collective entity, one can speak of one's community—of one's family or tribe or nation, even one's species—as a sentient being, a being with a collective soul. What were America's conditions of awareness and political will after World War II? How did these conditions develop and progress through the 1950s and 1960s? And how were these conditions expressed and manifested in the popular culture of the period?

The British blues historian Paul Oliver wrote of the white blues emerging in the 1960s:

> It is unlikely that [the blues] will survive through the imitations of the young white college copyists . . . whose relation to the blues is that of the "trad" jazz band to the music of New Orleans: sterile and derivative.[44]

Derivative, yes, but sterile? Hardly. Witness what the first and most famous of the white blues bands did to American folk music when Bob Dylan went electric at the Newport Folk Festival in 1965, using Bloomfield and the Butterfield band's rhythm section as his backup band.

By 1967's Summer of Love, the generation arriving at maturity not only in America but worldwide was challenging entrenched power and was openly and expressly repudiating racism, sexism, and unjust war. Monterey Pop was exemplary of the extraordinarily high level of intercultural cross-fertilization that characterized the popular music of the 1960s, which poured forth an unprecedented array of new stylistic hybrids and pointed the way toward what is now called "world music." White blues bands were an integral part of this. One could make an argument that all of this stems directly from the American experiment in musical miscegenation that produced rock & roll and of which the Butterfield band and Mike Bloomfield's Electric Flag were further examples. In the short documentary film introducing the Smithsonian Institution's Memphis Rock and Soul Museum exhibition, legendary Memphian Jim Dickinson made this observation.

> "The" world was just about to change. . . . I think in the early 1950s the races were reaching for each other culturally in Memphis. It was happening right in front of our eyes. . . . We're talking about more than just white kids listening to black music. We're talking about the birth of Rock & Roll.[45]

Received mythology has it that rock & roll originated as the bastard offspring of the blues and hillbilly country music. And often this story is personified in Elvis, Buddy Holly, Jerry Lee Lewis, and Carl Perkins—young white men fascinated by African American music. But there is another side to this story. Chuck Berry remembers as the crucial turning point in his career the night that:

> Curiosity provoked me to lay a lot of that [country and western swing music] on our predominantly black audience, and some of the club-goers started whispering "Who is that black hillbilly at the Cosmo?" . . . After they laughed at me a few times, they began requesting the hillbilly stuff and enjoyed trying to dance to it. If you ever want to see something that is far out, watch a crowd of colored folk, half high, wholeheartedly doing the hoe-down, barefooted.[46]

Notice how this turns rock & roll's racialized origination myth, according to which rock & roll happens when a white singer tries to sound black to a white audience, on its head. In a similar vein, we might note that black Memphian O. B. McClinton recorded four albums of straight country music for Stax's subsidiary label Enterprise Records, placing fifteen singles on the country charts.

Thus we return to the critical consensus that the stylistic merger between gospel music and the secular forms of popular music—blues, rhythm & blues, and rock & roll—that became known as soul music transcended mere (disposable) pop fashion, serving rather as the forceful and integral musical soundtrack to the American civil rights struggle of the 1950s and 1960s. For me, and many of my generation, the performances of Otis Redding, Janis Joplin, the Who, Jimi Hendrix, the Electric Flag, Ravi Shankar, and company at Monterey Pop established a high-water mark—a stirring of consciousness in the collective soul. But darker forces were also stirring in the struggle over America's political will. Nine months after Monterey Pop, Dr. Martin Luther King Jr., having come out against the American invasion of Vietnam, was assassinated in

Memphis while lending his support to the struggle for improved working conditions for the city's largely black garbage workers.

As we shall see in the next chapter, the struggle for America's soul is deep and treacherous and ongoing. And it continues, of course, to this day. The inauguration of America's first president of color was followed also by a surge in hysterical reactionary political rhetoric and a likewise predictable uptick in what appear to be politically motivated violence and hate crimes.[47]

CHAPTER 7

Speaking in Tongues
(Isn't This All Too Straussian?)

But the gist of it was that Socrates was forcing them to admit that the same man might be capable of writing both comedy and tragedy—that the tragic poet might be a comedian as well. —PLATO, SYMPOSIUM, 223D

For a man of independent thought can utter his views in public and remain unharmed, provided he moves with circumspection. He can even utter them in print without incurring any danger, provided he is capable of writing between the lines. —LEO STRAUSS, PERSECUTION AND THE ART OF WRITING

The blues will forever be here. Just like gospel. You can't get rid of something that is true. —JIMMY MCCRACKLIN

The scene is Agathon's house at dawn, amid the wreckage of an all-night drinking party. The three individuals who remain conscious enough to carry on a conversation are Agathon (who represents tragedy), Aristophanes the comedian, and Socrates—the comic figure and tragic hero of the Platonic corpus, who represents, in this exquisitely contrived context, a style or mode of communication unique in its capacity to embody the cleansing and therapeutic effects of both tragedy and comedy in a single text: irony. Thus the passage quoted in the epigram may be read as a veiled piece of Platonic self-disclosure and as exemplary of itself.

I had my "midlife career crisis" in the early 1980s. In my twenties, I had managed to secure a position as a junior faculty member in the Department of Philosophy at Dartmouth College but did not achieve tenure or promotion beyond the rank of assistant professor. And so, in 1980, as America took a hard right turn, welcoming to Washington a

Hollywood production of political "conservatism" in the person of California's governor Ronald Reagan, I went the other way, returning to my hometown on the left coast with no career prospects and no plan other than to join a rock & roll band and play the white-boy baby-boomer blues.

To break my fall, I had managed to gain admission to a summer seminar sponsored by the National Endowment for the Humanities on the topic of the philosophy of Socrates. The seminar was led by the preeminent classics scholar Gregory Vlastos and was to take place at the University of California in Berkeley. This was perfect for me in so many ways! I got really commodious interim transitional housing right in the middle of the San Francisco Bay Area at no cost—a summer house-sit in the north Berkeley hills arranged through the UC Faculty Club. I had a summer stipend, so there was no immediate need to search for a "day job." I had three or four morning meetings and an occasional afternoon or evening function per week that I was expected to attend. But there was also a fair amount of time available to check out bands, answer musician-wanted ads, attend auditions, go to jam sessions, and generally try to get hooked up musically.

Everybody in the seminar was expected to present a piece of scholarly work at some point during the ten-week course. My plan was to investigate Socratic irony. More specifically, I proposed to explore certain Platonic passages I thought contained important "ironic" dimensions. One of these passages is in *Republic* Book III, where I think I see a deliberate and strategically placed instance of the famous Epimenedes Paradox.[1] I call it Plato's Paradox of Mimetic Writing. It occurs during the discussion of the education of the guardians. Starting in Book II, the guardians' educational curriculum is considered in stages, beginning with what we may call the "content." The stories themselves must be carefully selected to present the guardians with only good role models.[2] After the content of the literature has been cleansed, next comes "form" or "style" or "mode of presentation." It matters not just what the stories are but also how they are told. Socrates distinguishes two forms or styles or modes of narration, simple and "mimetic" (imitative), which sometimes come mixed or blended together. What is "mimetic" narration? Socrates offers an example from Homer's *Iliad* to illustrate.

> Then you know that up to these lines, "And he entreated all the Acheans, but especially Atreus' two sons . . ." the poet himself speaks and doesn't attempt to turn our thought elsewhere, as though someone other than he were speaking. But in what follows he speaks as though

he himself were Chryses and tries as hard as he can to make it seem to us that it's not Homer speaking, but the priest, an old man.[3]

Mimetic narrative, then, is narrative in which the author does not address the reader in his own voice, instead deploying the voices of dramatis personae. In the ensuing discussion it is decided that mimetic narrative and all forms of presentation based upon it (all forms of imitation, acting, for example) are to be excluded from the curriculum, and mimetic artists will not be allowed to enter the model city.[4] This, by the way, is a primary source of the traditional reading of Plato as an enemy of the mimetic arts.[5] The prohibition gets further support in Book VII in the famous Allegory of the Cave (where mimetic illusions effectively pass for reality) and is reiterated at the beginning of Book X.[6]

All of this invites the question, "What are we to make of the fact that, according to the distinction as just presented, the *Republic* itself is a mimetic narrative?" Therein lies the paradox. When I went to my tutorial with Professor Vlastos, he heard me out but then, to my complete surprise, told me I would not be allowed to present these ideas before the assembled seminar. I was dumbfounded. When I asked why not, he told me, "It's all too 'Straussian.'" I was still dumbfounded. At the time I had not yet read anything by or even about Leo Strauss.

While I was in Berkeley that summer, I had an opportunity to visit with rock critic and historian Greil Marcus, who was also living in Berkeley at the time. I told him I was on my way out of the academy proper but still reading philosophy while I looked for gigs. In my state of "academic disaffection," I told him I thought Socrates had more in common with Lenny Bruce and Frank Zappa than with most of the professional academics I had encountered in my career. I told him that I had a mischievous "conceptual art" project in mind—a rock & roll musical entitled *The Song and Dance of Socrates—in Which the Love of Wisdom Leads to the Discovery That "The Unlived Life Ain't Worth Examining"* (to be sung to the tune "The Old Gray Mare").[7] He told me, "You should read some Leo Strauss." What a coincidence!

The Ideas and Influence of Leo Strauss

Who is (or was) Leo Strauss? A more obscure but intriguing figure in the history of ideas would be hard to identify indeed! Strauss's published work is comprised almost entirely of dense commentaries on difficult texts by other figures, particularly in the history of political philosophy. Strauss presents himself essentially as a scholarly *interpreter* of other philosophers' political writings. Strauss's own philosophy, then, is first and foremost a hermeneutic (a systematic approach to interpretation) with a set of corollary implications deriving from the application of that hermeneutic approach to classic texts of political philosophy.

Strauss's work would almost certainly be gathering much dust in the library stacks as obscure secondary source material were it not for the fact that during his tenure at the University of Chicago, where he taught from 1949 to 1968, he managed to spawn a sort of "cult" of followers and disciples, who eventually came to occupy positions of considerable influence in American neoconservative politics. Indeed, by the turn of the millennium a small number of so-called Straussians had climbed to the very pinnacle of power on the world stage, operating influentially not very far behind the scenes, especially during the administration of George W. Bush.[8]

Arguably the most important of these individuals is Paul Wolfowitz. As deputy secretary of defense under Donald Rumsfeld during the first term of the Bush administration, Wolfowitz was a major architect and proponent of the Iraq War. Then in 2005, as Iraq descended into chaos, Wolfowitz parachuted out of the Department of Defense into the presidency of the World Bank—a position he lasted in for two years before being hounded back to the think tanks. As a graduate student at the University of Chicago, Wolfowitz studied Plato and Montesquieu under Leo Strauss. What led Wolfowitz in that direction was his undergraduate encounter at Cornell University with another of Strauss's students, the political philosopher Allan Bloom. In molding the Bush administration's Iraq policies, Wolfowoitz was supported and assisted by yet another Straussian, Abram Shulsky, who directed the Pentagon's Office of Special Plans, an agency created by Wolfowitz and Donald Rumsfeld as a kind of "short-order intelligence kitchen." In that capacity Shulsky reported to Wolfowitz in the Department of Defense. Still another Straussian, Leon Kass, became the chairman of the President's Council on Bioethics and in that capacity helped define the Bush administration's policies on stem-cell research and birth control. And of course we are already well aware of Allan Bloom, who studied the classics with Leo Strauss at the University of Chicago, taught political philosophy to Wolfowitz and others at Cornell during the tumultuous 1960s, published the translation of Plato's *Republic* that informs this essay, and in his best-selling book *The Closing of the American Mind* bitterly denounced baby-boom American popular culture, especially rock & roll, as morally, intellectually, and spiritually decadent.

What really pumps up the intrigue, while elevating this discussion above the level of guilt-by-association gossip, is the notion that behind the American political movement called neoconservatism, and the approach to policy formation that came to define the George W. Bush administration and the policy agendas it pursued during the first eight years of the twenty-first century, there might lie an actual political philosophy—and not only that but one claiming to contain an ancient secret teaching. This is, as it turns out, exactly what self-identified "Straussians"—as well as some of their most strident critics—have been saying in the intersection of the scholarly academic and public policy discourses. What might that political philosophy be? And in what might its crucial ancient secret teaching possibly consist? With questions like *these* now before us, we will do well to proceed with great caution.

It would be sensible to consult Leo Strauss's own writings. But given the intrigue and the controversy surrounding the topic, Strauss's oeuvre now sits like a forbidden planet at the center of a dark and cloudy atmosphere—a swirling fog of intimidating interpretive commentary and controversy. According to some commentators, Strauss's own writings pose legendary and nearly insurmountable obstacles to understanding. The historian Theodore Roszak observes:

> His scholarship is pedantic in the extreme—dense subtle, complex—as indeed are all the works he spent his lifetime elucidating. Even as academic literature, Strauss is among the most demanding (and fatiguing) of writers.[9]

Writing for *Harper's* magazine near the end of Bush's first term in office, contributing editor Earl Shorris gave this assessment.

> Strauss is more difficult to read than almost anyone, including Wittgenstein, Heidegger. And Joyce. . . . [Strauss] believed in what you and I would call bad writing. He buttered it with the word "esoteric," but "bad" is the right word, unless you prefer "lousy." Here was a man who did not want to be understood by any but the few, his disciples. . . . In the only book he wrote in anything close to plain English, *Persecution and the Art of Writing*, Leo Strauss advised his readers not to write in plain English. Strauss followed his own advice. Convoluted, contradictory, arcane, clubfooted writing was his game. He worked at it. He skulked in the dark corners of exposition, making it all but impossible for anyone to discern exactly what he thought. In all the history of the English language there had never been a man—not merely a man, a professor at a great university—who so publicly opposed clarity and so brilliantly demonstrated his talent for obfuscation. In his chosen field he was a giant.[10]

Obviously Shorris is no Straussian. In a commentary published in *The Public Interest,* two rather well established Straussians, Steven Lenzner and the ubiquitous conservative pundit William Kristol, admonish their readers:

> The only way to begin to understand Leo Strauss's political thought is by studying his writings. This may seem a simple rule of common sense. Yet a glance at the current controversy of Strauss's supposed influence on contemporary American politics and foreign policy suggests that this rule is easily ignored.[11]

They then go on to interpret those writings for their unfortunate readers to a length of twenty pages of dense scholarly commentary—providing in effect a guided tour of the history of political theory as understood by Strauss (according to these two of his leading contemporary "apologists") with stops at Xenophon, Weber, Hobbes, Locke, Rousseau, Burke, and Machiavelli—thereby contributing considerable additional fog to the atmosphere. Roszak observes ironically:

> There is something almost comic about the fear that Straussians have of revealing the hidden teachings of their mentor. There are few writers who are as well protected from popularity as is Strauss. If there are esoteric messages in his work, they are safely sequestered from the public.[12]

What Was Leo Strauss *Really* Up To?

There is certainly a pervasive dark perversity about Straussianism. Academic Straussians do conduct and express themselves very much in the manner of a cult. There are code words galore and insiders and outsiders and, for all I know, a secret handshake. It can, of course, be plausibly argued that the perversity of Straussianism comes directly from Strauss himself and that the perversity of the intellectual content of Straussianism is what drives and informs the twisted behavior. Professor Vlastos certainly held to this view, a view presented in persuasive detail by Myles Burnyeat.[13] On this reading of Strauss and his followers it becomes especially difficult to appreciate *anything* of value in the constellation of ideas that comprise the intellectual content of Straussianism. However, there is also the possibility that Strauss had ideas and interests that differed in important ways from those of his followers, so that something of intellectual value, especially to my own topics, might be lost or obscured by simply submerging him in his rather twisted legacy. This is the possibility I will explore now.

By their very nature as academic interpretations of difficult and diverse classical sources of political theory, Strauss's actual writings would be by any measure relatively inaccessible. But he is certainly nowhere near as bad a writer as Shorris makes him out to be. Consider, for example, this passage, the opening lines of Strauss's commentary on Plato's *Republic.*

> Generally speaking, we can know the thought of a man only through his speeches oral or written. We can know Aristotle's political philosophy through his *Politics.* Plato's *Republic* on the other hand, in contradistinction to the *Politics,* is not a treatise but a dialogue among people other than Plato. Whereas in reading the *Politics* we hear Aristotle all the time, in reading the *Republic* we hear Plato never. In none of his dialogues does Plato ever say anything. Hence we cannot know from them what Plato thought. If someone quotes a passage from the dialogues in order to prove that Plato held such and such a view he acts about as reasonably as if he were to assert that according to Shakespeare life is a tale told by an idiot, full of sound and fury, signifying nothing.[14]

Strauss's point is just that Plato's writings, like Shakespeare's plays, are mimetic texts—dramas that therefore do not disclose their author's actual views in any direct and straightforward way. Although some may find this point challenging and hard to swallow, Strauss's presentation of it is in any case quite clear and straightforward.[15]

Reading "Between the Lines"

So much for "bad" writing. But this brings us to the brink of Strauss's central interpretive idea: the concept of "esoteric" writing. A text written "esoterically" is one that presents a relatively accessible, superficial, or popular "exoteric" teaching as a facade behind which lies buried, or veiled, a secret "esoteric" teaching—the hidden or forbidden truth. As Strauss elaborates in *Persecution and the Art of Writing,* literary devices and strategies for "writing between the lines" naturally arise under conditions of political repression and persecution. Strauss's account of this process is framed within an analysis of authoritarian orthodoxy. How is it possible for an authoritarian regime to accomplish large-scale indoctrination and maintain thought control over a repressed population? It cannot be by direct compulsion.

> For compulsion does not produce conviction. It merely paves the way for conviction by silencing contradiction.[16]

In other words you cannot compel belief. Belief will be and must be chosen voluntarily. Human beings do not easily surrender their "intellectual independence."[17] Thus, as Strauss goes on to argue, thought control on a mass scale can be accomplished only to the extent that the regime can control the boundaries within which the people may exercise their freedom of thought, that is to say, by controlling the spectrum of opinion expressible in public discourse. This can be an effective means of controlling public opinion because in most cases intellectual independence is exercised in choosing from among a "menu of options" and only in the rare case to create new options "outside the box."

> What is called freedom of thought in a large number of cases amounts to—and even for all practical purposes consists of—the ability to choose between two or more different views presented by the small minority of people who are public speakers or writers. If this choice is prevented, the only kind of intellectual independence of which many people are capable is destroyed, and that is the only freedom of thought which is of political importance.[18]

So the crucial idea is that the regime must control the spectrum of opinion expressed in public in order to effectively herd public opinion into orthodox alignment.

But there will always be a few whose thinking will not be herded. In any population under any political regime in any age there will be at least a few whose thinking will not be confined within the limitations imposed upon public discourse. Even in the most authoritarian regimes willing to use the most violent and repressive of measures to silence dissent, as in the Spanish Inquisition, there will be some who dissent from official orthodoxy. And those of truly independent mind will find artful ways to express themselves.

> Persecution, then, cannot prevent independent thinking. It cannot prevent even the expression of independent thought. For it is as true today as it was more than two thousand years ago that it is a safe venture to tell the truth one knows to benevolent and trustworthy acquaintances, or more precisely, to reasonable friends. Persecution cannot prevent even public expression of heterodox truth, for a man of independent thought can utter his views in public and remain unharmed, provided he moves with circumspection. He can even utter them in print without incurring any danger, provided he is capable of writing between the lines.[19]

An esoteric text, then is composed very deliberately and carefully, the author being mindful that it may come into the hands of more than one kind of reader. It may at some point come to the attention of the authorities, and so its heterodoxy must be encrypted. But these encrypted heresies are the most crucial of the meanings the text has to convey, and so clues and hints and guidance to them are also built into the text. The author will make use of literary devices such as pseudonyms, irony, mimetic dialogue, apparent contradictions, crucial omissions, inexact repetitions, and other "obtrusively enigmatic features" to alert the careful reader.[20]

Thus an esoteric composition will actually sort its audience into those who can find their way to the forbidden truths and those who fail to do so. Strauss reads Plato as a paradigm example of an esoteric writer. In the 1980s, when I finally came to read and understand Strauss's theory of esoteric writing, I could also understand why Professor Vlastos didn't want to touch it. The notion of a text that sorts its readers into categories according to whether they get the secret hidden messages or not arguably sets up an a priori and unverifiable interpretive litmus test: any reader who doubts the esoteric reading thereby discredits himself as a reader. What will stop this from degenerating into or begetting a credulous conspiracy cult led by a priesthood of haughty charlatans?[21]

Still I could not and cannot deny that Plato presents some remarkably artful challenges as a writer. Of the clever literary devices that seem particularly well suited to presenting while at the same time obscuring one's meaning, three in particular—mimetic writing, paradox, and irony—are apparent, and deployed crucially, throughout Plato's work. For me it follows from the undeniable presence of these devices in Plato's writing that Plato's meaning is not readily available on its surfaces. Once one recognizes that the central character, Socrates—the only credible candidate for the role of Plato's mouthpiece—is a master of irony, and is indeed so often and so unmistakably ironic in tone as he converses with his interlocutors that it becomes difficult to tell when he is *not* being ironic, one cannot help but be puzzled. One can no longer hope to find Plato's meaning straightforwardly expressed in the speeches of *any* of his characters. Once one has recognized that Plato deploys characters in his dialogues and indeed that nearly everything Plato wrote is, according to the account presented in *Republic* Book III, mimetic, and once that very mode of presentation has been called into question as untrustworthy, again one cannot help but be puzzled. One is *forced* to deal with these literary artifacts. Indeed it is *in these very puzzles* that one comes finally into contact with the author, Plato. The puzzles are not attributable to the characters. They are the work of the author.

The moment one begins to talk about secret teachings, in Plato or anywhere else, people will immediately want to know what the content of the secret teachings might possibly be. However, if in approaching Plato we seek guidance from Strauss, here is what we get. Strauss counsels patience.

> One cannot separate the understanding of Plato's teaching from the understanding of the form in which it is presented. One must pay as much attention to the How as to the What. At any rate to begin with one must pay even greater attention to the "form" than to the "substance," since the meaning of the "substance" depends on the "form." One must postpone one's concern with the most serious questions (the philosophic questions) in order to become engrossed in the study of a merely literary question.[22]

Strauss says that before we can satisfy our urge to know the secret teaching we must go back to the literary question and patiently apply ourselves to solving the puzzle posed by the composition we are trying to understand. Only then can we expect it to disclose to us its hidden teaching. Exasperating perhaps—but basically sound advice. Then Strauss offers an interesting tidbit of encouragement.

> Still, there is a connection between the literary question and the philosophic question. The literary question, the question of presentation, is concerned with a kind of communication.[23]

The literary question, in other words, is not tangential to the central philosophical questions, themes, and teaching. If Plato is communicating in an artful and indirect way, his compositional strategies and tactics may very well pertain to his subject matter and to what he has to say about it. And indeed, Plato may be artfully and indirectly *explaining himself* as an author in his use of puzzling literary strategies and devices. This oblique self-referential turn occurs, I believe, in the passage from the *Symposium* quoted at the beginning of this chapter, as well as in the Paradox of Mimetic Writing, and of course elsewhere in Plato's work. At this juncture it is important to note that while such literary devices make the writing challenging to our understanding they don't add up to or boil down to "bad writing." Plato is not an *easy* writer, but he is surely one of the *great* writers. Strauss explains further.

Communication may be a means of living together; in its highest form, communication *is* living together. The study of the literary question is therefore an important part of the study of society. Furthermore, the quest for truth is necessarily, if not in every respect, a common quest, a quest taking place through communication. The study of the literary question is therefore an important part or the study of what philosophy is. The literary question properly understood is the question of the relation between society and philosophy.[24]

But when Strauss then turns to the literary question in his commentary on the *Republic* he turns in a very strange direction. He turns to the question of writing as distinct from conversation—the question of "literate versus oral communication" as discussed in Plato's later dialogue the *Phaedrus*.[25] Strangely, what Strauss does *not* pause to remark is the literary question posed in the *Republic* itself: Plato's Paradox of Mimetic Writing. Strauss has already made clear that the literary question that vexes the study of Plato's *Republic* cannot ("properly understood") be the question of literate versus oral communication (the *Phaedrus'* question of writing versus speech) because Strauss is talking about a particular *kind of writing*. The distinction between literate and oral systems of communication is irrelevant to a distinction between strategic varieties of *writing*. Why, then, does Strauss pass over without comment (studiously ignore) a self-referential puzzle focused upon precisely the distinction he *is* concerned with in the very text upon which he is commenting? And isn't this just the sort of thing Strauss would expect a careful reader to notice? It would appear, then, that Strauss's commentary on Plato's *Republic* contains an esoteric teaching. That would be ironic—also just what one might expect.

Why in attempting to elucidate a difficult work would Strauss encumber his own commentary with the same or similar difficulties? Let us return to the earlier point: literary devices and strategies for "writing between the lines" naturally arise under conditions of political repression and persecution. Strauss observes that repression and persecution can take a variety of shapes and forms.

> The term persecution covers a variety of phenomena, ranging from the most cruel type, as exemplified by the Spanish Inquisition, to the mildest, which is social ostracism. Between these extremes are the types which are most important from the point of view of literary or intellectual history. Examples of these are found in the Athens of the fifth and fourth centuries B.C., in some Muslim countries of the early Middle Ages, in seventeenth century Holland and England, and in eighteenth

century France and Germany—all of them comparatively liberal periods. But a glance at the biographies of Anaxagoras, Protagoras, Socrates, Plato, Xenophon, Aristotle, Avicenna, Averroes, Maimonides, Grotius, Descartes, Hobbes, Spinoza, Locke, Bayle, Wolff, Montesquieu, Voltaire, Rousseau, Lessing and Kant, and in some cases even a glance at the title pages of their books is sufficient to show that they witnessed or suffered, during at least part of their lifetimes, a kind of persecution which was more tangible than social ostracism.[26]

Plato had seen his own mentor, Socrates, put to death—in a *democracy*— for questioning official orthodoxy. Strauss, a Jew, who had studied in Germany under Edmund Husserl, also a Jew, and under Husserl's protégé Martin Heidegger, was certainly aware of the persecution Husserl suffered under the Nazis and that the Nazi Heidegger had distanced himself from his teacher and advanced his own academic career in Nazi Germany at his teacher's expense.[27] Strauss fled rising totalitarian fascism in Europe. Did he *escape* it in America? What might Strauss have been referring or alluding to in the opening lines of the title essay in *Persecution and the Art of Writing*, when he said:

> In a considerable number of countries which, for about a hundred years, have enjoyed a practically complete freedom of public discussion, that freedom is now suppressed and replaced by a compulsion to coordinate speech with such views as the government believes to be expedient, or holds in all seriousness.[28]

To a European reader in the early 1950s when this passage was published, it would have been obvious that the description applied about as well to the country in which Strauss was then living as to any other country in the world. In the immediate aftermath of World War II a wave of political repression swept the United States that was every bit as virulent as any in twentieth-century Europe. Federal law enforcement agencies conducted intrusive and unwarranted domestic surveillance and investigations. These intrusive and repressive measures of course targeted perfectly legitimate groups of citizens engaged in peaceful and lawful political organizing on behalf of workers, the poor, and black people. Law-abiding citizens were dragged before congressional committees and compelled to testify as to their own and their families' and neighbors' political activities and affiliations. Loyalty oaths were imposed in government service and the public universities. If American readers fail to notice this reference in Strauss to the witch hunts and blacklists of McCarthyism, it simply underscores the degree to which the official orthodoxy of the United States as an unparalleled bastion of freedom of thought and expression remains entrenched in America.

In this connection it's worth noting the striking similarity between Strauss's analysis of the natural mechanisms of mass indoctrination and Noam Chomsky's more recent and complementary Orwellian analysis of what he calls "brainwashing under freedom."

> In a totalitarian state, it's required only that official doctrine be obeyed: but in a democratic system of thought control more is required. It's . . . necessary to take over the entire spectrum of opinion . . . so that nothing can be thinkable apart from the party line.[29]

Strauss understood that doctrinal discipline under *authoritarian* repression and persecution depends upon controlling the spectrum of opinion within which "freedom of thought" may be exercised. Chomsky, following Orwell, understood that the same principle applies *especially* under a "democratic" regime such as the one that was evolving and has continued to evolve in the United States of America since World War II. I think it is more than reasonable to suppose that Strauss anticipated Chomsky's critique of American brainwashing under freedom, that he had witnessed enough harassment of intellectuals in fascist Europe to know the score, and that he applied his own theories about writing between the lines to his own circumstances as a thinker and writer in cold war America. In so doing he was publicly contradicting official cold war American orthodoxy—publishing what Chomsky would later call an "unthinkable thought." This is a main reason why it goes unnoticed.[30]

Strauss and the "Straussians"

Under conditions of intellectual repression and persecution, an independent thinker's disciples are among the most treacherous and dangerous of his potential enemies. Shorris, quoted earlier, completely misses this point.[31] But I think it not unlikely that Strauss fully understood it. Socrates had his disastrous student in Alcibiades, not the least of his troubles at trial.[32] And Heidegger's betrayal of Husserl surely reinforced for Strauss this "Lesson for All Teachers in Times of Political Turmoil": beware especially of the student who comes to you as a disciple. Strauss of all people would surely have understood the relevance of this lesson for a teacher of political theory, whose students come, like Alcibiades came to Socrates, eager to learn the secrets of political power. What, then, shall we make of the "Straussians" and their representations of

Strauss's political philosophy? Do they faithfully and accurately represent Strauss's own philosophy or have they misunderstood, or worse, betrayed, their teacher and systematically misrepresented his teaching?

To read the critiques of Straussianism that have been published over the last few years is a chilling experience.[33] To read the writings of the political Straussians is even more so.[34] One gets the impression of a nest of protofascist vermin, devoid of all integrity, especially intellectual integrity, possessed above all else by the will to power, who having infested the government of the most powerful nation on earth were willing to propagate any falsehood and deny all truth in clinging to power, driven by a delusional faith in the righteousness of their quest. This faith flows from a sense the political Straussians seem to have that they alone truly understand the secret teachings of ancient philosophy, these having been revealed and entrusted to them by their revered teacher, Leo Strauss, whose insights again they alone are capable of understanding. Bullshit.

Here is a representative example. At the close of the lengthy essay quoted earlier, Lenzner and Kristol credit Strauss with the rehabilitation of the very language of social and political science by reintroducing certain crucial but forgotten or discredited terms and concepts (like "tyranny" and "natural right") into the professional literature in these subject areas. And in this connection they say:

> One particularly timely example is Strauss's rehabilitation of the classical understanding of "regime." . . . The concept of regime, properly understood, is one that avoids the unhealthy extremes of utopian universalism and insular nationalism. President Bush's advocacy of "regime change"—which avoids the pitfalls of a wishful global universalism on the one hand, and a fatalistic cultural determinism on the other—is a not altogether unworthy product of Strauss's rehabilitation of the notion of regime.[35]

Well, this (properly understood) is just "nonsense on stilts"—an example par excellence of the doctrine of the "noble lie," the notion that when used by the power elite, lies are not just legitimate but *virtuous* instruments of *wise* policy management. This doctrine, as practiced by the Straussians in the Bush administration and as rationalized by the think tank Straussians, holds that those who are fit to rule in the city (or nation) may legitimately lie to the citizens in order to maintain political order and manage policy for the good of the city (or nation). They claim for this doctrine a philosophical pedigree traceable through Strauss all the way back to Plato. But a close and careful reading of Plato, the kind of reading Strauss supposedly stood for, makes it clear that Plato said no such thing.

The Platonic presentation and supposed defense of this doctrine is in Book III of the *Republic*,[36] Plato's famous Allegory of the Metals. In the allegory, the guardians of the model city are told a fable (a "noble lie") about their genesis within the earth and how their natural fitness for either leadership or auxiliary military service was engendered in them: those born with an admixture of gold in their souls were naturally fit to rule, those with silver were fit for military service, those with bronze were to engage in economic production. In Plato's *Republic,* let us not forget, the Allegory of the Metals is presented as a *lie*. To read it, then, as a *defense* of lying, and indeed a defense available only to those in power, is not just circular but turns the text inside out and its meaning upside down.[37]

It is also arguably a cynical perversion of Strauss's theory of esoteric writing, although I've been able to find only one commentator who has recognized this possibility, political scientist Anne Norton, who says, I think reasonably:

> *Persecution and the Art of Writing* described the ways in which people who loved learning and wished to preserve it for others evaded the control of those who would persecute them. They wrote and taught carefully in times of danger, and their learning lived on. In this understanding, secret teachings and esoteric writings are intended to preserve learning, so that knowledge may be passed to many others. Those who wrote in this way did not intend to keep teachings *from* those who wished to learn, but to keep teachings *for* them.[38]

The essential point to keep in mind is this. Philosophy is the love of wisdom, and as such it is committed to the search for truth, which, as Strauss pointed out, is the common quest of all mankind. Let us suppose, then, that Strauss understood that the truth sometimes needs a disguise to get around in the world. In times of political repression, such as both Plato and Strauss witnessed, when the powers that be are prepared to persecute and punish and even kill those who express politically unsettling truths in public, the philosopher must find ways of expressing the truth so that it can be recognized by those who will treasure it and yet travel under cover when necessary. Contrary to what the political Straussians say, the philosopher does not "write between the lines" so as to keep secrets from all mankind, as though the truth were "too dangerous" for general consumption and to be known only by those in power. As Norton reasonably observes:

> Nor were these strategies of concealment used by and for the good of those in power. Jews in the Inquisition, the freethinking in religious realms, the disenfranchised, the excluded, the persecuted, employed these strategies against the powerful, against their rulers, against those who would persecute them. The art of writing, as Strauss described it, was a weapon of the [vulnerable]. The forms of esoteric teaching advocated by the Straussians work in exactly the opposite way: to prevent the circulation of ideas, to preserve the powerful against criticism, to serve the strong and keep the weak vulnerable.[39]

Backlash in the Sixties

In his bitter screed *The Closing of the American Mind* the Straussian Allan Bloom, writing as a self-appointed guardian of the culture, summed up the student movements of the 1960s as a full-scale calamity comparable to the "dismantling of the structure of rational inquiry in the German universities of the 1930s."[40] The moral Bloom was trying to draw was that just as Europe's descent into fascism was the predictable consequence of the collapse of German rationalist idealism, the same fate was awaiting America as a result of the cultural upheavals and student movements of the 1960s, with all their relativist intellectual implications. As a student in the 1960s I lacked the vocabulary and conceptual apparatus to theorize the enthusiasm with which I joined in the spectacle and the struggle. But I nevertheless recognized such reactionary criticisms as Bloom's for what they were. There was nothing "relativistic" about our politics. We were right—about *some* things, anyway.[41] Forty years on I continue to regard the student movements and other popular cultural revolutions of the 1960s as a great blooming renaissance of culture in all of its manifestations, as well as a general raising of political consciousness (all in naive, clumsy, and excessive fits and starts, to be sure). And if America did descend into some form of protofascism during the cold war, or after the collapse of the Soviet Union, this can hardly be attributed to the student or civil rights or antiwar movements of the 1960s, as flawed and imperfect as they were.

And so, whether or not Strauss himself would approve of it, it is in any case clear that tyrants have now taken over Strauss's teaching and turned it to their own sinister purposes. Although they will deny it through their teeth, the so-called Straussians in the American neoconservative political movement are the political proponents in America of a fascist world order. In practice, as in the theoretical justifications they offer for the approaches to policy management they prefer, they manifest nothing other than tyranny. As in Nazi Germany, these people came into power through the manipulation and corruption of democratic institutions, just as Plato predicted, by the way.

Blues Is Truth

The blues has, as art forms go, an uncommonly close relationship with the truth. Blues people often assert an equation between the two, expressing the relationship as a kind of identity. They will tell you that the blues *is* the truth. Listen, for example, to what Brownie McGhee has to say.

> I don't write anything from imagination. Blues is not a dream. Blues is truth. I can't write about something I haven't seen or experienced. Whiskey, women, money, maybe politics—these are my leading topics. The highway has been my home. I haven't been in prison for murder, but I do know what a jailhouse is. And I do know about gambling, and I know all about riding in the back of the bus. I tell people about this.[42]

At the same time, the relationship between the blues and the truths expressed therein is also an uncommonly artful one—neither simple nor entirely straightforward but characterized by semantic and syntactic encryption and misdirection and not least by cryptic irony.[43] Indeed, if one is looking for good literary examples to illustrate the special kind of covert communication strategies that Leo Strauss theorized as "writing between the lines," one will find few better than the blues.

It is obvious that the social and political circumstances into which the blues were born were violently repressive of the black population—a paradigm of persecution. Thus it is also widely understood and well documented that covert communication strategies have been developed and employed throughout African American history. For example, the evolution of "Black English," as well as a number of its salient characteristics, such as crucial ambiguity, understatement, irony, and inversion of meaning ("bad" means "good" and so on), may best be explained as the development of cryptic communicative strategies under repression.

> Blacks clearly recognized that to master the language of whites was in effect to consent to be mastered by it through the white definitions of caste built into the semantic/social system. Inversion therefore be-

comes the defensive mechanism which enables blacks to fight linguistic, and thereby psychological, entrapment. . . . Words and phrases were given reverse meanings and functions changed. Whites, denied access to the semantic extensions of duality, connotations, and denotations that developed within black usage, could only interpret the same material according to its original singular meaning . . . enabling blacks to deceive and manipulate whites without penalty. This protective process, understood and shared by blacks, became a contest of matching wits . . . [and a] form of linguistic guerilla warfare [which] protected the subordinated, permitted the masking and disguising of true feelings, allowed the subtle assertion of self, and promoted group solidarity.[44]

The pattern continues, of course, to this day. Writing in 2006 about current developments in hip-hop, pop music critic Sasha Frere-Jones observes:

Hip-hop has always been driven by an imperative to employ the most vibrant words possible. . . . The result is complex poetry: Songs that simultaneously broadcast and hide their meaning.[45]

Ethnomusicologists, working independently and apparently absent any familiarity with Strauss's work in political philosophy or sociolinguistic studies of Black English, have arrived at strikingly similar conclusions regarding the origins, functions, and stylistic features of jazz and blues.[46]

One important commonality between the blues and spirituals is cryptic lyrical content—messages communicated in code. Lyrically the blues are rife with more or less covert allusions to the oppressive conditions of black life in America. The relatively overt reference in Jimmy Reed's "Big Boss Man,"

Big boss man, can't you hear me when I call (twice)?
Well you ain't so big, you just tall, that's all.

recalls a more covert tradition central to the blues. As Paul Oliver observes:

An appreciation of the part African Americans have played in United States society and of the rights and other aspects of living that were denied them is of major assistance in understanding the blues. But there are barriers to appreciation presented by the manner of delivery, of speech, and of form, and when these are overcome the full significance of the blues to the black audience still remains elusive. . . . Many black terms arose through the deliberate intention to conceal meaning . . .

[and] innocuous words were often given secondary meanings which were closed to all but the initiated and by their use the singer could be more outspoken in the blues than might otherwise be prudent. Some of these became traditional terms recognized and used throughout the states by blacks, for whom the colored man was the "monkey," the white man the "baboon." With comparative immunity Dirty Red could sing:

> Monkey and the baboon playing Seven-Up,
> Monkey win the money, scared to pick it up.
> The monkey stumbled, the baboon fell,
> Monkey grabbed the money an' he run like hell![47]

Similarly, Samuel Charters writes about the difficulties that characterized early white attempts to appreciate blues performances, exemplified by a review of a nightclub performance by a young Champion Jack Dupree.

> Jack Dupree was thirty when Duncan Scheidt saw him in Indianapolis, playing his first full-time job as a musician. He had already had so much of life that he could sing blues about almost anything and still be singing about himself—and he managed to give the feeling that he was always a little distant from it. It was his quick move back out of reach. He'd suddenly bang out some chords on the piano—start laughing as he was singing—do a little dance when he had to introduce his next number. He was giving his audience the truth, but not in a way that they'd be left uncomfortably holding it.[48]

Here the irony suffusing the performance is understood as a diplomatic nicety—the hard truth politely presented, as it were. These readings of blues irony by Charters and Oliver actually put the point rather mildly. Although blues irony indeed functions well enough on this level, deeper and more militant ironies resonate in the blues as well. Thus we find somewhat more radical analyses in blues scholarship of hidden meanings and covert communication in the blues, for instance, tracing the development of a mythology of active resistance against racist repression and violence, personified in legendary "superheroic" figures such as Railroad Bill and Stagolee, and theorizing the blues

> as a social response to the grievous spiritual pressures exerted upon working class black southerners by the sudden eruption of lynching-as-spectacle . . . [S]uch violence helped to form . . . a "blues subject," who then found ways more or less covert, to sing back to that ever hovering threat.[49]

Truth and Reconciliation

Let us return now to our main questions about the role of music in the life of the soul. Throughout this essay I have wondered at the capacity music appears to have to affect the health of the human soul in both positive and negative ways—to both heal and harm the soul. Following Plato's moral psychology, in chapter 4 we reframed the question of music's healing and harmful effects on the soul as follows: how does music enhance and contribute to, or undermine and detract from, the soul's healthy condition of balanced intonation and inner harmony? In chapter 6 we consciously expanded these questions to comprehend collective consciousness and agency. In what ways has the music we've been considering affected the "soul of the nation," so to speak, or of the world? Just as countless individual human souls have been traumatized in various ways, and just as these spiritual wounds have been treated in various ways, we may also consider spiritual trauma suffered collectively by a people or a nation or by humanity as a whole, as well as available means of treatment for such trauma. This orientation opens a way of understanding and appreciating the significance of the musical movements with which we have been concerned. Situated within their historical contexts, how have the spirituals, the blues, gospel, and soul music contributed to the health of the nation's soul? This is a way of examining what the spirituals, the blues, gospel, and soul music have meant to the history of culture in America.

Trauma—the suffering of a wound, whether physical, emotional (as with the loss of a loved one), or spiritual (as in cases of grievous injustice)—leaves one in deep trouble with the truth. On the one hand, speaking one's truth as a traumatized individual is a matter of excruciating difficulty—the deeper and more serious the wound, the greater the difficulty. To tell the story of one's trauma is in a sense to relive the experience. Thus, in extreme cases, what we call atrocities are also often called "unspeakable." Familiar psychological coping strategies of denial reflect this understanding. "I can't talk about it! I don't want to *think* about it! Perish the thought! I banish it from my consciousness." On the other hand, no healing can take place in denial of the truth. Like the cleansing of a physical wound, speaking one's truth as a traumatized individual is a painful necessity of the recovery process. Until this necessity is faced the wound just festers.

Furthermore, those who inflict trauma are also traumatized by the experience and find themselves in their own deep trouble with the truth. A burden of guilt can be as unspeakably painful to bear as the victim's experience is to relive—and its admission every bit as necessary to the healing process for all parties. In traumatized societies these mutually reinforcing difficulties become even more deeply entangled. Unspeakable truths and festering wounds are transmitted from generation to generation, perpetuating social divisions and reinforcing cycles of resentment, revenge, and violence. Thus, to heal a traumatized society it is both painfully difficult and absolutely essential to break through barriers to unspeakable truths. This was the central insight underlying the establishment of the Truth and Reconciliation Commission in postapartheid South Africa, which its chairman, Archbishop Desmond Tutu, described as having established a world-historic benchmark.

> We are deeply grateful to the thousands of South Africans who came to the Commission to tell us their stories. They have won our country the admiration of the world: wherever one goes, South Africa's peaceful transition to democracy, culminating in the Truth and Reconciliation process, is spoken of almost in reverent tones, as a phenomenon that is unique in the annals of history, one to be commended as a new way of living for humankind.[50]

In the absence of an officially sanctioned truth and reconciliation process like the one modeled in South Africa, what responsive strategies are available to a people or society that has been traumatized or is suffering ongoing trauma? Well, it comes out in the culture. It comes out in the movies and the literature, in the video games, in the music.

And here I return to irony, which I first introduced in this chapter as a style or mode of communication uniquely capable of embodying the cleansing and therapeutic effects of both tragedy and comedy in a single text. As we have seen, Leo Strauss explains the use of irony as a covert communication strategy for conveying politically unutterable truths "between the lines." Similarly irony can function as a therapeutic strategy to break through barriers to unspeakable truths, to "look up at down," to "laugh to keep from crying." These are blues expressions, by the way, and they represent the crucial importance of irony as an African American coping strategy.[51]

Thus far in our short history, we in America haven't become very comfortable as a nation with soul-searching. We like to celebrate much more than we like to engage in sober, let alone grave, reflection. We much prefer to think of the glories than of the traumas in our past. This is why some of our best music has had to be so ironic.[52]

CHAPTER 8

Music as a Healing Art
(*Music and Medicine, Body and Soul*)

One must first believe, on a fundamental level, in the ability of music to do more than just entertain.
— ANDREW A. STEWART

Blues is a Healer.
— JOHN LEE HOOKER

You can't make spiritual progress in a drugged state. You have to be sober.
— ROBERT CRUMB

The use of music as therapy is a growing clinical practice in health care today. Music has been used to treat clinical depression, autism, stroke, Parkinson's and Alzheimer's diseases, and for the regulation and modulation of physiological functions, including respiration, heart rate, and blood pressure.[1] A recently published review study indicates beneficial therapeutic applications of music in neonatal care.[2] This movement grows at the expense of the bemused skepticism of mainstream Western medical science. Scientists, of course, are professional and methodical skeptics. After all, science basically *is* method, and skepticism is crucial to the method. As a scientist, you may acknowledge the commonplace that music "can make you feel better." But you're going to want to know how to objectively measure these "good feelings," and you're going to hold out for rigorous demonstrations that they correlate significantly with specific therapeutic outcomes. And if you find such evidence you're still going to want to know that it is the music, not some other variable, that accounts for the correlation. And if you can manage to control all the other variables experimentally you're still going to wonder how to explain the causal connection before you assert it. How does the music therapy work? Is the causal mechanism physiological, psychological, a mixture of both, electromagnetic, hormonal, or what?[3]

Western medical science is interested in music therapy, just as it is in other "alternative therapies" both new and ancient. While medical science is too scrupulous to endorse knowledge claims in advance of the unfinished research, practicing musicians and music therapists "know" from their own experience that music works therapeutically. This by itself does not make their and their clients' knowledge claims unscrupulous—just unscientific. To put it diplomatically, it makes such claims "speculative" from the point of view of the sciences, which would rather investigate them as experimental hypotheses.

Scientific interest in music therapy is encouraged by music's measurability in terms of both formal features (musicology) and acoustics (the physics of sound) and by impressive advances in the neurosciences. Oliver Sacks, who first became interested in the "profound effects of music on deeply parkinsonian patients" in 1966, notes that while

> there was virtually no neuroscience of music prior to the 1980s . . . [t]here is now an enormous and rapidly growing body of work on the neural underpinnings of musical perception and imagery and the complex and often bizarre disorders to which these are prone.[4]

Research is ongoing in places like Harvard Medical School's Institute for Music and Brain Science, directed by a neurologist who is also a composer, Dr. Mark Jude Tramo. Here is Dr. Tramo's assessment of the state of the science available now to guide and support the clinical use of music as therapy.

> What evidence we have in hand really does show that music makes a difference. [But] the cold, hard, randomized multi-center large population, statistically sound clinical trials—that's what's lacking. [And] if we can understand how it is that music communicates emotion and meaning, if we can understand all the computations the brain has to do to recognize that you're hearing the same melody in a different key . . . we're getting fundamental information about how the brain works.[5]

In other words, what we have is a promising but still unfinished research agenda recalling several of our unanswered questions from chapters 1, 4, and 5. At the present pace of scientific research, even if it is accelerating, resolving these questions could take a while.

In the meantime, if you want to pursue a career in music therapy, the American Music Therapy Association identifies various courses of education and training, mostly areas of concentration in accredited music schools, leading to baccalaureate, masters, and doctoral degrees, and to board certification to practice music therapy as an "allied health profession."[6]

Like other healing modalities and practices still more or less mysterious to Western science (acupuncture, aromatherapy), music therapy is suspended somewhere between the domain of the sciences (physics, biology, chemistry, neurology, psychology) and the domains of ancient folk wisdom and New Age spirituality (astrology, crystals, healing touch, magnets, pyramids, ritual exorcism, past life regression). A recent issue of the quarterly journal *Music Therapy Today* includes scholarly articles on topics ranging from shamanism and biomedicine in Nepal, to traditional oriental and Islamic music therapy and its adaptations in modern Europe, to contemporary rave culture.[7]

Therapeutic Music by Design

The average music lover or seeker of health care may wonder how to navigate and make sense of this field as a layperson. As a philosopher who is also a musician, I wonder the same thing. Let me offer a preliminary distinction. The term *music therapy* can refer to treatment that on the one hand engages the patient or client in music-making activities and on the other involves the patient or client simply as a listener. Clearly the former is of great interest to therapists working with conditions such as stroke, autism, and communication disorders because the activity of music making engages the patient's perceptual, mental, and responsive motor-functional capacities in a holistic way. This presents complexities several orders of magnitude greater than the latter form of music therapy in which music is administered to the patient as a listener. Let us therefore begin with the latter.

A leading example of this latter kind of music therapy is the Musica Humana project—an ongoing program of controlled experimentation in the therapeutic applications of music in hospitals. The researchers are trying to find out whether and how the addition or alteration of music in the ambient hospital environment can be used to promote healing and how music played in the hospital environment may affect therapeutic outcomes. There are some for whom the word *promote* raises a skeptical flag as too vague to function other than as a weasel word for purposes of marketing. But healers of all stripes, including hard-nosed Western physicians, understand that healing is a process that happens in the patient. The body—or body/mind—heals itself, and the practice of medicine is directed toward assisting, enabling, facilitating, supporting, promoting that well-known yet deeply mysterious (some would even say "miraculous") process.

On its face the Musica Humana project clearly seems to satisfy the methodological criteria scientists such as Dr. Tramo are looking for. First of all the research program is already ten years old and ongoing. It involves a large international patient population. The research is conducted in and under the cooperating auspices of accredited hospitals in Denmark, Norway, Sweden, and the United States. Also worthy of note, the music to be studied in the hospital environment has been especially designed for the project by a trained and accomplished musician, the oboist and composer Niels Eje.[8]

Among the many parameters to consider in designing experiments in this area is the type of music to "prescribe" for different treatable conditions. Should the same music be used in the premature nursery as in the physical therapy room or the oncology chemotherapy infusion center or the cardiac intensive care unit? Dr. Per Thorgaard has been studying the use of music in the ambient environment of treatment rooms where patients undergo invasive procedures under mild sedation or local anaesthetic (i.e., while awake) and also in postoperative recovery rooms where patients awaken from full anaesthesia. Explaining the appropriateness of the dreamy ambient music Eje has designed for these applications, Thorgaard is quoted as saying, "We guessed it should not be Jimi Hendrix or Pearl Jam."[9] *Designed* is the pivotal word here. The music in Thorgaard's and other similar projects is "designed" more than "composed." This distinction highlights the fact that the musical elements—the melodies, harmonies, rhythms, timbres, and so on—are selected for desired psychological and physiological effect. The research presupposes and focuses on the important role of the mind in the healing process. Eje's musical design objectives are "to have a soothing and physically relaxing effect" and to "stimulate the mind in a positive way, creating experiences and images." The design process is outcome driven and informed by the research, in which patient (and caregiver) responses to music are collated and then correlated with physiological measures such as blood pressure, heart rate, and level of Immunoglobulin A in saliva. Eje's music, having been thus tested and refined through clinical trials over a period of several years, was first made available commercially through Danish pharmacies in 2003, later also through Norwegian pharmacies, and is now available worldwide online.

The Psychopharmacology of Music

In northern California, where I live, there are quite a few health spas offering a variety of treatments (mineral baths, volcanic mud baths, Japa-

nese enzyme baths, many modalities of massage, and so on). Music is almost always an ingredient in the ambient environment where these services are delivered. The music is intentionally chosen as part of an "inte-
rior design" process. Often CDs of the music are available for sale in the
lobby or reception area. And almost all of this music is "designed music"
for therapy. Web sites offering this kind of music for sale, and there are a
good many, often pointedly refer to it as "designed (or designer) music."
Search the Internet for massage music or meditation music or relaxation
music—you'll find a large market of essentially very similar material.

As with any stylistic category of music (baroque, jazz, blues, funk,
rockabilly, you name it), there are both similarities and differences between any two passages or pieces of music in the category. And as with
most (if not all) such categories, sensitivity to the differences between
one piece of music and the next in a given style is a matter of nuance and
detail and is therefore highly correlated with interest and close studious
attention. (People who say, for example, that all jazz "sounds the same"
give a good indication of how little interest they have in studying or paying close attention to jazz music.)

However, although there is surely a wide enough variety among
pieces of designed relaxation music, as a category it is especially easy,
even inviting, to stereotype. If a given piece of designed relaxation music
is a composition unique unto itself, its unique identity as a work of art is
quite beside the point. As designed relaxation music it isn't really meant
to arrest the listener's attention or distinguish itself in the listener's
mind. In the spa environment, for example, it seems primarily intended
to "blend in" with other ambient factors—the colors, the lighting, the
fragrances—to enhance the overall "healing arts ambience" of the place,
whereas in the hospital environment it seems rather intended to neutralize noise and other ambient stress factors. We hear a breathy wooden
flute with natural sound (a distant gentle surf, a quiet brook, birdsong)
floating through a serene dreamscape of vague orchestral washes. Or a
series of deeply resonant gongs is sounded and allowed to gradually decay into the background of gentle natural sound. There are no dynamics. There is minimal if any formal compositional structure. There's not
much there to "think about" (that's by design, of course). And of course
that's not exactly correct, either. Because there's actually quite a lot to
think about, but if you think about it in the spa environment during
treatment you're defeating the designed purpose of the music. With relaxation music, if the client goes into a deeply relaxed state of semicon-
sciousness or sleep during the massage, that's what we *want* to happen!
Of course, in the postoperative recovery room we expect the patient to

wake up, not go to sleep. But we still want to minimize the trauma and stress. We want the patient to emerge as from a reverie. So Eje's music may want to be an ever so slightly more stimulating strain of soothing relaxation music. Discerning the difference is, well, let's just say a matter of considerable subtlety.

This also raises a question essentially similar to the one we wondered about in chapter 4 regarding music's apparent emotional power: how does the music do its therapeutic work? One fairly plausible story is that the music supplies a pleasant distraction for the patient's mind in an otherwise stressful situation. The music gives the patient something to pay attention to besides his or her own fear and physical discomfort and the cold sterility, noise, and high-strung stress levels of the busy hospital environment. But if that were the whole story there would be no reason not to use Hendrix or Pearl Jam. You could just turn on the radio. But not just any old music will do. Some music *adds* stress to the environment. Suitable music, like the right medicine, must be prescribed. So the design process seems to presuppose an additional premise about music, namely, that music, in its variety, makes available an array of determinate psychoactive properties that may be selectively invoked by design to promote healing. Hence the woodwinds and the gently falling water, the low-frequency gongs, the largo rubato—and the importance of those elusive and subtle musical differences.

It is no mere coincidence that the music developed through the Musica Humana project was originally brought to market and is still sold through pharmacies. The conceptual framework within which many of these research and treatment programs are pursued assimilates music therapy to drug therapy, in other words to pharmacology, specifically psychopharmacology, which studies the action of drugs upon the mind.[10] One imagines eventually a psychopharmacological desk reference manual for the practicing music therapist, with musical instruments, natural sound sources, and formal musical features all classified and listed with their known effects, recommended medical indications, and ranges of application.

The Dark Side of Musical Psychopharmacology

The same psychopharmacological set of assumptions also underlies some darker trends in the use of music. Here are a few examples. In 1989, when the United States invaded Panama, the embattled dictator Manuel Noriega took refuge in the Vatican embassy. U.S. marines surrounded, and bombarded, the embassy for several days—with hard rock and heavy metal music. Music is also being used by several nations, including the United States, as an "enhanced interrogation technique" (a euphemism for torture). In this application, loud music is used in combination with strobe lights and other irritants to deprive the interrogation subject of sleep and inculcate a "sense of futility."[11]

These "experiments," if you can call them that, with the use of music in military combat and the interrogation of prisoners are less rigorous and responsible scientifically, for a host of reasons, than the therapeutic experiments just mentioned. If in these pursuits the military is genuinely interested in results (surrender and disclosure), it apparently cares far less about arriving at precise understandings of the mechanisms whereby these results are obtained. So, for example, interrogation teams heap irritant on top of irritant with little or no regard for isolating and controlling variables for experimental purposes. From the military point of view it scarcely matters whether the enemy complies as a result of the kind of music played or because of the volume at which it is played or how long or repetitive the exposure to it is. The "torture playlist" is reported to include not just the usual suspect list of aggressive heavy metal and rap but the *Barney the Dinosaur* theme song and a Meow Mix commercial, as well as music chosen for thematic or lyrical content expected to offend the interrogation subject's presumed religious and moral sensibilities. Still, the assumption that music has determinate psychoactive properties that can be selectively used to promote an agenda operates here as well, at least at the crude level of identifying music likely to be irritating.

A further military application of music as a form of "self-medication" among active duty troops in the theater of combat also illustrates this assumption. *Rolling Stone* magazine reports that soldiers deployed in Iraq and Afghanistan are using their iPods to download music and create "war mixes" specifically designed to psych them up for battle and alternatively to enable them to sleep. The statements of the soldiers are quite revealing.

> You can't put a Dashboard Confessional song on and expect to go out there and kill somebody. When you're getting ready, grabbing your gear, putting the bullets where you need to put them and getting in the mind-set, like, "OK, we're going to war"—that's when I listen to 50 Cent. (twenty-three-year-old marine sergeant Brandon Welsh)
>
> People use heroin or smoke pot to get through things, and that's what music is over here: It helps pump you up or mellow you out, as needed. (twenty-five-year-old Travis Steele)[12]

Again the operative assumption is that music has determinate psychoactive properties that may be used selectively and combined by design to achieve specific desired effects on oneself as well as others. The soldier's explicit comparison and association between music and psychoactive drugs echoes a commonplace understanding in society at large, reflected, for instance, in the title of Daniel Levitin's landmark study of the emerging science of musical perception, *This Is Your Brain on Music*.[13]

Is Pharmacology the Right Model?

Let us entertain the assumption that music *does* offer in its variety an array of psychoactive properties that may be used selectively and combined by design for specific therapeutic and other purposes. This leads us to wonder what are the psychological and physiological processes involved in music's psychoactivity. To what extent are the psychoactive properties of music determined by its formal musical and objectively measurable acoustic properties? Can we identify "receptors" in the human organism that account for the effects of music? To what extent are such properties and effects culturally determined? To what extent are they just "in the ear (or mind) of the beholder"?

In chapter 4 we reviewed the history of formalist attempts to explain the emotional power of music, concluding that no theory has yet succeeded or is likely to succeed in linking music's purely formal features with its emotional power in a fully satisfying explanatory account. Is there any reason to expect formalism to fare better in explaining the psychoactive properties of music?

In the military applications the prospects are dim. Even though there are some relatively obvious patterns discernible in the collection of music selected for such applications (lots of crunchy power chords and screaming), overall it's still pretty much a grab bag of music off the shelf—whatever somebody thinks is going to work. And again, there is (God help us!) little interest in rigorous experimentation in this area. And if there *is* any rigorous experimentation going on, it is highly classified and unavailable to international peer review.

Music designed for therapeutic applications is by and large purely instrumental and without text (although it does sometimes come with associated visual imagery). So perhaps its purely formal features are easier to isolate and more available to systematic study. Broad generalities are plausible enough. If the objective is relaxation, the tempo of the music's pulse should be relatively slow, melodic movement should be gradual and minimal, volume should be low, and the dynamics relatively even. But even here the prospects for purely formal in-depth comprehension and scientific validation in detail seem limited. Beyond subtle differences between individual pieces of designed relaxation music, here, too, one can select from among a wide variety of composed music fitting the general design profile. Brahms's "Lullaby" (Opus 49) and Bach's "Air on a G String" and George Winston's "Walking in the Air" are each quite distinct in formal compositional terms, although they would all be great candidates for inclusion on a relaxation mix tape. Perhaps the precise qualitative nature of the relaxation can be mapped onto the formal details of the compositions, but then again this may well vary from patient to patient and day to day, who knows? It's an open empirical question.

But here I want to raise instead a bottom-line theoretical question. How illuminating overall is the pharmacological model? Pharmacology is essentially the study of medical chemistry. It is the science that studies the effects in living organisms of chemical agents other than food.[14] As a conceptual framework for understanding, developing, and assessing music as a therapeutic agent in health care, the pharmacological model therefore has some important limitations. You get a glimpse of these as soon as you ask how to rule out the placebo effect. What would a musical placebo sound like? Is a musical placebo even possible? But the most important limitations manifest at the level of explanation. Although there are no doubt interesting things to learn about the neurochemistry of listening to and hearing music, the agent in this case is not a chemical one. Music is energy. Music enters the body not as a substance to be metabolized but as waves of sound energy. If we are to understand music's effect on the organism, this must be central to the explanation. We're in the realm of physics.

Physics, Acoustics, Resonance

Specifically, we're in the realm of acoustics, the branch of physics that has to do with sound. In physics, sound is a form of energy that expresses itself through the displacement of molecules of some elastic medium (normally air) caused by something vibrating. When something starts vibrating, this disturbs the air molecules right next to it. These molecules disturb the molecules next to them, which disturb the ones next to them, and so on. This sets in motion a traveling "wave" of disturbances radiating outward from the vibration. We call these "sound waves."[15] Human beings, like many other animals, have evolved specialized tissues (auditory nerves) and organs (ears, eardrums) that enable us to register and interpret this kind of energy as a means of orienting ourselves in our environment. We call this "hearing."

Sound waves travel pretty fast (the "speed of sound" = 770 miles per hour in dry air at 68 degrees Fahrenheit) and pretty far (if a tree falls in the forest, the sound can be heard for miles). And they travel through any elastic medium. An elastic medium is any stuff in which the molecules, when they are disturbed, disturb other molecules. So sound travels through air, water, wood, human bodies. Sound waves don't go nearly as fast through us as they go through the air, but they don't just stop when they hit us. They go right into us. Not just into our ears. The entire body absorbs sound. This is the basis of sonography (ultrasound), a medical imaging technology used to gain information about conditions inside the body.

Human beings have also evolved ways of organizing, controlling, and manipulating sound energy for many purposes, including communication (and medical imaging, just mentioned). If we think of music as "sound art," or the use of sound energy for artistic purposes, we may understand a "musical instrument" (including the human body) as a tool for organizing and controlling sound energy for artistic purposes. Among the first things to notice about musically organized sound is its abundant "regularity."[16] We find regularity in rhythms, harmonies, melodies, and musical pitches and at the most basic and fundamental level in musical "tone" itself. With certain musical instruments (the violin, the trumpet, and certain reed instruments are good examples) probably the biggest challenge facing the beginning student is getting a clear, sustained, musical tone to come out of the instrument. Getting noises to come out is not the hard part. We start by causing vibrations—on the violin by rubbing the bow across the string, on the trumpet by forcing the air through our own vibrating lips, on the clarinet by blowing a column of air past a reed. The difficulty of getting a tone is essentially the challenge of getting the vibrations regular enough and under enough control to "resonate" in the instrument.

In acoustics, *resonance* is the technical term for an observable and measurable phenomenon—"the intensification and prolongation of sound energy, produced by sympathetic vibration." The concept originates in acoustics (cf. "resound" = re-sound) but is extended throughout physics generally to mean "the enhancement of a system's response to a periodic driving force whose frequency is equal to the natural frequency of the system." Here's how this works, for example, in a violin. The strings are stretched out over a box (the resonator) formed out of some elastic material (like wood) in a complex shape with multiple curves. When one of the strings starts vibrating, the air molecules around it are disturbed and sound waves are created, causing the air molecules around and inside the resonator and the resonator itself to be disturbed. Based on certain factors, including the thickness and density of the wood they are made of and the complex geometry of their shape, the resonator and its individual surfaces have natural resonant frequencies at which they vibrate when they are disturbed. When the frequency of the string's vibration matches up with a natural frequency in the resonator, the sound energy is amplified (gets louder) and sustained (lasts longer) because now the string and the resonator are vibrating "in sympathy" (are synchronized) with each other.

Now let us look at resonance in terms of the Law of Conservation of Energy, one of the fundamental laws of physics, which states that energy can neither be created nor destroyed, only converted from one kind of energy to another. When we rub the bow across the string we are using a certain amount of kinetic energy to get the string to vibrate, and our kinetic energy is converted into sound energy. When we achieve resonance on a musical instrument the kinetic energy we spend is matched by the potential energy stored in the resonator in the form of its responsive elasticity, and this multiplies the sound energy we produce. This is the most important reason why the production of a steady musical tone, based on the achievement of a relatively steady state of resonance with an instrument, *feels* so special. It's as if we "got the attention" of the resonator, which then "joined in" (as in call-and-response). It feels so much more "effortless" because in effect we've engaged a part of the world as a partner, and the sound energy we produce together is so much more than we're able to produce on our own without the resonator's sympathetic contribution.

The "Law of Entrainment"

A closely related phenomenon, now commonly referred to as the "Law of Entrainment," is that two independent oscillators or sources of vibrating energy will tend to "fall into sympathy" or synchronize with each other. The seventeenth-century mathematician and clock maker Christian Huygens is generally credited as the first to report this phenomenon. In a letter to his father dated February 26, 1665, and the next day in a letter to the secretary of the Royal Society, Huygens wrote:

> I have noted an impressive effect which no one has yet been able to explain. This is that two clocks, hanging side by side and separated by one or two feet, keep between them a consonance so exact that the two pendula always strike together, never varying.[17]

Huygens observed that two independent pendulum clocks would actually *alter* each other's frequency of vibration (pendulum swings) in order to *achieve* resonance.

If that's not fascinating enough all by itself, now consider the wide range of phenomena where the Law of Entrainment appears to function and apply. Take the complex interaction between horse and rider in which the rider must adapt to the motion of the horse while directing it. And speaking of horses, draft horses can learn to entrain in teams, becoming smoother and more efficient in harness. Horses seem to be able to figure this out all by themselves. And they seem to *like* working this way! Similarly in team sports such as rowing: when the crew entrains, the effort is rewarded handsomely. Resistance is overcome, and the boat moves so much more smoothly and efficiently. Athletes learn to entrain their breathing with their other exertions, enabling their bodies likewise to perform more smoothly and efficiently.

It makes sense to look for entrainment phenomena functioning wherever things are organized or behave rhythmically. This means throughout biology because all of life is rhythmic. And indeed we do find entrainment phenomena at many biological levels. At the global level, biological entrainment can be seen to function in the seasonal migration patterns of many species, in cycles of biological fertility, and in circadian rhythms of activity and rest characteristic of organic life generally, all entrained to the rhythms of planetary motion. At the level of the individual organism, physical coordination as in walking, running, skipping, swimming, dancing, making music, and so on involves neuromuscular entrainment. Research into biological entrainment at the cellular and subcellular level is ongoing and fruitful in several scientific specialties.[18]

And of course we find entrainment phenomena in music. Ensemble work of any kind involves entrainment at several levels. It would be impossible to establish, find, or maintain a rhythmic groove or harmonize in a vocal ensemble without entrainment. Entrained musicians find themselves moving together and breathing together. Entrainment also characterizes the complex exchange of energy between the musicians and the audience. The audience often seems to move and be moved as one as it bounces and sways and moshes and claps hands and taps toes in time with the music. Couples' dancing involves entrainment between the partners, of course, and with the music.[19]

Scientific Uncertainty, Skepticism, and Snake Oil

All of this suggests the concepts of resonance and especially entrainment as good candidates for consideration in explaining the therapeutic effects of music on the listener.

But we need to be careful here because there is still a good deal of scientific uncertainty about how music is received and processed in our bodies and minds and about how our bodies are able to mend themselves. Equally pertinent, with matters as mysterious and important as health and healing there is a good deal of hopeful and wishful thinking abroad and to be expected. So, to put it bluntly but also mildly, there's a market for snake oil. And this attracts snake oil salesmen—who are only too eager to sell us boring music as potent (patent) medicine on the basis of exaggerated claims of scientific validation or fancy-sounding pseudo-scientific mumbo jumbo. And this quite rightly offends and alarms skeptics. Unfortunately that's where we seem to be today with music and entrainment.

It's the human potential music market, more than the massage therapy and relaxation music market that bothers the skeptics. Search under "brainwave entrainment" or "binaural beats," and you will find a good many Web sites selling music designed to entrain the brain for spiritual growth and peak performance. If you happen across some slick Web site that looks like it was produced for a major pharmaceutical corporation, all in understated whites and cheery pastels, with a tanned and lithe supermodel posed in the lotus position wearing earphones and an expression of blissful serenity, you might be in the snake oil zone. But then, if you're told that the patented and unique sonic materials (which you may add to your online shopping cart and download for the special reduced, one-time-only, introductory rate of $$$.99—*if you act now!*) is *GUARAN-TEED* to give you instant effortless access to deep and superpleasurable meditative states within the first few seconds, minutes, hours, days, or weeks; and that it will eliminate anxiety, depression, fear, worry, and addiction while unlocking your infinite creative potential literally at the touch of a button; and then if you're offered the comforting reassurance that this is all proven by the latest in cutting-edge science, but first read these personal testimonials from people just like you with initials for last names, you're *definitely* in the snake oil zone. Hold onto your wallet.

This would not be the first time that exaggerated claims have been made on behalf of music in the human potential market. Probably the most famous such episode is the so-called Mozart Effect, which claimed that listening to Mozart resulted in immediate significant gains in spatial reasoning.[20] The problems with the study on which this still lingering craze was based had to do with flaws in the experimental design and gaps in the explanatory account, as explained here by Daniel Levitin.

The experimental controls were inadequate, and the tiny difference in spatial ability . . . turned on the choice of a control task. Compared to sitting in a room and doing nothing, music listening looked pretty good. But if the subjects in the control [group] were given the slightest mental stimulation—hearing a book on tape, reading, etc.—there was no advantage for music listening. Another problem with the study was that there was no plausible mechanism proposed by which this might work—how could music listening increase spatial performance?[21]

It wasn't that the guiding intuition (listening to good music supports intellectual growth and development in other areas) was wrong. The Mozart Effect was an example of hopeful and wishful thinking getting ahead of itself. One factor undermining the study was that the performance gains that were sought and "measured" were in the immediate short term. The experimenters were apparently so pleased with their findings that they didn't bother to make comparisons over extended periods of exposure to music, where real benefits indeed have been demonstrated and can be more plausibly explained.[22]

Snake oil sales pitches lack integrity and are not to be trusted. But this does not mean that they are necessarily based entirely on falsehoods. We know, scientifically, that there are measurable electromagnetic brain waves and that identifiable states of consciousness (deep dreamless sleep, meditative trance, relaxed awareness, fully alert awareness, mental hyperactivity, and so on) can be correlated with measurable patterns and frequency ranges of brain wave activity. It is also well established empirically that brain waves can be influenced by means of strobe lights and sound. We know further—and this is confirmed everywhere in the human experience of music from indigenous tribal drumming to classical Indian raga to Tibetan and Gregorian chant to Tuvan throat singing to reggae to contemporary techno-rave culture—that there is a profound connection of some kind between musical entrainment and trance (and other states of consciousness), just as there is between trance and meditation. But we do not yet understand the causal mechanisms well enough scientifically to make the kinds of stated and implied causal claims that fuel the snake oil market.

Metaphysics, Science, and Spirituality

The proper scientific balance point between credulous enthusiasm and a priori denial is open-minded scientific (and therefore skeptical) curiosity. I was rather surprised (I must confess) to find this balance reflected in the writings of one Valerie V. Hunt, whose research into the electromagnetic energy fields (or auras) surrounding living organisms is widely cited in the growing literature on alternative energy medicine. A few months ago I would have relegated any and all talk of "auras" to the category of carnival cargo-cult pseudo science. But, as Hunt persuasively points out, quoting Margaret Mead, "to believe without questioning or to dismiss without investigation is to comport oneself unscientifically." And so now, having read at least a bit of her work on vibrations, electromagnetic energy, and consciousness, I'm suddenly quite curious about bioelectromagnetics as an emerging field on the common frontiers of biology, medicine, and physics.[23] How might sound energy impact a person's electromagnetic energy field? It's an interesting research question and one that poses a number of challenging methodological issues, as we'll see further in a moment.

Given our interest in the causal mechanisms linking musical entrainment and the life of the conscious body/mind, another area of research both highly relevant and deeply interesting is the neuroscience of meditation. What measurable changes occur in the brains of people when they meditate? And what are the cumulative effects upon the brain of years of daily practice in meditation? Among the hypotheses preliminary research has opened up to further investigation is the possibility that people might be able to alter brain function by the deliberate voluntary practice of meditation. Buddhists believe and teach that one can cultivate compassion in oneself through disciplined meditation over time and that this is a way to make spiritual progress. Can compassion be measured electromagnetically as a condition of consciousness? Can spiritual progress be documented empirically?

At the University of Wisconsin, Richard Davidson, a Harvard-trained neuropsychologist, has been pursuing these questions by studying the brain states of both advanced and novice practitioners of Tibetan Buddhist meditation with the interested support of the Dalai Lama.[24] Here, too, of course, the science is unfinished and faces a number of complex challenges. Among these are the importance within the spiritual contemplative traditions of introspection and first-person phenomenal descriptive reports as indicators of conditions of consciousness, coupled with the fact that the traditional accounts of the goals and practices of the contemplative disciplines are often couched in "poetic" metaphysical terms that do not lend themselves easily to empirical investigation. How does one design an empirical test for "the cleansing of all mental afflictions through the sustained cultivation of insight penetrating the ultimate nature of reality, the innate purity of the mind—which Nagarjuna calls the 'ultimate expanse' "?[25] A further challenge is posed by the wide variety of discreet practices and states of consciousness associated with the generic label "meditation." For the sake of scientific rigor, as well as from the point of view of the spiritual disciplines themselves, it is important to distinguish carefully between particular meditative practices—such as chanting, reciting a mantra, movement and posture, focused attention on the breath, and visualizations of specific deities or energy flowing in and around one's body—and study these individually and in comparison with each other.[26]

It takes a good deal of patience to follow the science. A craving for answers can make the pace of ongoing scientific inquiry seem painfully slow. How frustrating to be forever waiting for the science to be finished before forming an opinion! But impatience will only make us more vulnerable to peddlers of snake oil. Scientists, like philosophers, are used to living with unanswered questions. The scientist is too busy doing the science to get frustrated about how unfinished it is.

We seem to be arriving at the heart of the labyrinth we entered in chapter 1. There we began talking of the soul as the locus of consciousness and the agent of voluntary action in any sentient being. Here we find neuroscientists investigating the effects of deliberate voluntary action upon the consciousness of the agent. We have transcended physics. We're now clearly in the realm of the metaphysical.

Healing Music for the Dying

Science and philosophy both begin in wonder. As a philosopher I find the unfinished research initiatives in alternative energy medicine and the neuroscience of meditation especially exciting because they reflect an open-minded scientific interest in the metaphysics of spirituality and because they pertain so directly to my interest in music and the health care of the soul. Besides the many as yet unanswered questions about music as therapy, there remains a threshold or horizon beyond which science and philosophy can only conjecture. And yet it is a horizon we all face and a threshold we are all bound to cross. And so we find it inevitably compelling to contemplation. But here we must contemplate in a spirit of the deepest humility. With characteristic wit, the Dalai Lama put the problem this way.

> My own teacher Ling Rinpoche remained in the clear light of death for thirteen days; although he was clinically dead and had stopped breathing, he stayed in the meditation posture and his body showed no sign of decomposition. Another realized meditator remained in this state for seventeen days in the tropical heat of high summer in eastern India. It

would be most interesting to know what was happening at the physio-logical level during this period, and if there might be any detectable signs at the biochemical level. When Richard Davidson's team came to Dharamsala, they were keen to do some experiments on this phenome-non, but when they were there—I am not sure whether I should say for-tunately or unfortunately—no meditators died.[27]

In his 1941 composition "Going Down Slow," James Burke Oden ("St. Louis Jimmy") sings from the point of view of a man contemplating his own imminent death.

> I have had my fun, if I don't get well no more. (2x)
> My health is failing me, and I'm going down slow.
> Please write my mother, tell her the shape I'm in. (2x)
> Tell her to pray for me, forgive me for my sin.
> Tell her don't send no doctor, doctor can't do no good. (2x)
> It's all my fault, didn't do the things I should.
> Mother please don't worry, this is all in my prayer. (2x)
> Just say your son is gone, out in this world somewhere.

Oden wrote this lyric in his thirty-eighth year with nearly half of his life yet ahead of him. But the lyric speaks eloquently to the complex physical and spiritual needs of the dying. How can music be of service to the dy-ing patient?

Harpist Therese Schroeder-Sheker has developed a practice of music in hospice care she calls music-thanatology, which she describes as a clin-ical application of music distinct from but closely allied with music ther-apy. Music-thanatology belongs to palliative as opposed to therapeutic medicine. A therapeutic care modality presupposes a reserve of energy in the patient and seeks to engage the patient in interactions that sup-port continued living and the patient's return to improved health. By contrast a palliative care modality is indicated where therapeutic means have been exhausted and is intended to ease and support the patient's completion of and passage from this life.

> The dying person should not spend energy making new connections. In music-thanatology, the patient only receives. . . . The sole focus is to help the person move toward completion and to unbind from anything that prevents, impedes, or clouds a tranquil passage."[28]

Schroeder-Sheker derives her practice from the eleventh-century Bene-dictine Cluniac tradition of monastic medicine. For the monks at Cluny the infirmary was considered not only a clinic where the bodies of the sick were treated medically and nursed back to health but also a sanctuary dedicated to providing for the souls of the dying.[29]

Schroeder-Shecker's practice has attracted scientific interest. In a comparative study of the clinical use of music in the treatment of end-stage Alzheimer's disease, music was divided into two categories: sedative and palliative. In this study, sedative music, as music designed for a therapeutic application, was identified as "sustained melodic music" with a pulse somewhere within the normal range of the human heart at rest but with no pronounced use of percussion or strong rhythms. Following the Cluniac tradition, the palliative music selected was modal plainchant with highly developed melodic content but no rhythmic accents. A population of patients with end-stage Alzheimer's dementia was randomly divided into three groups, one group receiving sedative music, another receiving palliative music, and a control group receiving no music. The hypotheses under investigation were that the palliative music would be more deeply relaxing than the sedative music and that either would be more relaxing than no music. End-stage Alzheimer's patients are generally unresponsive and certainly uncommunicative and can therefore only be monitored physiologically, by measuring heart rate, respiratory rate, body temperature, and so on. Differences in physiological response between the three groups were not statistically significant. The results were inconclusive.[30] Again science is humbled before the mystery of life and death.

For the philosopher, however, nothing stands in the way of further thoughtful consideration and conjecture. Schroeder-Shecker notes as a fundamental tenet of her practice that each individual person's death is a process unique unto itself. Accordingly, she approaches her work reverently, offering only live (never recorded) music specifically chosen for and addressed to the dying person as an individual. This highlights what is surely among the biggest challenges facing science in its investigations. Science cannot rely here on the repeatability of experiments and the replication of results to meet rigorous standards of verification and confirmation (as is rightly to be expected, for example, in the testing of synthetic pharmaceutical drugs). The uniqueness of each individual person's end of life process and experience and the concomitant commitment to tailoring the music to the individual need combine to make strict replication impossible.[31] But we should notice that this is not by itself an insurmountable obstacle to the development of a responsible medical practice. Each individual birth is a unique process and experience for both mother and child. That hasn't prevented midwifery or obstetrics from accumulating a large body of reliable experience and understanding of childbirth. The lesson here would seem to be that the responsible practice of music as a healing art will have to lead the science.

Sex and Drugs and Rock & Roll

Coming of age in the 1950s and 1960s, my musical sensibilities and tastes were shaped to a great extent by rock & roll. Over the last twenty to thirty years as popular music culture has evolved, I've found myself less and less interested in following out every new trend and more and more interested in exploring the antecedent musical roots of rock & roll—what some people call American "roots music." But whether you look back or forward from the 1950s and 1960s, it is striking throughout the twentieth century how closely so much of this music, root *and* branch, has been entangled with social conditions and patterns of behavior manifestly damaging to the human being, body *and* soul. Quite apart from the social conditions of slavery and Reconstruction discussed in chapters 2 and 3, and other, similar historical, social, and political circumstances that vernacular music has responded to and expressed, here I'm referring to the toxic conditions that tend to surround the music as an entertainment industry commodity.

I have come to believe that the highest calling for a musician is the spiritual practice of music as a healing art and that serious musicians have always understood this at some level. Music is a wonderful but extremely difficult and endlessly challenging discipline. I marvel at the dedication it takes to develop oneself as a musician, especially over an extended period of time. On any instrument at any level of attainment the practicing musician is always confronted by his or her limitations. There is always so much more to learn. I cannot imagine how a person could sustain the effort if there were not something inherently nourishing and healing about music and the activity of making it and the gift of sharing it with others.[32]

But sooner or later the serious musician confronts the question of making a living. And for musicians who play jazz or blues or soul or funk or rock & roll or country music, the opportunities for "gainful employment" have always been more or less confined within the entertainment industry, an often shady world that is generally structured at cross-purposes with the spiritual practice of music as a healing art. This unfortunate association has created some deep challenges and conflicts with which working musicians must wrestle.[33] To this day, if you are a musician and want to play the blues for an audience (or if you simply want to hear the blues performed live), chances are you will soon find yourself in a public space with a liquor license. Alcohol is a challenging constant. And even though you are surrounded by souls in need of healing (why else would they be there?), it's very easy to lose sight of your higher calling as a musician in an environment that is all about intoxication. Even if you don't drink, you do come under the influence.[34] This is to say nothing of the kinds of drugs that seem to be forever lurking behind the scenes of major touring rock acts. By the time you get to "Guns N' Roses" or "Mötley Crüe" the quicksand is very deep.

Nonetheless, watching a blues shaman like John Lee Hooker work, one realizes that deep healing does get accomplished in these settings despite the toxic conditions. This is often the result of genuinely creative musical solutions to the challenges and conflicts inherent in the context—solutions that can wind up opening whole new vistas of musical possibility for future generations. Let me illustrate with one final example.

Case Study: Parlor Professors of the Piano

All journeys in search of the roots of American popular music must eventually go to New Orleans, where sure enough one finds one of the richest sources anywhere of vernacular keyboard inspiration in the New Orleans piano tradition. This lineage is crucial to the history of rock & roll. Fats Domino belongs to this lineage, as does Mac Rebennak (Dr. John), Harry Connick Jr., Professor Longhair, Huey "Piano" Smith, Allen Touissaint, and the great James Booker.

To understand the development of the New Orleans piano tradition, we must go back at least to the New Orleans of the late 1800s and early 1900s. Although jazz and New Orleans piano music developed simultaneously under the same general historical and cultural conditions, the two nevertheless developed as separate and distinct entities. One important difference is basically a matter of technology. Jazz, as ensemble music, developed out of parade music for brass bands. The instruments typically used are, naturally, portable. The piano is a large piece of furniture—a parlor instrument. It belongs in a room large enough to entertain a gathering of people. At the turn of the twentieth century, according to Ferdinand "Jelly Roll" Morton:

> New Orleans was the stomping grounds for all the greatest pianists in the country. We had Spanish, we had colored, we had white, we had Frenchmens. We had Americans, we had them from all parts of the

world, because there were more jobs for pianists in New Orleans than in any other ten places in the world. The sporting houses needed professors.[35]

A "sporting house" is a brothel. And "the professor" was the house piano player.

The history of prostitution in the city of New Orleans is complex, with many contributing factors, not least the colonial French government's response to a scarcity of marriageable females among the colonists, which was to send over boatloads of indigent women partly as a way to relieve overcrowding in the Paris jails. Suffice to say that the trade reached a scale and level of prosperity sufficient to establish it as a pillar of the New Orleans economy. In 1896, with prostitution threatening to engulf the entire city of New Orleans, Alderman Sidney Story promulgated an ordinance creating a district outside of which it would be unlawful to engage in prostitution. In what Alderman Story perhaps came to regard as a cruel irony, the district became known as Storyville. Jelly Roll continues:

> They had everything in the district from the highest class to the lowest—creep joints and cribs that rented for $5/day, small time houses where the price was 50 cents to a dollar and they put on naked dances and jive. Then of course we had the mansions. These houses were filled up with the most expensive furniture and paintings. Three of them had mirror parlors where you couldn't find the door for the mirrors. It was in these mansions that the best of the piano players worked.[36]

Now I want to highlight a crucial dimension of the style of music that comes out of this situation. So let's reflect on the circumstances. First of all, there is an abundance of employment opportunity for pianists. An abundance of talent flocks to the city from all over the world. The branch of the entertainment/hospitality industry that employs the talent is highly stratified economically (and otherwise). This produces a competitive environment in the talent community. A significant premium is attached to excellence in all aspects of the performing art—technical mastery, creative originality, stylistic range and flexibility, showmanship, and so on. Finally, now consider the reward that comes to the pianist who, like Jelly Roll Morton, rises to the top of this competitive field. One gains tenure, as "the Professor" at one of the top two or three houses of prostitution in the most renowned city of leisure of its day. What this means in practice is that one works as an entertainer, mostly for tips, in an environment where patrons of the most magnificent means go to enjoy themselves. These patrons, again from all over the world, expect to be entertained in a grand manner and to be surrounded by the symbols and amenities of highest culture. Quoting from a souvenir booklet of the period:

> The most famous establishment on Basin Street, Mahogany Hall, over-seen by Madame Lula White, has four stories, five grand parlors on the ground floor, 15 bedrooms on the upper floors all with private baths. . . . Within the great walls of this mansion will be found the work of great artists from Europe and America. . . . As an entertainment Miss Lula stands foremost, having made a lifelong study of music and litera-ture. She's well read and one that will interest anybody and make a visit to her place a continued round of pleasure.[37]

So here we see the values of colonial European "high culture" deployed strategically for commercial purposes of high-end sexual entertain-ment—hence, the academic title bestowed upon the piano player. "Ah, Professor. Here's a handsome tip. Now, how's about playing us a little Chopin!" Consider now the musical challenge that must have presented itself on a regular basis to a piano player working in such circumstances: What sort of music to make so as to uphold the respectability of the pa-trons, who are in each other's presence in the parlor enjoying the com-pany of hired women (your coworkers, by the way), while at the same time you remain truthful about just what sort of congregation they are and about what kind of transaction is actually going down. I think I now understand what Wynton Marsalis meant when he said:

> You have a war going on out here where your ammunition is your imag-ination and your technique. When you bring off a good piece of work, you have taken a victorious position in the struggle with falsehoods.[38]

Jelly Roll Morton's musical solution to the challenge, typical of the style, was to "rag the tune," to use syncopations and other embellishments and variations in a playful and subversively ironic spirit.

> I transform a lot of those numbers into jazz time. And from time to time introduce little variations and ideas in it that would no doubt have a tendency to "detract" or "masquerade" the tune.[39]

This is a strategy we have seen before—the use of irony both to "say things between the lines" and to release emotional energy. Listen to James Booker's rendition of Chopin's "Minute Waltz"—a consummate example of the style highlighting this strategy in particular.[40]

The piano music in this tradition is as playful, juicy, and mischievous as any music in my experience. It is my favorite kind of music. And it reminds me, as I reflect on its importance to the history of world music and especially on its genesis in the New Orleans sex trade, of an important principle for the spiritual practice of music as a healing art in situations that are toxic and compromised by other agendas. Your audience may be sorely in need of healing, but that's likely not what's on their minds. Maybe they're interested in getting laid or getting wasted. Let them be. They're not really listening anyway. You transform the situation by first healing yourself.

Notes

INTRODUCTION

1. See Alex Ross, "Voice of the Century," *New Yorker*, April 13, 2009, 78–79; Raymond Arsenault, *The Sound of Freedom: Marian Anderson, the Lincoln Memorial, and the Concert That Awakened America* (New York: Bloomsbury, 2009). Compara- ble moments include Paul Robeson's 1952 performance before an audience of 40,000 at Peace Arch Park on the border between Canada and the United States in protest against the revocation of his passport and right to travel. See Paul Robeson, *Here I Stand* (New York: Othello Associates, 1958), 63.

2. Phil Cousineau, ed., *Soul—An Archaeology: Readings from Socrates to Ray Charles* (New York: HarperCollins, 1994). Cousineau is a poet, screenwriter, ad- venture travel guide, and host of *Global Spirit,* a new Link TV series.

CHAPTER 1

The three chapter-opening epigraphs are from, respectively: George Robinson Ricks, *Some Aspects of the Religious Music of the United States Negro: An Ethnomusico- logical Study with Special Emphasis on the Gospel Tradition* (New York: Arno, 1977), 139; Quoted in Ben Sidran, *A Life in the Music* (New York: Rowman & Littlefield, 2003), 248; and Dick Hebdige, "What Is Soul?" in *Video Icons and Values,* ed. Alan M. Olson, Christopher Parr, and Debra Parr (Albany: State University of New York Press, 1991), 121.

1. Ray Charles and David Ritz, *Brother Ray: Ray Charles' Own Story* (New York: Dial Press, 1978), 151.

2. Amiri Baraka (LeRoi Jones), "The Phenomenon of *Soul* in African-Ameri- can Music," in *The Music* (New York: Morrow, 1987), 268–76.

3. See Samuel A. Floyd, Jr., *The Power of Black Music: Interpreting Its History from Africa to the United States* (New York: Oxford University Press, 1995), 203. Cf. Baraka, "The Phenomenon of *Soul* in African-American Music."

4. *Rhythm & blues* was the coinage of Jerry Wexler, then writing for *Billboard Magazine,* later to become a major figure in record production with Atlantic Records. Cf. Portia K. Maultsby, "Soul," in *African American Music: An Introduction,* ed. Mellonee V. Burnim and Portia K. Maultsby (New York: Routledge, 2006), 272–73.

5. Peter Guralnick, *Sweet Soul Music: Rhythm and Blues and the Southern Dream of Freedom* (New York: HarperCollins, 1988).

6. Ibid., 1–2.

7. Ibid., 6.

8. Ibid., 5.

9. Rob Bowman, "Stax," in *African American Music: An Introduction,* ed. Mellonee V. Burnim and Portia K. Maultsby (New York: Routledge, 2006), 452.

10. Guralnick, *Sweet Soul Music,* 8.

11. Guralnick, *Sweet Soul Music,* 339–44. Cf. Craig Werner, *Higher Ground* (New York: Three Rivers Press, 2004), 130–35.

12. Gene Santoro, "Sweet Soul Music," in *Highway 61 Revisited: The Tangled Roots of American Jazz, Blues, Rock & Country Music* (New York: Oxford University Press, 2004), 135–49.

13. Brian Ward, *Just My Soul Responding: Rhythm and Blues, Black Consciousness, and Race Relations* (Berkeley: University of California Press, 1998), 3–7.

14. Portia Maultsby, "Soul," in Burnim and Maultsby, 271–91.

15. Nelson George, *The Death of Rhythm & Blues* (New York: Pantheon, 1988), 93.

16. Rob Bowman, *Soulsville U.S.A.: The Story of Stax Records* (New York: Schirmer, 1997), 11.

17. Mark A. Humphrey, "Holy Blues: The Gospel Tradition," in *Nothing But the Blues,* ed. Lawrence Cohn (New York: Abbeville, 1993), 107.

18. Humphrey, 107 (emphasis added).

19. Ibid.

20. "Soul," in Dictionary.com, *Online Etymology Dictionary,* Douglas Harper, historian, http://dictionary,reference.com/browse/soul (accessed March 10, 2007).

21. Compiled from *Merriam-Webster's Online Dictionary;* Dictionary.com Unabridged (vol. 1.1), Random House, http://dictionary,reference.com/browse/soul (accessed March 10, 2007); *The American Heritage Dictionary of the English Language* (New York: American Heritage, 1970); *The American Heritage Dictionary of the English Language,* 4th ed. (Boston: Houghton Mifflin, 2004), http://dictionary,reference.com/browse/soul (accessed March 10, 2007).

22. Three additional meanings are given as slang or derivative:

(1) An aggregate of elemental qualities that enables one to be in harmony with oneself and to convey to others the honest and unadorned expression of the hard side of life;

(2) A strong positive feeling (as of intense sensitivity and emotional fervor) conveyed especially by black American performers;

(3) Negritude, the essence of blackness.

These reflect the views of Amiri Baraka discussed above: that Soul (as essence, rather than as an entity) is the condition of authentic blackness.

23. "Supreme being" stands in here for the more cumbersome "being than which none greater can be conceived." St. Anselm wrote in the *Proslogium,* as translated by Jonathan Barnes: "Therefore, Lord, who grant understanding to faith, grant me that, in so far as you know it beneficial, I understand that you are as we believe and you are that which we believe. Now we believe that you are something than which nothing greater can be imagined . . . And certainly that than which a greater cannot be imagined cannot be in the understanding alone.

For if it is at least in the understanding alone, it can be imagined to be in reality too, which is greater. Therefore if that than which a greater cannot be imagined is in the understanding alone, that very thing than which a greater cannot be imagined is something than which a greater can be imagined. But certainly this cannot be. There exists, therefore, beyond doubt something than which a greater cannot be imagined, both in the understanding and in reality."

24. This means that when you add zero to any other number, the sum equals the other number.

25. See "Folk Psychology as a Theory," in *Stanford Encyclopedia of Philosophy*, http://plato.stanford.edu/entries/folkpsych-theory/ (accessed June 11, 2009). Another source of this view is the work of the twentieth-century Viennese philosopher Ludwig Wittgenstein. In his "later period" as a lecturer at the University of Cambridge, Wittgenstein would "attack" philosophical problems and try to "clear them up" and get rid of them by showing how they were generated by some idiom, or conventional way of speaking. So, for example, I speak of my "soul," as though there is some "thing" separate from but related to me. Then I start to wonder where it is, and what it is, and why I can't catch even a glimpse of it. And when I can't find answers to these questions, rather than critique the questions and their presuppositions, I get increasingly mystified and tied up in philosophical knots of confusion. Or perhaps I simply ignore the philosophical problems generated by my "soul talk" and relax into mushier and mushier metaphysical mumbo jumbo about a mere word.

CHAPTER 2

The three chapter-opening epigraphs are from, respectively: Andrew Fletcher, *Conversation Concerning a Right Regulation of Government for the Common Good of Mankind* (1703); *Progressive*, August 2005, 41; and Mark Twain, *Pudd'nhead Wilson's New Calendar* (1897), chap. 51, "Following the Equator."

1. Allan Bloom, *The Closing of the American Mind* (New York: Simon and Schuster, 1987), 71.

2. *Republic, Book IV,* 424c.

3. *Philosophical Fragments.*

4. William McDonald, "Søren Kierkegaard," in *The Stanford Encyclopedia of Philosophy*, ed. Edward N. Zalta, Summer 2006 ed., http://plato.stanford.edu/archives/sum2006/entries/kierkegaard/ (accessed January 11, 2010).

5. David Evans, "Goin' Up the Country: Blues in Texas and the Deep South," in *Nothing But the Blues*, ed. Lawrence Cohn (New York: Abbeville, 1993), 74.

6. Francis Davis, *The History of the Blues* (Cambridge, MA: Da Capo, 1993), 124.

7. Robert Santelli, "A Century of the Blues," in *Martin Scorsese Presents: The Blues—A Musical Journey*, ed. Peter Guralnick, Robert Santelli, Holly George-Warren, and Christopher John Farley (New York: HarperCollins Amistad, 2003), 27–28.

8. Peter Guralnick, *Searching for Robert Johnson* (New York: Dutton, 1989), 1–5.

9. Eric Clapton, "Discovering Robert Johnson," *Robert Johnson: The Complete Recordings* (New York: CBS Records, 1990), 23.

10. References to stabbing can be found attributed to Son House, who reports it as an early unconfirmed rumor; in Guralnick, *Searching for Robert Johnson,* 49; and in an interview with Michael Bloomfield published by Ed Ward in Ward, *Michael Bloomfield: The Rise and Fall of an American Guitar Hero* (New York: Cherry Lane, 1981), 7–9. The poisoning account is generally accepted as best confirmed.

11. Griel Marcus, *Mystery Train: Images of America in Rock 'n' Roll Music* (New York: Dutton, 1975), 28.

12. Ward, Bloomfield interview. The interview is said to have been conducted just two days before Bloomfield's own death by accidental drug overdose in 1981. David Evans doubts the sources of Bloomfield's account because he cannot find corroborating testimony directly from Johnny Shines, Sunnyland Slim, or Elmore James, and he points out that Muddy Waters and Robert Johnson never met.

13. Cf. Alan Lomax, *The Land Where the Blues Began* (New York: Pantheon, 1993), 366–67.

14. Ibid.

15. Guralnick, *Searching for Robert Johnson,* 17–18.

16. Cf. Paul Garon, *The Devil's Son-in-Law: The Story of Peetie Wheatstraw and His Songs* (London: November Books, 1971), 64–65.

17. Guralnick, *Searching for Robert Johnson,* 18. Cf. David Evans, *Tommy Johnson* (London: Studio Vista, 1971). Guralnick, probably following Welding, also confirms the attributions of the legend as regards Robert Johnson to Son House and Johnny Shines and recycles speculation by "others" about "the black arts" at 49.

18. See Gayle Dean Wardlow, "Searching for the Robert Johnson Death Certificate (1965–1968)." On the back of the death certificate is a report of additional speculation as to the cause of death (syphilis) by the owner of the plantation where Johnson died. Also see "Robert Johnson: New Details on the Death of a Bluesman." Both sources are reprinted in *Chasin' That Devil Music: Searching for the Blues* (San Francisco: Backbeat Books, 1998), 86–93.

19. Keith Richards, "Well, This Is It," *Robert Johnson: The Complete Recordings* (New York: CBS Records, 1990), 21–22.

20. F. Davis, 129.

21. Santelli, 28.

22. Marcus, *Mystery Train,* 26.

23. Santelli, 28.

24. Evans, *Tommy Johnson.*

25. David Evans, "Early Deep South and Mississippi Basin Blues," in *The New Blackwell Guide to Recorded Blues,* ed. John Cowley and Paul Oliver (Cambridge, MA: Blackwell, 1996), 75.

26. Ibid., 76.

27. Robert M. W. Dixon and John Godrich, "Recording the Blues," in *Yonder Come the Blues,* ed. Paul Oliver, Tony Russell, Robert M. W. Dixon, John Godrich, and Howard Rye (Cambridge: Cambridge University Press, 2001), 316.

28. Rudi Blesh, *Shining Trumpets: A History of Jazz* (New York: Knopf, 1946).

29. Clapton, "Discovering Robert Johnson," 22. Cf. Guralnick, *Searching for Robert Johnson,* 3.

30. Marcus, *Mystery Train,* 22.

31. F. Davis, 124.

32. Dave Marsh, *The Heart of Rock & Soul: The 1001 Greatest Singles Ever Made* (New York: Penguin, 1989), 2, 103.

33. Humphrey, 107–8.

34. Evans, "Goin' Up the Country," 74. Cf. Samuel Charters, *The Country Blues* (New York: Da Capo, 1959).

35. Evans, "Early Deep South and Mississippi Basin Blues," 75–76.

36. But see also Marybeth Hamilton, *In Search of the Blues: Black Voices, White Visions* (London: Jonathan Cape, 2007); Barry Lee Pearson and Bill McCulloch, *Robert Johnson Lost and Found* (Urbana: University of Illinois Press, 2003); Elijah Wald, *Escaping the Delta: Robert Johnson and the Invention of the Blues* (New York: HarperCollins Amistad, 2004).

37. Marcus, *Mystery Train,* 28.

38. David Hume, "Of Superstition and Enthusiasm," in *Of the Standard of Taste and Other Essays* (Indianapolis: Bobbs Merrill Library of Liberal Arts, 1965), 146.

39. Paul Oliver, "The Jinx Is on Me," in *Blues Fell This Morning* (Cambridge: Cambridge University Press, 1960), 118–19.

40. Dick Waterman, *Between Midnight and Day* (New York: Thunder's Mouth Press, 2003), 37–41.

41. Stephen C. LaVere, "Liner Notes," *Robert Johnson: The Complete Recordings* (New York: CBS Records, 1990), 11.

42. Ibid., 13.

43. Ibid., 46–47; Wardlow, 200. Cf. Charters, *The Country Blues.*

44. Marcus, *Mystery Train,* 28.

45. Pete Welding, "Hell Hound on His Trail: Robert Johnson," *Down Beat's Music '66* (Chicago: Maher, 1966), 73–74, 76, 103; reprinted in *Blues Unlimited,* no. 81 (1971), 15; no. 82 (1971), 16–17; no. 83 (1971), 16–17.

46. Evans, *Tommy Johnson.*

47. Gayle Dean Wardlow and Edward Komara, "Stop, Look, and Listen at the Cross Road," in *Chasin' That Devil Music: Searching for the Blues* (San Francisco: Backbeat Books, 1998), 200–204.

48. Pearson and McCulloch, ix–x.

49. Ibid., 4.

50. E. Wald, 276.

51. See Robert Walser, *Running with the Devil: Power, Gender, and Madness in Heavy Metal Music* (Hanover, NH: Wesleyan University Press, 1993), especially chap. 5.

52. Mikal Gilmore, "The Long Shadow of Led Zeppelin (savaged by critics, adored by fans, the biggest band of the 70s took sex, drugs and rock & roll to epic heights before collapsing under the weight of its own heaviness)," *Rolling Stone* 1006, 66.

53. Ibid.

54. Ibid.

55. Robert Farris Thompson, *Flash of the Spirit: African and Afro-American Art and Philosophy* (New York: Random House, 1983), 18.

56. N. N. Puckett, *Folk Beliefs of the Southern Negro* (Chapel Hill: University of North Carolina Press, 1926), 554; cited by Floyd, 73–74.

57. See, for example, William Barlow, *Looking Up at Down: The Emergence of Blues Culture* (Philadelphia: Temple University Press, 1989), 49–50. Cf. the comment on Barlow's interpretive effort in Pearson and McCulloch, 49–50.

58. See Ted Gioia, *Delta Blues: The Life and Times of the Mississippi Masters Who Revolutionized American Music* (New York: Norton, 2008), 370–80.

59. Marcus, *Mystery Train,* 28.

60. Jim O'Neal, "BluEsoterica: Dealing with the Devil at the Crossroads," *Living Blues* 37, no. 2 (March–April 2006): 104.

61. Ibid.

62. Ibid.

63. Stevie Wonder, "Superstition," *Talking Book* (Tamla/Motown, 1972).

64. Ward, 9.

CHAPTER 3

The three chapter-opening epigraphs are from, respectively: Amiri Baraka, *Black Music* (New York: William Morrow, 1963), 183; The Neville Brothers, "Sermon," *Live On Planet Earth* (Hollywood: A&M Records, 1994); and Bob Dylan, "I and I," *Infidels* (Columbia Records, 1983).

1. George, 70.

2. Humphrey, 145.

3. David Whiteis, "The Devil Ain't Got No Music! Mavis Staples," *Living Blues* 175 (December 2004), 14. Thus, as oversimplified and unhelpful as the familiar dichotomous categories and conceptual frameworks may be, they cannot be blamed entirely on the flawed scholarship of ignorant academics using clumsy methodologies alien to African American cultural life, as some have argued. See, for example, Jon Michael Spencer, *Blues and Evil* (Knoxville: University of Tennessee Press, 1993), xi–xxv.

4. Humphrey, 143.

5. Angela Y. Davis, *Blues Legacies and Black Feminism* (New York: Pantheon, 1998), 124. Cf. Alice Walker, *The Same River Twice: Honoring the Difficult* (New York: Simon and Schuster, 1996), 142–43.

6. Oliver, *Blues Fell This Morning,* 117.

7. Lomax, *The Land Where the Blues Began,* 364.

8. Ibid,. 365.

9. Ibid.

10. Ibid.

11. Ibid.

12. I thank my colleague Steve Bernstein for triggering this line of thought.

13. Though they don't make this point explicitly, I find both Ben Sidran and Barry Pearson hinting at some such explanation. Cf. Ben Sidran, *Black Talk: How the Music of Black America Created a Radical Alternative to the Values of the Western Literary Tradition* (New York: Holt, Rinehart and Winston, 1971), 20; and Barry Pearson, "Jump Steady: The Roots of R & B," in *Nothing But the Blues,* ed. Lawrence Cohn (New York: Abbeville, 1993), 339.

14. Mellonee V. Burnim, "Religious Music," in Burnim and Maultsby, 57.

15. John F. Watson, "Methodist Error" (1819); reprinted in Eileen Southern,

comp and ed., *Readings in Black American Music,* 2nd ed. (New York: Norton, 1983), 62–64; quoted in Burnim, "Religious Music," 57.

16. Miles Mark Fisher, *Negro Slave Songs in the United States,* 2nd ed. (New York: Citadel, 1963), 35; quoted in Burnim, "Religious Music," 57.

17. Daniel Alexander Payne, "Recollections of Seventy Years" (1888); reprinted in Eileen Southern, comp. and ed., *Readings in Black American Music,* 2nd ed. (New York: Norton, 1983), 69. Cited in Burnim, "Religious Music," 56–58.

18. James H. Cone, *The Spirituals and the Blues* (Maryknoll, NY: Orbis, 1991), 114 (emphasis in the original).

19. Ibid.

20. A. Y. Davis, 131.

21. Ibid., 123.

22. W. E. B. DuBois, "Of Our Spiritual Strivings," *The Souls of Black Folk* (1903), in *The Oxford W. E. B. DuBois Reader,* ed. Eric J. Sundquist (New York: Oxford University Press, 1996), 103.

23. Harry T. Burleigh, *The Spirituals of Harry T. Burleigh* (Miami: Belwin Mills, 1984), 4.

24. W. E. B. DuBois, "The Sorrow Songs," *The Souls of Black Folk* (1903), in Sundquist, 232. So profound is this double consciousness that it arguably poses a problem even for DuBois's hopes for the development of a talented tenth through education.

25. Ibid.

26. Ibid., 238.

27. Ibid., 103–4.

28. J. H. Cone, 101.

29. Ibid., 99.

30. Alan Young, *Woke Me Up This Morning: Black Gospel Singers and the Gospel Life* (Jackson: University Press of Mississippi, 1997), x.

31. J. H. Cone, 100.

32. Cf. Robert C. Solomon, *Spirituality for the Skeptic* (New York: Oxford University Press, 2002), 12.

33. Bob Dylan, "I and I," *Infidels* (Columbia Records, 1983). A lot of the retrospective "appreciations" of Dylan's work overlook this album or write it off as part of his (wayward) "born-again Christian phase," but for me his work on this album, well exemplified by this song, ranks with his best and most profound.

34. Many spiritual traditions have functionally analogous rituals of purification and describe them in similarly poetic ways. See, for example, George Morgan, "Recollections of the Peyote Road," in *Psychedelic Reflections,* ed. L. Grinspoon and J. Bakalar (New York: Human Sciences Press, 1983).

35. Rory Block, whose CD *The Lady and Mr. Johnson* was honored as the acoustic blues album of the year at the 2007 Blues Music Awards, has positioned herself as a contemporary custodian of Robert Johnson's body of work. In 2006, during the recording of the album, she became acquainted with Johnson's surviving relatives in Mississippi, including a grandson, Elder Steven Johnson of the Straightway Ministries Church and Gospel Choir. Together they conceived a concert presentation bringing Robert Johnson's blues together with gospel music

and have taken the concert on tour throughout the South. In this context they are presenting Robert Johnson's "devil music" as "anointed spiritually healing music."

36. Spencer, *Blues and Evil,* 68–98.

37. J. H. Cone, 112.

38. Cf. Amiri Baraka, interviewed in *The Story of Gospel Music: The Power of the Voice* (British Broadcasting Corporation, 1996).

39. Leon Litwack, *Trouble in Mind: Black Southerners in the Age of Jim Crow* (New York: Knopf, 1998), 387; quoted in Gayle F. Wald, *Shout, Sister, Shout! The Untold Story of Rock-and-Roll Trailblazer Sister Rosetta Tharpe* (Boston: Beacon Press, 2007), 12.

40. Paul Garon, *Blues & the Poetic Spirit* (New York: Da Capo, 1978), 134–36.

41. Cf. Allan Moore, "Surveying the Field: Our Knowledge of Blues and Gospel Music," in *The Cambridge Companion to Blues and Gospel Music* (Cambridge: Cambridge University Press, 2002), 1; and Floyd, 5; see also Dr. John for the converse point that church music is crucial to blues piano, *Sanctifying the Blues: Dr. John Teaches New Orleans Piano,* vol. 3 (Milwaukee: Hal Leonard, 1997).

42. *Sacred Steel: Live!* (El Cerrito, CA: Arhoolie Records 472, 1999), track 14; or *Can You Feel It?* (Ropeadope Records, 2005), track 9.

43. Robert Fontenot, "Robert Randolph: The Second Coming of Sacred Steel?" *Blues Revue* 80 (February–March 2003): 8–14; and Eric Fine, "Heavenly Hitmakers: The Rise of Sacred Steel," *Blues Revue* 80 (February–March 2003): 11–13. Cf. Robert L. Stone, *Sacred Steel: Live!* (El Cerrito, CA: Arhoolie Records 472, 1999), liner notes.

44. McKinley Morganfield (Muddy Waters), *Hard Again* (New York: Columbia Records 34449, 1977).

45. See Michael W. Harris, *The Rise of Gospel Blues: The Music of Thomas Andrew Dorsey in the Urban Church* (New York: Oxford University Press, 1992); see also Lulie Haddad, *This Far by Faith* (PBS Video, 2003).

46. Eskew Reeder, Jr. (who recorded and performed as "Esquerita," "Professor Eskew Reeder," "S. Q. Reeder," "The Magnificent Malochi," and "the Voola"), was a self-taught piano player who began his musical career as a teenager in a Baptist church in Greenville, South Carolina, then graduated to the gospel group the Heavenly Echoes ("Didn't It Rain," 1953), and then crossed over to rock & roll. "Little Richard" Penniman's flamboyant performance style and stage persona, adopted when he began recording for Art Rupe's New Orleans–based Specialty Records label, are evidently influenced by Reeder. For a detailed and analytical survey of gospel crossover history, see Young, 233–52; and Humphrey, 107–49.

47. Harris, 96.

48. Ibid., 96–97.

49. Ibid., 106–9.

50. See John Cowley and Paul Oliver, eds., *The New Blackwell Guide to Recorded Blues* (Cambridge, MA: Blackwell, 1996), 18, 22, 144, 146, 198, 206, 292.

51. See Haddad, episode 3. Cf. Harris, 150, 216–17.

52. Edward H. Boatman, choir director at Ebenezer Baptist Church, quoted in Harris, 198.

53. George, 70–71.

54. Robert Neff and Anthony Connor, *Blues* (Boston: David R. Godine, 1975), 8–9.

55. Ibid., 9.

56. David Evans, private correspondence.

57. Both were born in 1915 in the Mississippi Delta; both migrated to Chicago in the mid-1930s.

58. Mavis Staples, *We'll Never Turn Back* (Los Angeles: Anti-Records, 2007). Cf. Bowman, *Soulsville U.S.A.,* 157.

CHAPTER 4

1. Jacqueline L. Tobin and Raymond G. Dobard, *Hidden in Plain View: A Secret Story of Quilts and the Underground Railroad* (New York: Random House, 1999). Tobin, who teaches literature and women's studies at the University of Denver, enlisted Dobard, who teaches African American art history at Howard University and is himself a quilt maker, to coauthor an account based on an oral history offered to Tobin by an African American quilt maker named Ozella McDaniel Williams (now deceased) whom she encountered in a South Carolina bazaar. Tobin and Dobard's book got an early boost from Oprah Winfrey and is cited rather widely but has also attracted some detailed criticism.

2. Gerhard Kubik, *Africa and the Blues* (Jackson: University Press of Mississippi, 1999), 84.

3. Bruno Nettl, *The Study of Ethnomusicology: Twenty-nine Issues and Concepts* (Urbana: University of Illinois Press, 1983), 25.

4. John Dewey, *Art as Experience* (New York: Minton, Balch, 1934), 330.

5. Ibid., 330–31.

6. Ibid., 334.

7. Ibid.

8. Kubik, 118.

9. Hip-hop has of course demonstrated that even a tonal reference point is not strictly necessary.

10. Kubik, 119.

11. Ibid., 83.

12. Zora Neal Hurston, "Spirituals and Neo-Spirituals," in *Voices from the Harlem Renaissance,* ed. Nathan Huggins (New York: Oxford University Press, 1976), 344.

13. Cf. David Evans, "Hill Country Blues," *Living Blues* 189 (April 2007): 78.

14. Cf. Giles Oakley, *The Devil's Music* (Cambridge, MA: Da Capo, 1997), 68–73; Mike Rowe, "Piano Blues and Boogie Woogie," in *The New Blackwell Guide to Recorded Blues,* ed. John Cowley and Paul Oliver (Cambridge, MA: Blackwell, 1996), 155–83.

15. The classic philosophical critique is O. K. Bouwsma's "The Expression Theory of Art," in *Philosophical Essays* (Lincoln: University of Nebraska Press, 1965).

16. Peter Kivy, *The Corded Shell: Reflections on Musical Expression* (Princeton: Princeton University Press, 1980), 22–23. Cf. Edward Bullough, "'Psychical Distance'as a Factor in Art and as an Aesthetic Principle," *British Journal of Psychology* 5 (1912–13): 87–118.

17. Cf. Peter Kivy, "Experiencing the Musical Emotions," *New Essays on Musical Understanding* (New York: Oxford University Press, 2001), 118.

18. For a summary of the controversy over the nature of musical expressiveness see Stephen Davies's entry "Music" in *The Oxford Companion to Aesthetics,* ed. Jerrold Levinson (Oxford: Oxford University Press, 2003), 502–8.

19. Peter Kivy, "Auditor's Emotions: Contention, Concession, and Compromise," in *New Essays on Musical Understanding,* 75. I will use Kivy's theory as my example and stalking horse. Although there are other theories extant in the literature, most of these are either variations on, intended refinements of, or reactions to Kivy's.

20. Edward Lippman, ed., *Musical Aesthetics: A Historical Reader,* vol. 1, *From Antiquity to the Eighteenth Century* (New York: Pendragon Press, 1986), quoted in Kathleen M. Higgins, "Music and Emotions: The History," in *The Music of Our Lives* (Philadelphia: Temple University Press, 1991), 87; the "explanatory model" of vital fluids animating the body is a Cartesian invention.

21. Derek Matravers, *Art and Emotion* (Oxford: Clarendon Press, 1998). Cf. Peter Kivy's critique of Matravers in "The Arousal Theory of Musical Expression: Rethinking the Unthinkable," in *New Essays on Musical Understanding,* 119–51.

22. Kivy, "Experiencing the Musical Emotions," 95. Kivy also finds Schopenhauer's insight anticipated in eighteenth-century composer Johann Mattheson's writings. See Kivy, "Mattheson as Philosopher of Art," in *The Fine Art of Repetition: Essays in the Philosophy of Music* (Cambridge: Cambridge University Press, 1993), 229–49.

23. Kivy, "Experiencing the Musical Emotions," 95.

24. Ibid.

25. Peter Kivy, "Something I've Always Wanted to Know about Hanslick," *Journal of Aesthetics and Art Criticism* 46, no. 3 (Spring 1988): 413–18; "On Hanslick's Inconsistency," in *New Essays on Musical Understanding,* 39–43.

26. Peter Kivy, "Mood and Music: Some Reflections for Noel Carroll," *Journal of Aesthetics and Art Criticism* 64, no. 2 (Spring 2006): 271. Kivy's way of solving this problem, while remaining consistent with his theory of musical expressiveness, is to argue that we are moved emotionally as listeners not by the emotionally expressive properties we may recognize in the music (be it sad, joyful, angry, or whatever) but by its beauty. We may be reduced to tears, we should notice, even by certain passages of *joyful* or *triumphant* music. Thus even when we are reduced to tears while listening to sad music, these should not be confused with tears of sadness or understood as having been aroused by the sadness in the music. Rather, it is that we are overcome by the sheer beauty of the music and these are tears of, for want of a better label, aesthetic joy or aesthetic appreciation. See Peter Kivy, *Music Alone* (Ithaca: Cornell University Press, 1990), chap. 8, "How Music Moves," 146–72.

27. Kivy, "Auditor's Emotions," 72.

28. Arguably Kivy's focus is narrower still, since he seems to have nothing to say about jazz, much of which is pure instrumental music, though not part of what he identifies as "absolute music" or "music alone."

29. Cf. Edward T. Cone, *The Composer's Voice* (Berkeley: University of California Press, 1974).

30. Aaron Copland, quoted in Roy A. Prendergast, "The Aesthetics of Film

Music," in *A Neglected Art: A Critical Study of Music in Films* (New York: New York University Press, 1977), 204.

31. The word *philosophy,* meaning "love of wisdom," derives from the Greek *philia* (love) and *sophia* (wisdom). This coinage is credited to Pythagoras. See W. K. C. Guthrie, *The Encyclopedia of Philosophy* (New York: MacMillan Publishing Co.): 443.

32. This was suggested to me by Arnie Cox in private correspondence. It is worth noting, though, that this "aversion," while it may be understandable, even in some sense "normal," is by no means inevitable. Some listeners may be, indeed *are,* drawn to dissonant harmonies and melodies, perhaps because they like the challenge.

33. See Ernest G. McClain, *The Myth of Invariance: The Origins of the Gods, Mathematics and Music from the RG Veda to Plato* (Stony Brook, NY: Nicolas Hays, 1976); and McClain, *Meditations through the Quran: Tonal Images in an Oral Culture* (Stony Brook, NY: Nicolas Hays, 1981).

34. Musicologist Ernest McClain is one of the very few writers to have explored these connections thoroughly and in depth. See Ernest G. McClain, *The Pythagorean Plato: Prelude to the Song Itself* (Stony Brook, NY: Nicolas Hays, 1978). But see also Eva T. H. Brann, "The Music of the *Republic,*" *St. John's Review* 39 (1989–90): 1–103.

35. *Republic,* bk. 9, line 587e. Cf. McClain, *The Pythagorean Plato,* chap. 3, "The Tyrant's Allegory," 33–39.

36. *Republic,* bk. 8, lines 546a–547a. Cf. McClain, *The Pythagorean Plato,* chap. 2, "The Marriage Allegory," 17–31.

37. *Republic,* bk. 7, lines 530d–e.

38. *Republic,* bk. 4, lines 432a, 443d–e.

39. Cf. the complementary image of the soul as a winged charioteer driving a pair of winged horses presented in Plato's *Phaedrus* 248a–257b.

40. Bloom, *Closing of the American Mind,* 71.

41. Ibid., 71, 69.

42. Allan Bloom, *The Republic of Plato* (New York: Basic Books, 1968), vii.

43. *Republic,* bk. 2, lines 376e–377b. This is Bloom's own translation. See Bloom, *The Republic of Plato,* 54.

44. *Republic,* bk. 3, lines 401d–e. Again this is Bloom's own translation. See Bloom, *The Republic of Plato,* 80.

45. *Republic,* bk. 3, lines 398c–399e.

46. Kubik, 149–51.

47. McClain, *The Pythagorean Plato,* 4–5.

48. Cf. Ernest McClain, "Music's Discipline of the Means," *Parabola* 16 (Winter 1991): 87–89.

49. Jennifer Judkins tells me that the earliest prohibitive reference she can find to the tritone is in the hexachordal system of Guido D'Arezzo, the ninth-century Benedictine monk who invented both staff notation and solfeggio.

50. For a survey, both historical and critical, of the philosophical literature on music and the emotions, see Kathleen M. Higgins, *The Music of Our Lives* (Philadelphia: Temple University Press, 1991), 81–137. For a review of the current state of musical neuropsychology, see Daniel J. Levitin, *This Is Your Brain on Music: The Science of a Human Obsession* (New York: Dutton, 2006).

51. Malcolm Gladwell, "The Formula," *New Yorker,* October 16, 2006, 138–49.

52. Recent work in experimental psychology and the neurosciences has suggested a new conceptual approach to the emotions according to which emotions are complex processes involving more or less automatic embodied affective responses overlaid with cognitive monitoring and processing. See Jenefer Robinson, *Deeper than Reason: Emotion and Its Role in Literature, Music, and Art* (New York: Oxford University Press, 2005). In my view, one of the most promising implications of this approach is that it integrates the body as an intelligent and responsive organism into the picture. We explore this further in chapter 5.

53. See Levitin, *This Is Your Brain on Music;* and Oliver Sacks, "A Bolt from the Blue," in *Musicophilia: Tales of Music and the Brain* (New York: Knopf, 2007), 3–17.

54. Levitin, *This Is Your Brain on Music,* 4.

55. Douglas Hofstadter, *MetaMagical Themas* (New York: Basic Books, 1985), xxv.

CHAPTER 5

1. See, for example, Peter Kivy, "Platonism in Music: A Kind of Defense," "Platonism in Music: Another Kind of Defense," and "Orchestrating Platonism," all in *The Fine Art of Repetition: Essays in the Philosophy of Music,* 35–94. For a critical survey of musical Platonism, see Higgins, 28–46.

2. *Republic,* bk. 2, lines 375d–376c.

3. *Republic,* bk. 3, line 398d.

4. *Republic,* bk. 3, line 400a.

5. *Republic,* bk. 3, line 400d.

6. *Republic,* bk. 3, lines 389e–399c.

7. *Republic,* bk. 3, lines 399d–e.

8. *Republic,* bk. 3, lines 400a–e.

9. Someone should test the system of prosody on hip-hop. Cf. Tricia Rose, *Black Noise: Rap Music and Black Culture in Contemporary America* (Hanover, NH: Wesleyan University Press, 1994), 66.

10. *Republic,* bk. 3, line 399e.

11. Cf. Higgins, 82–84; and Peter Kivy, *Introduction to a Philosophy of Music* (New York: Oxford University Press, 2002), 15–16.

12. In addition to Allan Bloom, see, for example, Paul Friedlander, *Plato: The Dialogues . . . Second and Third Periods* (London: Routledge and Kegan Paul, 1969), 87–88; G. M. A. Grube, *Plato's Thought* (Indianapolis: Hackett, 1980), 182–87; Theodore Gracyk, *Rhythm and Noise* (Durham, NC: Duke University Press, 1996), 127ff.; and Higgins, 82.

13. *Republic,* bk. 3, line 399e.

14. Leonard Meyer, *Emotion and Meaning in Music* (Chicago: University of Chicago Press, 1956), chap. 3 passim, and 135.

15. Ibid., 93.

16. Ibid.

17. James Brown, "Get Up (I Feel Like Being a) Sex Machine (Parts I and

II)," originally released on King Records in 1970; compiled in *Star Time* (New York: Polygram Records, 1991). Brothers William "Bootsy" Collins and Phelps "Catfish" Collins played bass and rhythm guitar, respectively, in James Brown's backup band, the JB's, from 1969 to 1971.

18. Meyer, 102.

19. Ibid., 103; See also Grosvenor W. Cooper and Leonard B. Meyer, *The Rhythmic Structure of Music* (Chicago: University of Chicago Press, 1960).

20. Wynton Marsalis, "Why Toes Tap," *Marsalis on Music* (New York: Norton, 1995), 20.

21. Ibid., 20–22.

22. Meyer, 102.

23. Meters can of course get more challenging. Learning to count in multiples of 5 and 7 and 13 is required for fluency in some jazz contexts. In classical Indian music the talas (rhythmic patterns) are quite long by Western standards.

24. Meyer, 103–10. Cf. Victor L. Wooten's observation, "Rhythm can be looked at as harmony slowed down," in *The Music Lesson: A Spiritual Search for Growth through Music* (New York: Berkeley Books, 2006), 37–38.

25. Marsalis, 26–27.

26. Cf. Grateful Dead percussionist Mickey Hart, who says, "One of the first laws of rhythm is repetition. . . . There is no rhythm without repetition." *Drumming at the Edge of Magic* (New York: HarperCollins, 1990), 119.

27. Kivy, *The Fine Art of Repetition*, 328.

28. Ibid., 343–45.

29. Ibid., 349–59.

30. Susanne K. Langer, *Feeling and Form* (New York: Scribners, 1953), 126. Cf. Dewey, 163; see also Hart, 117–22.

31. Langer, 127. Cf. Dewey, 150.

32. Langer, 129.

33. Ibid., 126. Cf. Dewey, 163–64.

34. Langer, 126.

35. The renowned percussionist Evelyn Glennie, who is severely hearing impaired, argues quite persuasively for an expanded understanding of and approach to *listening* involving the whole body, an approach she applies to all of sound, not just rhythm.

36. Dewey, 13–15.

37. Ibid., 144–51.

38. Richard Shusterman, *Pragmatist Aesthetics* (Cambridge, MA: Blackwell, 1992), 6–7.

39. Richard Shusterman, "Somaesthetics: A Disciplinary Proposal," *Journal of Aesthetics and Art Criticism* 57, no. 3 (Summer 1999): 299–313. See also Richard Shusterman, *Body Consciousness: A Philosophy of Mindfulness and Somaesthetics* (Cambridge: Cambridge University Press, 2008). Cf. Charles Keil, "Motion and Feeling through Music," in Keil and Steven Feld, *Music Grooves* (Chicago: University of Chicago Press, 1994), 56–57.

40. Alexander Baumgarten, *Aesthetica,* secs. 1 and 14, translated and quoted by Richard Shusterman in "Somaesthetics: A Disciplinary Proposal," *Journal of Aesthetics and Art Criticism* 57, no. 3 (Summer 1999): 300, 311n6.

41. Noting that rhythm has been particularly neglected in Western theory of music in large part due to its relation to the body, Robert Walser posits culturally entrenched misogyny as a possible explanation. He writes, "Denial of the body, related to the common fear of music's 'feminizing' effects, is a recurrent anxiety of Western music criticism (and Western culture more generally). It is connected with suspicion of the sensual subversion of reason, and it is often invoked in the context of the reactionary projection of innovative threats onto the most immediate—and therefore dangerous of others: women." Walser, 48.

42. See "The Flesh and the Spirit" section of chapter 3; J. H. Cone, 114 (emphasis in the original).

43. See Robinson.

44. Kivy, *The Corded Shell*, 55 (emphasis in the original).

45. For a wonderful example see the award-winning documentary *Piano Players Rarely Ever Play Together* by Stevenson Palfi (1980). Since there is usually only one piano in a given performance space, it is *only on the rarest of occasions* that piano players ever get to play *with each other*. So a concert is arranged in which three generations of New Orleans piano players will perform together as a trio: The central figure is Henry Roland Byrd (aka "Professor Longhair"). The film documents the series of rehearsals, during which comes Byrd's untimely death. The climax of the film is the funeral.

46. "Swing," Glossary, Jazzinamerica.org, the Thelonious Monk Insititute of Jazz, *Jazz in America*, http://www.jazzinamerica.org/l_glossary.asp (accessed November 18, 2007).

47. Taj Mahal, *An Evening of Acoustic Music* (Ruf Records, 1996).

48. Robert Palmer, *Rock and Roll: An Unruly History* (New York: Harmony Books, 1995), 59–60.

49. Cf. Rick Coleman, *Blue Monday: Fats Domino and the Lost Dawn of Rock 'N' Roll* (Cambridge, MA: Da Capo, 2006), 5–7.

50. Meyer, 12off. Cf. Marsalis, 48–49; Gracyk, 134.

51. Kubik, 57.

52. Gracyk, 135.

53. Gunther Schuller, *The History of Jazz*, vol. 1, *Early Jazz: Its Roots and Musical Development* (Oxford: Oxford University Press, 1968), glossary, 376.

54. Ibid., 8 (emphasis added).

55. Ibid., 9–12.

56. Lomax, 260–61.

57. Schuller, 10. Cf. Gracyk, 134.

58. In his 1965 hit "Papa's Got a Brand New Bag." See Gerri Hirshey, "Funk's Founding Father," *Rolling Stone* 1018 (January 25, 2007), 42.

59. Santoro, 137.

60. Cf. references to John Dewey and Gerhard Kubik in chapter 4.

61. Cf. Michael Ventura, "White Boys Dancing" and "Hear That Long Snake Moan," in *Shadow Dancing in the USA* (Los Angeles: Jeremy P. Tarcher, 1985), 42–51, 103–62.

62. Guitarist and ethnomusicologist Bob Brozman made this point in an interview with John Ytsdie, *All Things Considered*, National Public Radio, June 4, 2002. Regarding on-beat accentuation, marching, and regimentation, cf. Walser, 49.

CHAPTER 6

The chapter opening epigraphs are from, respectively: Amiri Baraka (Leroi Jones), *Blues People: The Negro Experience in White America and the Music that Developed from it* (New York: William Morrow, 1963), 148; Johnny Otis, "The Bassackwards Blues," *Upside Your Head: Rhythm and Blues on Central Avenue* (Hanover, NH: Wesleyan University Press, 1994), 107–8; Elaine Lipworth, "In the Court of the King," *The Independent,* March 29, 2006; Charlie Yardbird Parker online, http://www.cmgww.com/music/parker/about/quotes.html (accessed May 9, 2010); Griel Marcus, *Mystery Train* (New York: Dutton: 1975), 3.

1. Unfortunately, and I think unfairly, Bloomfield is reduced to footnote material in Steve Waksman's account of this development in *Instruments of Desire: The Electric Guitar and the Shaping of Musical Experience* (Cambridge, MA: Harvard University Press, 1999).

2. Genevieve Williams, "Robben Ford: Blue Moon Rising," *Blues Revue* 79 (January 2003): 11.

3. Jan Mark Wolkin and Bill Keenon, *Michael Bloomfield: If You Love These Blues—An Oral History* (San Francisco: Miller-Freeman, 2000), vii–viii.

4. Ralph J. Gleason, "Perspectives: Stop This Shuck, Mike Bloomfield," *Rolling Stone,* May 11, 1968, 10.

5. Joel Rudinow, "Race, Ethnicity, Expressive Authenticity: Can White People Sing the Blues?" *Journal of Aesthetics and Art Criticism* 52, no. 1 (Winter 1994): 127–37.

6. Ralph J. Gleason, "Can the White Man Sing the Blues?" *Jazz and Pop* (August 1968): 28–29.

7. Amiri Baraka, "The Great Music Robbery," in *The Music,* 328–32.

8. Amiri Baraka, "Jazz Writing: Survival in the Eighties," in *The Music,* 259.

9. Amiri Baraka, "Where's the Music Going and Why?" in *The Music,* 179.

10. Branford Marsalis, *I Heard You Twice the First Time,* liner notes by Delfeayo Marsalis (New York: SONY Music Entertainment, Columbia Records, 1992), 1.

11. See the third epigraph to this chapter.

12. Amiri Baraka (Leroi Jones), *Blues People: The Negro Experience in White America and the Music That Developed from It* (New York: William Morrow, 1963), 147–48.

13. Lee B. Brown, "Postmodernist Jazz Theory: Afrocentrism, Old and New," *Journal of Aesthetics and Art Criticism* 57, no. 2 (Spring 1999): 235–46. Cf. Krin Gabbard, *Jazz among the Discourses* (Durham, NC: Duke University Press, 1995).

14. Cf. Lee B. Brown, "Marsalis and Baraka: An Essay in Comparative Cultural Discourse," *Popular Music* 23 (2004): 241–55; Lee B. Brown, "Jazz: America's Classical Music?" *Philosophy and Literature* 26, no. 1 (April 2002): 157–72.

15. Kwame Anthony Appiah, "Racisms," in *Anatomy of Racism,* ed. David Theo Goldberg (Minneapolis: University of Minnesota Press, 1990), 3.

16. Ibid., 4.

17. Ibid.

18. Paul C. Taylor, " . . . So Black and Blue: Response to Rudinow," *Journal of Aesthetics and Art Criticism* 53, no. 3 (Summer 1995): 315; reprinted in David Boonin and Graham Oddie, eds., *What's Wrong: Applied Ethicists and Their Critics* (New York: Oxford University Press, 2005), 415–21.

19. Ibid., 314.

20. Howard Winant, *Racial Conditions: Politics, Theory, Comparisons* (Minneapolis: University of Minnesota Press, 1994), 24. Cf. David Theo Goldberg, *Racist Culture: Philosophy and the Politics of Meaning* (Oxford: Blackwell, 1993).

21. Joel Rudinow, "Reply to Taylor," *Journal of Aesthetics and Art Criticism* 53 , no. 3 (Summer 1995): 316–18; reprinted in David Boonin and Graham Oddie, eds., *What's Wrong: Applied Ethicists and Their Critics* (New York: Oxford University Press, 2005), 421–22. Cf. Paul Garon, "White Blues," *Race Traitor* 4 (Winter 1995): 4, 7ff.

22. Garon, "White Blues."

23. "Abolish the White Race—by Any Means Necessary," *Race Traitor* 1 (Winter 1993).

24. See Walter Benn Michaels, "Autobiography of an Ex-White Man: Why Race Is Not a Social Construction," *Transition* 73 (1997): 122–43.

25. Amiri Baraka, "Class Struggle in Music," in *The Music,* 319.

26. Ibid.

27. Gleason, "Perspectives," 10.

28. This is the idea of "authenticity" at the heart of philosopher Charles Taylor's work on personal and cultural identity formation. See Charles Taylor, *The Ethics of Authenticity* (Cambridge: Harvard University Press, 1991).

29. Gleason, "Can the White Man Sing the Blues?"

30. See David Borgo, "Can Blacks Play Klezmer? Authenticity in American Ethnic Musical Expression," *Sonneck Society for American Music Bulletin* 24, no. 2 (Summer 1998).

31. David Whiteis, "Singing through the Rain" (profile of folk singer Rosalie Sorrells), *No Depression* 58 (July–August 2005): 90.

32. Ibid.

33. Greil Marcus, *Invisible Republic: Bob Dylan's Basement Tapes* (New York: Henry Holt, 1997), ix–x.

34. Ben Sidran, "Expand, Expand, Keep Expanding," in *Ben Sidran—A Life in the Music,* 68.

35. A selection from the Flag's performance is captured as an "outtake" in D. A. Pennebaker's concert documentary *The Complete Monterey Pop Festival* (2002).

36. Wolkin and Keenon, 146.

37. Ibid.

38. Robert Johnson, "Me and the Devil Blues"; Eric Clapton, *Me and Mr. Johnson* (New York: Warner Reprise, 2004). In her rendition Rory Block changes the line to "Well I got to love my baby 'till I get satisfied." Cf. Rory Block, *The Lady and Mr. Johnson* (New York: Rykodisc, 2006).

39. Ted Cohen, *Jokes* (Chicago: University of Chicago Press, 1999), 84–85.

40. See Andy Austin, *Rule 53: Capturing Hippies, Spies, Politicians and Murderers in an American Courtroom* (Chicago: Lake Claremont Press, 2008).

41. Cohen, *Jokes* (emphasis added).

42. This is clearly part of a much larger psychological set of tendencies. The pop music critic Sasha Frere-Jones noted a discussion in the British press in which the epithet "Mockney" is used to describe singers who pitch their accents down a few class levels so as to sound "tougher" or more "authentic." Sasha Frere Jones, "Full Exposure: Making it on MySpace," *New Yorker* (January 14, 2008): 85.

43. I'm paraphrasing Cavell, who actually wrote, "A measure of the quality of

a new text is quality of the texts it arouses." *The Claim of Reason: Wittgenstein, Skepticism, Morality, and Tragedy* (Oxford: Clarendon Press, 1979), 5.

44. Paul Oliver, *Blues Off the Record,* the second epigram in my "Race, Ethnicity, Expressive Authenticity: Can White People Sing the Blues?" *Journal of Aesthetics and Art Criticism* 52, no. 1 (Winter 1994): 127.

45. Jim Dickinson, "Introductory Video," Memphis Rock and Soul Museum, Memphis, TN.

46. Chuck Berry, *The Autobiography* (New York: Harmony Books, 1987), 89–90.

47. See Chip Berlet, *Toxic to Democracy: Conspiracy Theories, Demonization, & Scapegoating* (Somerville, MA: Political Research Associates, 2009).

CHAPTER 7

1. The Epimenedes Paradox is a famous "paradox of self-reference." When Epimenedes of Crete said, "All Cretans are liars," it was impossible to take his statement as either true or false.

2. *Republic,* bk. 3, lines 377b–392c.

3. *Republic,* bk. 3, lines 393a–b.

4. *Republic,* bk. 3, line 398a.

5. This tradition is canonical throughout academic scholarship. For example, see Iris Murdoch, *The Fire and the Sun: Why Plato Banished the Artists* (Oxford: Clarendon Press, 1977).

6. *Republic,* bk. 7, lines 514a–517a; *Republic,* bk. 10, line 595a.

7. I wasn't just kidding either. I had gone so far as to sketch out a couple of tunes and even referenced this piece of musical/theatrical vaporware in the author's biographical note to one of my scholarly papers, "Duchamps' Mischief," *Critical Inquiry* 7, no. 4 (Summer 1981): 747–60.

8. Cf. Peter Singer, *The President of Good and Evil: The Ethics of George W. Bush* (New York: Dutton, 2004), 220–24; James Mann, *Rise of the Vulcans: The History of Bush's War Cabinet* (New York: Viking, 2004), 25–29. See also Seymour M. Hersch, "Selective Intelligence," *New Yorker,* May 12, 2003; and Ronald Bailey, "Origin of the Specious: Why Do Neoconservatives Doubt Darwin?" *Reason* (July 1997).

9. Theodore Roszak, *World, Beware! American Triumphalism in an Age of Terror* (Toronto: Provocations/Between the Lines, 2006), 142.

10. Earl Shorris, "Ignoble Liars: Leo Strauss, George Bush, and the Philosophy of Mass Deception," *Harper's Magazine,* June 2004, 66, 68.

11. Steven Lenzner and William Kristol, "What Was Leo Strauss Up To?" *Public Interest* 153 (Fall 2003): 19.

12. Roszak, 141–42.

13. Myles Burnyeat, "Sphinx without a Secret," *New York Review of Books,* May 30, 1985, 30–36. I owe this reference to Ted Cohen.

14. Leo Strauss, *The City and Man* (Chicago: University of Chicago Press, 1964), 50.

15. Burnyeat, for example, objects to Strauss's interpretive inference from the literary form of Plato's dialogues to the obscurity of Plato's exposition. But he has no doubt about Strauss's interpretive premise. "Sphinx without a Secret," 35.

16. Leo Strauss, *Persecution and the Art of Writing* (Chicago: University of Chicago Press, 1952), 22–23.

17. This highlights one of underappreciated functions of the philosophical view known as "relativism," which says in effect that there's no such thing as the truth, or the Truth (with a capital *T*), because all opinion is relative to a particular point of view, so what's "true for me" may not be "true for you." The view functions thus as a defense against and refuge from intellectual criticism and especially harassment. "Leave me alone. It's just an *opinion*. I'm entitled to my own opinion."

18. Strauss, *Persecution and the Art of Writing*, 23.

19. Ibid., 23–24.

20. Ibid., 73–75.

21. Cf. Burnyeat, 30–31.

22. Strauss, *The City and Man*, 52.

23. Ibid., 52.

24. Ibid.

25. Ibid., 52–54.

26. Strauss, *Persecution and the Art of Writing*, 32–33.

27. See Jonathan Glover, *Humanity: A Moral History of the Twentieth Century* (New Haven, CT: Yale University Press, 1999), 367–71.

28. Strauss, *Persecution and the Art of Writing*, 22.

29. Noam Chomsky, "1984: Orwell's and Ours," *Thoreau Quarterly* 16 (1984): 18. See also Edward S. Herman and Noam Chomsky, *Manufacturing Consent* (New York: Pantheon, 1988), chap. 1, "A Propaganda Model," 1–35.

30. Strauss was hardly alone in this regard. Consider the case of Thomas Mann, another of the prize refugee intellectuals (along with Albert Einstein) who came to America during the age of European fascism. Music critic Alex Ross writes, "He had come to America in 1938. Fearing that his adopted homeland was falling victim to the same totalitarian madness that had consumed Germany, he began to think about emigrating once again, and in 1952 he moved to Switzerland. Mann had come to America looking for freedom from demonic politics; he did not find it." Alex Ross, "Appalachian Autumn: Aaron Copland Confronts the Politics of the Cold War," *New Yorker*, August 27, 2007, 38.

31. When he says, "Here was a man who did not want to be understood by any but the few, his disciples."

32. Arguably among the most ambitious and treacherous of the political and military actors during the Peloponesian Wars, Alcibiades switched allegiances several times between Athens, Sparta, and Persia, making and betraying alliances repeatedly.

33. See, for example, William J. Leckey, "Stop the Straussians before They Lie Again," George Mason University, *History News Network*, June 9, 2003; Roszak, 139–44; Shorris, 65–71.

34. See, for example, Lenzner and Kristol, 19–39. Cf. Francis Fukuyama, "After Neo-Conservatism," *New York Times Magazine*, February 19, 2006.

35. Lenzner and Kristol, 38.

36. *Republic*, bk. 3, lines 414c–415d.

37. To better understand the Allegory of the Metals, remember to read it in the context of the governing analogy between the city and the individual human soul. The point of the allegory is really to establish the functional hierarchy of agencies within the soul and to say about reason that it is the agency most fit to do the job of deliberative decision making within the soul.

38. Anne Norton, *Leo Strauss and the Politics of American Empire* (New Haven, CT: Yale University Press, 2004), 102–3 (emphasis in the original).

39. Ibid., 103.

40. Bloom, *The Closing of the American Mind,* 313.

41. See Robert Cohen, *Freedom's Orator, Mario Savio and the Radical Legacy of the 1960s* (New York: Oxford University Press, 2009), pp. 1–13.

42. Neff and Connor, 1.

43. Cf. Russell Ames, "Protest and Irony in Negro Folksong," *Science and Society* 14 (1950): 193–213; Alain Locke, *The Negro and His Music* (Washington: Associates in Negro Folk Education, 1936), 32–33; Jeff Todd Titon, "Thematic Pattern in Downhome Blues Lyrics," *Journal of American Folklore* 90, no. 357 (1977): 316–30; Sherley Anne Williams, "The Blues Roots of Contemporary Afro-American Poetry," in *Afro-American Literature: The Reconstruction of Instruction,* ed. Dexter Fisher and Robert B. Stepto (New York: Modern Language Press Association of America, 1978), 75; and Paul Allen Anderson, *Deep River: Music and Memory in Harlem Renaissance Thought* (Durham, NC: Duke University Press, 2001), 181–82.

44. Grace Simms Holt, "'Inversion' in Black Communication," in *Rappin' and Stylin' Out,* ed. Thomas Kochman (Urbana: University of Illinois Press, 1972), quoted in Shusterman, *Pragmatist Aesthetics,* 221–22.

45. Sasha Frere-Jones, "Coke Is It: Rap's Drug Obsession," *New Yorker,* December 12, 2006, 146–47.

46. See Sidran, *Black Talk.* Cf. Roger Taylor's account of the origins and significance of jazz, blues, and in particular the New Orleans piano tradition in *Art, an Enemy of the People* (Sussex: Harvester, 1978), chap. 4. Worth noting is the analogous account of the origins of Yiddish, "Yiddish is the original jive, designed to keep Herr Charlie from knowing what we really think," in Michael Wex, *Born to Kvetch: Yiddish Language and Culture in All of Its Moods* (New York: St. Martin's, 2005), 18–23.

47. Oliver, *Blues Fell This Morning,* 265ff.

48. Samuel Charters, *The Legacy of the Blues: A Glimpse into the Art and Lives of Twelve Great Bluesmen* (New York: Da Capo, 1975), 125.

49. Adam Gussow, *Seems Like Murder Here: Southern Violence and the Blues Tradition* (Chicago: University of Chicago Press, 2002), 3–4. See also Cecil Brown, *Stagolee Shot Billy* (Cambridge, MA: Harvard University Press, 2003).

50. Archbishop Desmond Tutu, Chairperson's foreword to *Report of the Truth and Reconciliation Commission of South Africa,* http://www.info.gov.za/otherdocs/2003/trc/ (accessed June 12, 2008).

51. Cf. Alan Dundes, ed., *Mother Wit from the Laughing Barrel: Readings in the Interpretation of Afro-American Folklore* (Jackson: University of Mississippi Press, 1990).

52. Cf. Cornell West, *Democracy Matters: Winning the Fight against Imperialism* (New York: Penguin, 2004), 15–20.

CHAPTER 8

Chapter-opening epigraph from the home page for Careers in Music Therapy, Berklee College of Music, http://www.berklee.edu/careers/therapy.html (accessed May 29, 2008); third epigraph from Robert Crumb and Peter Poplaski, *The R. Crumb Handbook* (London: MQP, 2004), 45.

1. Early references to music therapy, for example in Robert Burton, *The Anatomy of Melancholy* (1621), seem to consider it as indicated primarily for the treatment of "mental" illness.

2. Julia Necheff, "Music May Improve Feeding, Reduce Pain in Premature Babies: U of A Study," *University of Alberta ExpressNews,* http://www.express news.ualberta.ca/article.cfm?id=10214 (accessed June 4, 2009).

3. Cf. Daniel J. Levitin, *The World in Six Songs* (New York: Dutton, 2008), 92–97.

4. Sacks, *Musicophilia,* xiii.

5. Carol M. Ostrom, "Music as Medicine," *Seattle Times,* May 25, 2005.

6. The American Music Therapy Association, http://www.musictherapy .org/ (accessed January 11, 2009). There are professional music therapy organizations now active worldwide. International organizations include the European Music Therapy Confederation and the World Federation of Music Therapy, http://www.musictherapyworld.de/ (accessed January 11, 2009). National organizations exist in Argentina, Australia, Austria, Belgium, Brazil, Canada, Denmark, Finland, France, Germany, Greece, Hungary, Iceland, Israel, Italy, Japan, Korea, Netherlands, New Zealand, Norway, Romania, Spain, Sweden, Switzerland, and the United Kingdom as well as in the United States.

7. *Music Therapy Today* 7, no. 3 (October 2006).

8. For a brief orientation to the Musica Humana research program go to http://www.musicahumana.org. For a biography of Niels Eje, go to http://www .musicure,com/ (accessed January 11, 2009).

9. Per Thorgaard, Ellen Ertmann, Vibeke Hansen, Anni Noergaard, Lene Spanggaard, "Designed Sound and Music Environment in Postanaesthesia Care Units—A Multicentre Study of Patients and Staff," *Progress in Natural Science* 21, no. 4 (August 2005): 220–25. Quotation given in Ostrom.

10. An interesting exception is based on research into "psychophysiology" and "neurocardiology," or the interaction between heart and brain. See the Institute of Heart Math, http://www.heartmath.org (accessed January 11, 2009).

11. Suzanne G. Cusick, " 'You Are in a Place That Is out of the World. . .': Music in the Detention Camps of the 'Global War on Terror,' " *Journal of the Society for American Music* 2, no. 1 (2008): 1–26. See also Jonathan Pieslak, *Sound Targets: American Soldiers and Music in the Iraq War* (Bloomington: Indiana University Press, 2009).

12. Evan Serpick, "Soundtrack to the War: From Rocking Hatebreed while on Patrol in Fallujah to iPods Rigged to Play in Soldiers' Helmets: What the Troops in Iraq Listen to as They Roll into Battle," *Rolling Stone* 1007 (August 24, 2006): 20–22.

13. Levitin, *This Is Your Brain on Music.* Levitin's analysis is by no means confined to the psychopharmacological model. But his title is obviously derived from the Reagan era antidrug advertising campaign "This is your brain on drugs" and is thus evidently intended to appeal to that popular association.

14. Stanley Scheindlin, "A Brief History of Pharmacology," *Modern Drug Development* 4, no. 5 (May 2001): 87.

15. For a brief and accessible survey of the physics underlying music theory,

see Catherine Schmidt-Jones, "Acoustics for Music Theory," *Connexions,* May 9, 2007, http://cnx.org/content/m13246/1.7/.

16. I'm talking here about *typical* music. Of course, *any* sound, even white noise, can be used for an artistic purpose and thus, according to the present formulation, qualifies as music when so used, and if the sound is not "regular" or "organized" in any other discernible way, it might pose a "counterexample."

17. C. Huygens, *Oeuvres Completes de Christian Huyghens,* vol. 5 (The Hague: M. Nijhoff, 1893), 243–44. My thanks to Professor Michael S. Mahoney, historian of science at Princeton University, for the reference.

18. Search under "Entrainment Cellular" or "Cellular Chrono-Biology."

19. For a discussion of entrainment in music, relating it to biology and spirituality, see Hart, 117–28.

20. F. H. Rauscher, G. L. Shaw, and K. N. Ky, "Music and Spatial Task Performance," *Nature* (1993).

21. Levitin, *This Is Your Brain on Music,* 220.

22. E. G. Schellenberg, "Does Exposure to Music Have Beneficial Side Effects?" in *The Cognitive Neuroscience of Music,* ed. I. Peretz and R. J. Zatorre (New York: Oxford University Press, 2003).

23. Valerie V. Hunt, *Infinite Mind: Science of the Human Vibrations of Consciousness* (Malibu: Malibu Publishing, 1989), 10. Cf. Beverly Rubik, "Bioelectromagnetics: Energy Medicine—A Challenge for Science"; Christian de Quincey, "Bioelectromagnetics: Old Roots of a New Science"; Jan Walleczek, "Bioelectromagnetics: The Question of Subtle Energies," all in *Noetic Sciences Review* 28 (Winter 1993).

24. Antoine Lutz, John D. Dunne, and Richard J. Davidson, "Meditation and the Neuroscience of Consciousness," in *Cambridge Handbook of Consciousness,* ed. P. Zelazo, M. Moscovitch, and E. Thompson (New York: Cambridge University Press, 2007): 499–554. Cf. The Dalai Lama, *The Universe in a Single Atom: The Convergence of Science and Spirituality* (New York: Morgan Road Books, 2005), 143–44, 157. One of the research subjects, Matthieu Ricard, earned his doctorate in molecular biology from the Institut Pasteur in Paris but has for over thirty years devoted himself to Buddhist practice and now serves as the Dalai Lama's French interpreter. For a fascinating dialogue between a father and son—the father a French philosopher, and the son a trained Western scientist and practicing Buddhist—about this ongoing conversation between spirituality and science, see Jean-Francois Revel and Matthieu Ricard, *The Monk and the Philosopher* (New York: Schocken, 1998). For reports on this research in the popular media see John Geirland, "Buddha on the Brain," *Wired Magazine,* February 2006; and David Biello, "Meditate on This: You Can Learn to Be More Compassionate," *Scientific American,* March 26, 2008.

25. Cf. The Dalai Lama, 148–50.

26. See Lutz et al.

27. The Dalai Lama, 157.

28. Therese Schroeder-Sheker, "Using Prescriptive Music in the Death-Bed Vigil," *Noetic Sciences Review* (Autumn 1994).

29. Frederick Paxton, *Christianizing Death: The Creation of a Ritual Process in Medieval Europe* (Ithaca: Cornell University Press, 1990).

30. Roseann E. Kasayka and Karen Hatfield, "A Comparison of Sedative vs. Palliative Music in Treatment of Persons in End-Stage Alzheimer's Disease," *Heather Hill Hospital* (1994), http://www.heatherhill.com/musicresearch02 .html (accessed, June 7, 2008).

31. Cf. Rubik.

32. Some guys will tell you that they got into music as a way to impress girls. It's an unreliable strategy at best, and if it works occasionally, you will soon discover that it's not enough to keep you going in the discipline.

33. For example, I believe it best explains why guys tend to think that music is a good way to impress girls.

34. Cf. Adam Gussow, *Journeyman's Road: Modern Blues Lives from Faulkner's Mississippi to Post-9/11 New York* (Knoxville: University of Tennessee Press, 2007), 20–22.

35. Alan Lomax, *Mister Jelly Roll* (Berkeley: University of California Press, 1950), 42–43.

36. Ibid., 50.

37. The "Blue Book," quoted in Roger L. Taylor, *Art, an Enemy of the People,* 101–2.

38. Wynton Marsalis, "Why We Must Preserve Our Jazz Heritage," *Ebony Magazine,* February 1986, 131.

39. Jelly Roll Morton, "Miserere," *The Complete Library of Congress Recordings* (Rounder Records, 2005), disc 1, track 7.

40. James Booker, "Black Minute Waltz," *Junko Partner* (Hannibal/Rykodisc, 1993).

Bibliography

Ames, Russell. "Protest and Irony in Negro Folksong." *Science and Society* 14 (1950): 193–213.

Anderson, Paul Allen. *Deep River: Music and Memory in Harlem Renaissance Thought.* Durham, NC: Duke University Press, 2001.

Appiah, Kwame Anthony. "Racisms." In *Anatomy of Racism,* edited by David Theo Goldberg. Minneapolis: University of Minnesota Press, 1990.

Arsenault, Raymond. *The Sound of Freedom: Marian Anderson, the Lincoln Memorial, and the Concert That Awakened America.* New York: Bloomsbury, 2009.

Austin, Andy. *Rule 53: Capturing Hippies, Spies, Politicians and Murderers in an American Courtroom.* Chicago: Lake Claremont Press, 2008.

Bailey, Ronald. "Origin of the Specious: Why Do Neoconservatives Doubt Darwin?" *Reason* (July 1997).

Baraka, Amiri. *Black Music.* New York: William Morrow, 1968.

Baraka, Amiri (Leroi Jones). *Blues People: The Negro Experience in White America and the Music the Developed from That.* New York: William Morrow, 1963.

Baraka, Amiri. *The Music: Reflections on Jazz and Blues.* New York: William Morrow, 1987.

Barlow, William. *Looking Up at Down: The Emergence of Blues Culture.* Philadelphia: Temple University Press, 1989.

Berlet, Chip. *Toxic to Democracy: Conspiracy Theories, Demonization, & Scapegoating.* Somerville, MA: Political Research Associates, 2009.

Berry, Chuck. *The Autobiography.* New York: Harmony Books, 1987.

Biello, David. "Meditate on This: You Can Learn to Be More Compassionate." *Scientific American,* March 26, 2008.

Blesh, Rudi. *Shining Trumpets: A History of Jazz.* New York: Knopf, 1946.

Bloom, Allan. *The Closing of the American Mind.* New York: Simon and Schuster, 1987.

Bloom, Allan. *The Republic of Plato.* New York: Basic Books, 1968.

Borgo, David. "Can Blacks Play Klezmer? Authenticity in American Ethnic Musical Expression." *Sonneck Society for American Music Bulletin* 24, no. 2 (Summer 1998).

Bouwsma, O. K. "The Expression Theory of Art." In *Philosophical Essays.* Lincoln: University of Nebraska Press, 1965.

Bowman, Rob. *Soulsville U.S.A.: The Story of Stax Records.* New York: Schirmer, 1997.

Bowman, Rob. "Stax." In *African American Music: An Introduction,* edited by Mellonee V. Burnim and Portia K. Maultsby. New York: Routledge, 2006.

Brann, Eva T. H. "The Music of the *Republic.*" *St. John's Review* 39 (1989–90): 1–103.

Brown, Cecil. *Stagolee Shot Billy.* Cambridge, MA: Harvard University Press, 2003.

Brown, Lee B. "Jazz: America's Classical Music?" *Philosophy and Literature* 26, no. 1 (April 2002): 157–72.

Brown, Lee B. "Marsalis and Baraka: An Essay in Comparative Cultural Discourse." *Popular Music* 23 (2004): 241–55.

Brown, Lee B. "Postmodernist Jazz Theory: Afrocentrism, Old and New." *Journal of Aesthetics and Art Criticism* 57, no. 2 (Spring 1999): 235–46.

Bullough, Edward. " 'Psychical Distance' as a Factor in Art and as an Aesthetic Principle." *British Journal of Psychology* 5 (1912–1913): 87–118.

Burleigh, Harry T. *The Spirituals of Harry T. Burleigh.* Miami: Belwin Mills, 1984.

Burnim, Mellonee V., and Portia K. Maultsby. *African American Music: An Introduction.* New York: Routledge, 2006.

Burnyeat, Myles. "Sphinx without a Secret." *New York Review of Books,* May 30, 1985, 30–36.

Burton, Robert. *The Anatomy of Melancholy.* 1621.

Cavell, Stanley. *The Claim of Reason: Wittgenstein, Skepticism, Morality, and Tragedy.* Oxford: Clarendon Press, 1979.

Charles, Ray, with David Ritz. *Brother Ray: Ray Charles' Own Story.* New York: Dial Press, 1978.

Charters, Samuel. *The Country Blues.* New York: Da Capo, 1959.

Charters, Samuel. *The Legacy of the Blues: A Glimpse into the Art and Lives of Twelve Great Bluesmen.* New York: Da Capo, 1975.

Cheseborough, Steve. *Blues Traveling: The Holy Sites of Delta Blues.* Jackson: University Press of Mississippi, 2001.

Chomsky, Noam. "1984: Orwell's and Ours." *Thoreau Quarterly* 16 (1984).

Cohen, Robert. *Freedom's Orator, Mario Savio and the Radical Legacy of the 1960s.* New York: Oxford University Press, 2009.

Cohen, Ted. *Jokes.* Chicago: University of Chicago Press, 1999.

Cohn, Lawrence, ed. *Nothing But the Blues.* New York: Abbeville, 1993.

Coleman, Rick. *Blue Monday: Fats Domino and the Lost Dawn of Rock 'N' Roll.* Cambridge, MA: Da Capo, 2006.

Cone, Edward T. *The Composer's Voice.* Berkeley: University of California Press, 1974.

Cone, James H. *The Spirituals and the Blues.* Maryknoll, NY: Orbis, 1991.

Cooper, Grosvenor W., and Leonard B. Meyer. *The Rhythmic Structure of Music.* Chicago: University of Chicago Press, 1960.

Cousineau, Phil, ed. *Soul—An Archaeology: Readings from Socrates to Ray Charles.* New York: HarperCollins, 1994.

Cowley, John, and Paul Oliver, eds. *The New Blackwell Guide to Recorded Blues.* Cambridge, MA: Blackwell, 1996.

Crumb, Robert. *R. Crumb Draws the Blues.* San Francisco: Last Gasp, 1993.

Crumb, Robert, and Peter Poplaski. *The R. Crumb Handbook.* London: MQP, 2004.

Cusick, Suzanne G. " 'You Are in a Place That Is out of the World. . .': Music in the Detention Camps of the 'Global War on Terror.'" *Journal of the Society for American Music* 2, no. 1 (2008): 1–26.

The Dalai Lama. *The Universe in a Single Atom: The Convergence of Science and Spirituality.* New York: Morgan Road Books, 2005.

Davis, Angela Y. *Blues Legacies and Black Feminism.* New York: Pantheon, 1998.

Davis, Francis. *The History of the Blues.* Cambridge, MA: Da Capo, 1993.

de Quincey, Christian. "Bioelectromagnetics: Old Roots of a New Science." *Noetic Sciences Review* 28 (Winter 1993).

Dewey, John. *Art as Experience.* New York: Minton, Balch, 1934.

Du Bois, W. E. B. *The Souls of Black Folk.* Chicago: A. C. McClurg, 1903.

Dunas, Jeff. *State of the Blues.* New York: Aperture, 1998.

Dundes, Alan, ed. *Mother Wit from the Laughing Barrel: Readings in the Interpretation of Afro-American Folklore.* Jackson: University Press of Mississippi, 1990.

Evans, David. "Early Deep South and Mississippi Basin Blues." In *The New Blackwell Guide to Recorded Blues,* edited by John Cowley and Paul Oliver. Cambridge, MA: Blackwell, 1996.

Evans, David. "Goin' Up the Country: Blues in Texas and the Deep South." In *Nothing But the Blues,* edited by Lawrence Cohn. New York: Abbeville, 1993.

Evans, David. "Hill Country Blues." *Living Blues* 189 (April 2007): 78.

Evans, David. *Tommy Johnson.* London: Studio Vista, 1971.

Fine, Eric. "Heavenly Hitmakers: The Rise of Sacred Steel." *Blues Revue* 80 (February/March 2003): 11–13.

Fisher, Miles Mark. *Negro Slave Songs in the United States.* New York: Citadel, 1963.

Fletcher, Andrew. *Conversation Concerning a Right Regulation of Government for the Common Good of Mankind.* 1703.

Floyd, Samuel A., Jr. *The Power of Black Music: Interpreting Its History from Africa to the United States.* New York: Oxford University Press, 1995.

Fontenot, Robert. "Robert Randolph: The Second Coming of Sacred Steel?" *Blues Revue* 80 (February/March 2003): 8–14.

Friedlander, Paul. *Plato: The Dialogues . . . Second and Third Periods.* London: Routledge and Kegan Paul, 1969.

Frere-Jones, Sasha. "Coke Is It: Rap's Drug Obsession." *New Yorker,* December 12, 2006, 146–47.

Frere-Jones, Sasha. "Full Exposure: Making it on MySpace." *New Yorker,* January 14, 2008, 84–85.

Fukuyama, Francis. "After Neo-Conservatism." *New York Times Magazine,* February 19, 2006.

Gabbard, Krin. *Jazz among the Discourses.* Durham, NC: Duke University Press, 1995.

Garon, Paul. *Blues & the Poetic Spirit.* New York: Da Capo, 1978.

Garon, Paul. *The Devil's Son-in-law: The Story of Peetie Wheatstraw and His Songs.* London: November Books, 1971.

Garon, Paul. "White Blues." *Race Traitor* 4 (Winter 1995).

Geirland, John. "Buddha on the Brain." *Wired Magazine,* February 2006.

George, Nelson. *The Death of Rhythm & Blues.* New York: Pantheon, 1988.

Gerard, Charley. *Jazz in Black and White: Race, Culture, and Identity in the Jazz Community.* Westport, CT: Praeger, 2001.

Gilmore, Mikal. "The Long Shadow of Led Zeppelin (savaged by critics, adored by fans, the biggest band of the 70s took sex, drugs and rock & roll to epic heights before collapsing under the weight of its own heaviness)." *Rolling Stone Magazine* 1006.

Gioia, Ted. *Delta Blues: The Life and Times of the Mississippi Masters Who Revolutionized American Music.* New York: Norton, 2008.

Gladwell, Malcolm. "The Formula." *New Yorker,* October 16, 2006, 138–49.

Gleason, Ralph J. "Can the White Man Sing the Blues?" *Jazz and Pop,* August 1968, 28–29.

Gleason, Ralph J. "Perspectives: Stop This Shuck, Mike Bloomfield." *Rolling Stone Magazine,* May 11, 1968, 10.

Glover, Jonathan. *Humanity: A Moral History of the Twentieth Century.* New Haven, CT: Yale University Press, 1999.

Goldberg, David Theo, ed. *Racist Culture: Philosophy and the Politics of Meaning.* Oxford: Blackwell, 1993.

Gordon, Robert. *Can't Be Satisfied: The Life and Times of Muddy Waters.* Boston: Little, Brown, 2002.

Gracyk, Theodore. *I Wanna Be Me: Rock Music and the Politics of Identity.* Philadelphia: Temple University Press, 2001.

Gracyk, Theodore. *Listening to Popular Music: Or How I Learned to Stop Worrying and Love Led Zeppelin.* Ann Arbor: University of Michigan Press, 2007.

Gracyk, Theodore. *Rhythm and Noise: An Aesthetics of Rock.* Durham, NC: Duke University Press, 1996.

Grube, G. M. A. *Plato's Thought.* Indianapolis: Hackett, 1980.

Guralnick, Peter. *Searching for Robert Johnson.* New York: Dutton, 1989.

Guralnick, Peter. *Sweet Soul Music: Rhythm and Blues and the Southern Dream of Freedom.* New York: HarperCollins, 1988.

Guralnick, Peter, Robert Santelli, Holly George-Warren, and Christopher John Farley. *Martin Scorsese Presents: The Blues—A Musical Journey.* New York: HarperCollins Amistad, 2003.

Gussow, Adam. *Journeyman's Road: Modern Blues Lives from Faulkner's Mississippi to Post-9/11 New York.* Knoxville: University of Tennessee Press, 2007.

Gussow, Adam. *Mister Satan's Apprentice: A Blues Memoir.* New York: Random House, 1998.

Gussow, Adam. *Seems Like Murder Here: Southern Violence and the Blues Tradition.* Chicago: University of Chicago Press, 2002.

Guthrie, W. K. C. "Pythagoras." In *The Encyclopedia of Philosophy,* Vol. 6. New York: MacMillan, 1976.

Hamilton, Marybeth. *In Search of the Blues: Black Voices, White Visions.* London: Jonathan Cape, 2007.

Harris, Michael W. *The Rise of Gospel Blues: The Music of Thomas Andrew Dorsey in the Urban Church.* New York: Oxford University Press, 1992.

Hart, Mickey. *Drumming at the Edge of Magic.* New York: HarperCollins, 1990.

Hebdige, Dick. "What Is Soul?" In *Video Icons and Values,* edited by Alan M. Olson, Christopher Parr, and Debra Parr. Albany: State University of New York Press, 1991.

Herman, Edward S., and Noam Chomsky. *Manufacturing Consent.* New York: Pantheon, 1988.

Hersch, Seymour M. "Selective Intelligence." *New Yorker,* May 12, 2003.

Higgins, Kathleen M. *The Music of Our Lives*. Philadelphia: Temple University Press, 1991.

Hirshey, Gerri. "Funk's Founding Father." *Rolling Stone* 1018 (January 25, 2007): 42.

Hofstadter, Douglas. *MetaMagical Themas*. New York: Basic Books, 1985.

Huggins, Nathan. *Voices from the Harlem Renaissance*. New York: Oxford University Press, 1976.

Hume, David. *Of the Standard of Taste and Other Essays*. Indianapolis: Bobbs Merrill Library of Liberal Arts, 1965.

Humphrey, Mark A. "Holy Blues: The Gospel Tradition." In *Nothing But the Blues*, edited by Lawrence Cohn. New York: Abbeville, 1993.

Hunt, Valerie V. *Infinite Mind: Science of the Human Vibrations of Consciousness*. Malibu: Malibu Publishing, 1989.

Hurston, Zora Neal. "Spirituals and Neo-Spirituals." In *Voices from the Harlem Renaissance*, edited by Nathan Huggins. New York: Oxford University Press, 1976.

Huygens, Christian. *Oeuvres Completes de Christian Huygens*. The Hague: M. Nijhoff, 1893.

Kasayka, Roseann E., and Karen Hatfield. "A Comparison of Sedative vs. Palliative Music in Treatment of Persons in End-Stage Alzheimer's Disease." *Heather Hill Hospital* (1994). http://www.heatherhill.com/musicresearch02.html.

Keil, Charles, and Steven Feld. *Music Grooves*. Chicago: University of Chicago Press, 1994.

Kennedy, Rick, and Randy McNutt. *Little Labels—Big Sound*. Bloomington: Indiana University Press, 1999.

Khan, Hazrat Inayat. *The Music of Life*. New Lebanon, NY: Omega, 1983.

Kivy, Peter. *The Corded Shell: Reflections on Musical Expression*. Princeton: Princeton University Press, 1980.

Kivy, Peter. *The Fine Art of Repetition: Essays in the Philosophy of Music*. Cambridge: Cambridge University Press, 1993.

Kivy, Peter. *Introduction to a Philosophy of Music*. New York: Oxford University Press, 2002.

Kivy, Peter. "Mood and Music: Some Reflections for Noel Carroll." *Journal of Aesthetics and Art Criticism* 64, no. 2 (Spring 2006): 271.

Kivy, Peter. *Music Alone*. Ithaca, NY: Cornell University Press, 1990.

Kivy, Peter. *New Essays on Musical Understanding*. New York: Oxford University Press, 2001.

Kivy, Peter. "Something I've Always Wanted to Know about Hanslick." *Journal of Aesthetics and Art Criticism* 46, no. 3 (Spring 1988): 413–18.

Kochman, Thomas. *Rappin' and Stylin' Out*. Urbana: University of Illinois Press, 1972.

Kubik, Gerhard. *Africa and the Blues*. Jackson: University Press of Mississippi, 1999.

Langer, Susanne K. *Feeling and Form*. New York: Scribners, 1953.

LaVere, Stephen C. "Liner Notes." *Robert Johnson: The Complete Recordings*, New York: CBS Records, 1990.

Leckey, William J. "Stop the Straussians before They Lie Again." George Mason University, *History News Network*, June 9, 2003.

Lenzner, Steven, and William Kristol. "What Was Leo Strauss Up To?" *Public Interest* 153 (Fall 2003).

Levinson, Jerrold, ed. *The Oxford Companion to Aesthetics.* Oxford: Oxford University Press, 2003.

Levitin, Daniel J. *This Is Your Brain on Music: The Science of a Human Obsession.* New York: Dutton, 2006.

Levitin, Daniel J. *The World in Six Songs.* New York: Dutton, 2008.

Lippman, Edward. *Musical Aesthetics: A Historical Reader, Vol. I: From Antiquity to the Eighteenth Century.* New York: Pendragon Press, 1986.

Lipsitz, George. *Dangerous Crossroads: Popular Music, Postmodernism and the Poetics of Place.* London: Verso, 1994.

Litwack, Leon. *Trouble in Mind: Black Southerners in the Age of Jim Crow.* New York: Knopf, 1998.

Locke, Alain. *The Negro and His Music.* Washington: Associates in Negro Folk Education, 1936.

Lomax, Alan. *The Land Where the Blues Began.* New York: Pantheon, 1993.

Lomax, Alan. *Mister Jelly Roll.* Berkeley: University of California Press, 1950.

Lutz, Antoine, John D. Dunne, and Richard J. Davidson. "Meditation and the Neuroscience of Consciousness." In *Cambridge Handbook of Consciousness,* ed. P. Zelazo, M. Moscovitch, and E. Thompson. New York: Cambridge University Press, 2007.

Mann, James. *Rise of the Vulcans: The History of Bush's War Cabinet.* New York: Viking, 2004.

Marcus, Greil. *Invisible Republic: Bob Dylan's Basement Tapes.* New York: Henry Holt, 1997.

Marcus, Griel. *Mystery Train: Images of America in Rock 'n' Roll Music.* New York: Dutton, 1975.

Marsalis, Wynton. *Marsalis on Music.* New York: Norton, 1995.

Marsalis, Wynton. "Why We Must Preserve Our Jazz Heritage." *Ebony Magazine,* February 1986.

Marsh, Dave. *The Heart of Rock & Soul: The 1001 Greatest Singles Ever Made.* New York: Penguin, 1989.

Matravers, Derek. *Art and Emotion.* Oxford: Clarendon Press, 1998.

McClain, Ernest G. *Meditations through the Quran: Tonal Images in an Oral Culture.* Stony Brook, NY: Nicolas Hays, 1981.

McClain, Ernest. "Music's Discipline of the Means." *Parabola* 16 (Winter 1991): 87–89.

McClain, Ernest G. *The Myth of Invariance: The Origins of the Gods, Mathematics and Music from the RG Veda to Plato.* Stony Brook, NY: Nicolas Hays, 1976.

McClain, Ernest G. *The Pythagorean Plato: Prelude to the Song Itself.* Stony Brook, NY: Nicolas Hays, 1978.

Melnick, Jeffrey. *A Right to Sing the Blues: African Americans, Jews, and American Popular Song.* Cambridge, MA: Harvard University Press, 1999.

Meyer, Leonard. *Emotion and Meaning in Music.* Chicago: University of Chicago Press, 1956.

Michaels, Walter Benn. "Autobiography of an Ex-White Man: Why Race Is Not a Social Construction." *Transition* 73 (1997): 122–43.

Moore, Allan. *The Cambridge Companion to Blues and Gospel Music.* Cambridge: Cambridge University Press, 2002.

Morgan, George. "Recollections of the Peyote Road." In *Psychedelic Reflections,* edited by L. Grinspoon and J. Bakalar. New York: Human Sciences Press, 1983.

Murdoch, Iris. *The Fire and the Sun: Why Plato Banished the Artists.* Oxford: Clarendon Press, 1977.

Neff, Robert, and Anthony Connor. *Blues.* Boston: David R. Godine, 1975.

Nettl, Bruno. *The Study of Ethnomusicology: Twenty-nine Issues and Concepts.* Urbana: University of Illinois Press, 1983.

Norton, Anne. *Leo Strauss and the Politics of American Empire.* New Haven, CT: Yale University Press, 2004.

Oakley, Giles. *The Devil's Music.* Cambridge, MA: Da Capo, 1997.

O'Neal, Jim. "BluEsoterica: Dealing with the Devil at the Crossroads." *Living Blues* 37, no. 2 (March–April 2006).

Oliver, Paul. *Blues Fell This Morning.* Cambridge: Cambridge University Press, 1960.

Oliver, Paul. *Blues Off the Record.* New York: Da Capo, 1988.

Oliver, Paul, Tony Russell, Robert M. W. Dixon, John Godrich, and Howard Rye. *Yonder Come the Blues.* Cambridge: Cambridge University Press, 2001.

Ostrom, Carol M. "Music as Medicine." *Seattle Times,* May 25, 2005.

Otis, Johnny. *Upside Your Head: Rhythm and Blues on Central Avenue.* Hanover, NH: Wesleyan University Press, 1994.

Palmer, Robert. *Deep Blues.* New York: Penguin Books, 1981.

Palmer, Robert. *Rock and Roll: An Unruly History.* New York: Harmony Books, 1995.

Paxton, Frederick. *Christianizing Death: The Creation of a Ritual Process in Medieval Europe.* Ithaca: Cornell University Press, 1990.

Payne, Daniel Alexander. "Recollections of Seventy Years." (1888) Reprinted in *Readings in Black American Music,* 2nd ed., ed. Eileen Southern. New York: Norton, 1983.

Pearson, Barry. "Jump Steady: The Roots of R & B." In *Nothing But the Blues,* edited by Lawrence Cohn. New York: Abbeville, 1993.

Pearson, Barry Lee, and Bill McCulloch. *Robert Johnson Lost and Found.* Urbana: University of Illinois Press, 2003.

Peretz, I., and R. J. Zatorre. *The Cognitive Neuroscience of Music.* New York: Oxford University Press, 2003.

Perry, Steve. "Ain't No Mountain High Enough: The Politics of Crossover." In *Facing the Music,* edited by Simon Frith. New York: Pantheon, 1989.

Phinney, Kevin. *Souled American: How Black Music Transformed White Culture.* New York: Billboard Books, 2005.

Pieslak, Jonathan. *Sound Targets: American Soldiers and Music in the Iraq War.* Bloomington: Indiana University Press, 2009.

Prendergast, Roy A. *A Neglected Art: A Critical Study of Music in Films.* New York: New York University Press, 1977.

Puckett, N. N. *Folk Beliefs of the Southern Negro.* Chapel Hill: University of North Carolina Press, 1926.

Rauscher, F. H., G. L. Shaw, and K. N. Ky. "Music and Spatial Task Performance." *Nature* (1993).

Revel, Jean-Francois, and Matthieu Ricard. *The Monk and the Philosopher.* New York: Schocken, 1998.

Ricks, George Robinson. *Some Aspects of the Religious Music of the United States Negro: An Ethnomusicological Study with Special Emphasis on the Gospel Tradition.* New York: Arno, 1977.

Robeson, Paul. *Here I Stand.* New York: Othello Associates, 1958.

Robinson, Jenefer. *Deeper than Reason: Emotion and Its Role in Literature, Music, and Art.* New York: Oxford University Press, 2005.

Rose, Tricia. *Black Noise: Rap Music and Black Culture in Contemporary America.* Hanover, NH: Wesleyan University Press, 1994.

Ross, Alex. "Appalachian Autumn: Aaron Copland Confronts the Politics of the Cold War." *New Yorker,* August 27, 2007.

Ross, Alex. "Voice of the Century." *New Yorker,* April 13, 2009, 78–79.

Roszak, Theodore. *World, Beware! American Triumphalism in an Age of Terror.* Toronto: Provocations/Between the Lines, 2006.

Rowe, Mike. "Piano Blues and Boogie Woogie." In *The New Blackwell Guide to Recorded Blues,* ed. John Cowley and Paul Oliver. Cambridge, MA: Blackwell, 1996, 155–83.

Rubik, Beverly. "Bioelectromagnetics: Energy Medicine—A Challenge for Science." *Noetic Sciences Review* 28 (Winter 1993).

Rudinow, Joel. "Duchamps' Mischief." *Critical Inquiry* 7, no. 4 (Summer 1981): 747–60.

Rudinow, Joel. "Race, Ethnicity, Expressive Authenticity: Can White People Sing the Blues?" *Journal of Aesthetics and Art Criticism* 52, no. 1 (Winter 1994): 127–37.

Rudinow, Joel. "Reply to Taylor." *Journal of Aesthetics and Art Criticism* 53, no. 3 (Summer 1995): 316–18.

Sacks, Oliver. *Musicophilia: Tales of Music and the Brain.* New York: Knopf, 2007.

Santelli, Robert. "A Century of the Blues." In *Martin Scorsese Presents: The Blues—A Musical Journey,* ed. Peter Guralnick, Robert Santelli, Holly George-Warren, and Christopher John Farley. New York: Harper-Collins Amistad, 2003.

Santoro, Gene. *Highway 61 Revisited: The Tangled Roots of American Jazz, Blues, Rock & Country Music.* New York: Oxford University Press, 2004.

Sartwell, Crispin. *Act Like You Know: African-American Autobiography and White Identity.* Chicago: University of Chicago Press, 1998.

Scheindlin, Stanley. "A Brief History of Pharmacology." *Modern Drug Development* 4, no. 5 (May 2001).

Schellenberg, E. G. "Does Exposure to Music Have Beneficial Side Effects?" In *The Cognitive Neuroscience of Music,* ed. I. Peretz and R. J. Zatorre. New York: Oxford University Press, 2003.

Schmidt-Jones, Catherine. "Acoustics for Music Theory." *Connexions,* May 9, 2007.

Schroeder, Patricia R. *Robert Johnson: Mythmaking and Contemporary American Culture.* Urbana: University of Illinois Press, 2004.

Schroeder-Sheker, Therese. "Using Prescriptive Music in the Death-Bed Vigil." *Noetic Sciences Review* (Autumn 1994).

Schuller, Gunther. *The History of Jazz.* Oxford: Oxford University Press, 1968.

Serpick, Evan. "Soundtrack to the War: What the Troops in Iraq Listen to as They Roll into Battle." *Rolling Stone* 1007 (August 24, 2006): 20–22.

Shorris, Earl. "Ignoble Liars: Leo Strauss, George Bush, and the Philosophy of Mass Deception." *Harper's Magazine,* June 2004.

Shusterman, Richard. *Body Consciousness: A Philosophy of Mindfulness and Somaesthetics.* Cambridge: Cambridge University Press, 2008.

Shusterman, Richard. *Pragmatist Aesthetics.* Cambridge, MA: Blackwell, 1992.

Shusterman, Richard. "Somaesthetics: A Disciplinary Proposal." *Journal of Aesthetics and Art Criticism,* 57. no. 3 (Summer 1999): 299–313.

Sidran, Ben. *Black Talk: How the Music of Black America Created a Radical Alternative to the Values of the Western Literary Tradition.* New York: Holt, Rinehart and Winston, 1971.

Sidran, Ben. *A Life in the Music.* New York: Rowman & Littlefield, 2003.

Singer, Peter. *The President of Good and Evil: The Ethics of George W. Bush.* New York: Dutton, 2004.

Solomon, Robert C. *Spirituality for the Skeptic.* New York: Oxford University Press, 2002.

Southern, Eileen. *Readings in Black American Music.* New York: Norton, 1983.

Spencer, Jon Michael. *Blues and Evil.* Knoxville: University of Tennessee Press, 1993.

Spencer, Jon Michael. *Protest and Praise: Sacred Music of Black Religion.* Minneapolis: Fortress Press, 1990.

Strauss, Leo. *The City and Man.* Chicago: University of Chicago Press, 1964.

Strauss, Leo. *Persecution and the Art of Writing.* Chicago: University of Chicago Press, 1952.

Sundquist, Eric J. *The Oxford W. E. B. Du Bois Reader.* New York: Oxford University Press, 1996.

Taft, Michael. *The Blues Lyric Formula.* New York: Routledge, 2006.

Taft, Michael. *Talkin' to Myself: Blues Lyrics, 1921–1942.* New York: Routledge, 2005.

Taylor, Charles. *The Ethics of Authenticity.* Cambridge: Harvard University Press, 1991.

Taylor, Paul C. ". . . So Black and Blue: Response to Rudinow." *Journal of Aesthetics and Art Criticism* 53, no. 3 (Summer 1995): 313–16.

Taylor, Roger. *Art, an Enemy of the People.* Sussex: Harvester, 1978.

Thompson, Robert Farris. *Flash of the Spirit: African and Afro-American Art and Philosophy.* New York: Random House, 1983.

Thorgaard, Per, Ellen Ertmann, Vibeke Hansen, Anni Noergaard, Lene Spanggaard. "Designed Sound and Music Environment in Postanaesthesia Care Units—a Multicentre Study of Patients and Staff." *Progress in Natural Science* 21, no. 4 (August 2005): 220–25.

Titon, Jeff Todd. "Thematic Pattern in Downhome Blues Lyrics." *Journal of American Folklore* 90, no. 357 (1977): 316–30.

Tobin, Jacqueline L., and Raymond G. Dobard. *Hidden in Plain View: A Secret Story of Quilts and the Underground Railroad.* New York: Random House, 1999.

Tutu, Desmond. *Report of the Truth and Reconciliation Commission of South Africa.* http://www.info.gov.za/otherdocs/2003/trc/.

Twain, Mark. *Pudd'nhead Wilson's New Calendar.* 1897.

Ventura, Michael. *Shadow Dancing in the USA.* Los Angeles: Jeremy P. Tarcher, 1985.

Waksman, Steve. *Instruments of Desire: The Electric Guitar and the Shaping of Musical Experience.* Cambridge, MA: Harvard University Press, 1999.

Wald, Elijah. *Escaping the Delta: Robert Johnson and the Invention of the Blues.* New York: HarperCollins Amistad, 2004.

Wald, Gayle F. *Shout, Sister, Shout! The Untold Story of Rock-and-Roll Trailblazer Sister Rosetta Tharpe.* Boston: Beacon Press, 2007.

Walker, Alice. *The Same River Twice: Honoring the Difficult.* New York: Simon & Schuster, 1996.

Walleczek, Jan. "Bioelectromagnetics: The Question of Subtle Energies." In *Noetic Sciences Review* 28 (Winter 1993).

Walser, Robert. *Running with the Devil: Power, Gender, and Madness in Heavy Metal Music.* Hanover, NH: Wesleyan University Press, 1993.

Ward, Brian. *Just My Soul Responding: Rhythm and Blues, Black Consciousness, and Race Relations.* Berkeley: University of California Press, 1998.

Ward, Ed. *Michael Bloomfield: The Rise and Fall of an American Guitar Hero.* New York: Cherry Lane, 1981.

Ward, Martha. *Voodoo Queen: The Spirited Lives of Marie Laveau.* Jackson: University Press of Mississippi, 2004.

Wardlow, Gayle Dean. *Chasin' That Devil Music: Searching for the Blues.* San Francisco: Backbeat Books, 1998.

Waterman, Dick. *Between Midnight and Day.* New York: Thunder's Mouth Press, 2003.

Watson, John F. "Methodist Error." (1819) Reprinted in *Readings in Black American Music,* 2nd ed., ed. Eileen Southern. New York: Norton, 1983.

Weiand, Jeffrey. "Duchamp and the Artworld (with a note from Joel Rudinow)." *Critical Inquiry* 8, no. 1 (Autumn 1981): 151–57.

Welding, Pete. "Hell Hound On His Trail: Robert Johnson." In *Down Beat's Music '66.* Chicago: Maher, 1966.

Werner, Craig. *Higher Ground.* New York: Three Rivers Press, 2004.

West, Cornell. *Democracy Matters: Winning the Fight against Imperialism.* New York: Penguin, 2004.

Wex, Michael. *Born to Kvetch: Yiddish Language and Culture in All of Its Moods.* New York: St. Martin's, 2005.

Whiteis, David. "The Devil Ain't Got No Music! Mavis Staples." *Living Blues* 175 (December 2004).

Whiteis, David. "Singing through the Rain" (profile of folk singer Rosalie Sorrells). *No Depression* 58 (July–August 2005).

Williams, Genevieve. "Robben Ford: Blue Moon Rising." *Blues Revue* 79 (January 2003): 11.

Williams, Sherley Anne. "The Blues Roots of Contemporary Afro-American Poetry." In *Afro-American Literature: The Reconstruction of Instruction,* edited by Dexter Fisher and Robert B. Stepto. New York: Modern Language Press Association of America, 1978.

Winant, Howard. *Racial Conditions: Politics, Theory, Comparisons.* Minneapolis: University of Minnesota Press, 1994.

Wolkin, Jan Mark, and Bill Keenon. *Michael Bloomfield: If You Love These Blues—An Oral History.* San Francisco: Miller-Freeman, 2000.

Wooten, Victor L. *The Music Lesson: A Spiritual Search for Growth through Music.* New York: Berkeley Books, 2006.

Wyman, Bill, with Richard Havers. *Bill Wyman's Blues Odyssey: A Journey to Music's Heart and Soul.* New York: DK, 2001.

Young, Alan. *Woke Me Up This Morning: Black Gospel Singers and the Gospel Life.* Jackson: University Press of Mississippi, 1997.

Young, James O. *Cultural Appropriation and the Arts,* Blackwell Publishing, 2008.

Zelazo, P., M. Moscovitch, and E. Thompson. *Cambridge Handbook of Consciousness.* New York: Cambridge University Press, 2007.

Recommended Listening and Viewing

CHAPTER 1

Ray Charles. *The Ray Charles Story.* Atlantic, ATC 2-900.

Ray Charles. *A Man and His Soul.* ABC-Paramount, ABCS-590X.

Phases 1 and 2 of Ray Charles' storied career. The Ray Charles Story surveys the recordings of his breakthrough period with Atlantic Records. Ray's move to ABC Paramount and his success at Atlantic gave him a then unparalleled level of artistic control—of which he took full advantage, moving in bold new directions.

Sam Cooke. *Portrait of a Legend—1951–1964.* Abkco, (2003) BoooogN1ZV.

Sam Cooke. *With the Soul Stirrers: The Complete Specialty Recordings.* Specialty Records, (2002) 3SPCD-4437-2.

Before crossing over to pop, Sam Cooke sang lead with the close harmony gospel quartet the Soul Stirrers. Portrait of a Legend surveys Cooke's body of work from the gospel period through the pop hits to the later work, including some blues (Willie Dixon's "Little Red Rooster" recorded for RCA).

Aretha Franklin. *Queen of Soul: The Atlantic Recordings.* 1992, Atlantic Records, Bo00003 2VS.

Aretha Franklin. *Amazing Grace.* 1972, Atlantic Records, 2-906-2.

Aretha established herself as the Queen of Soul during her Atlantic Records period. On Amazing Grace she is welcomed back in church with Reverend James Cleveland and the Southern California Community Choir.

Curtis Mayfield. *People Get Ready! The Curtis Mayfield Story.* 1996, Rhino/WEA, Bo00003 3PX.

Alan Slutsky et al. *Standing in the Shadows of Motown.* Lions Gate, (2003) Boooo8J2HC.

The film Standing in the Shadows of Motown documents the work of the Funk Brothers, the long unheralded Motown house band. A revealing look behind the scenes of the Motown hit machine. A must see.

Stevie Wonder. *Natural Wonder.* Motown, (1995) 31453-0546-2.

One of the most remarkable bodies of work in the history of recorded music, presented here live in international concert. The standards of production and performance are as high as the songwriting.

Various Artists. *Atlantic Rhythm & Blues 1947–1974.* Atlantic/WEA, (1991) B000021RS.

Various Artists. *Hitsville USA: The Motown Singles Collection 1959–1971.* Atlantic/WEA, (1991) B0000021QU.

Various Artists. *Love Train: The Sound of Philadelphia.* Sony Legacy, (2008) B001F290GM.

Various Artists. *The Complete Stax-Volt Singles 1959–1968.* Atlantic/WEA, (1991) B0000021QU.

Box-sets of the major soul labels.

CHAPTER 2

Robert Johnson. *The Complete Recordings.* 1990, CBS Records, C2K, C2T, C3: 46222.

Twenty nine titles, with alternate takes, published with notes and commentary by Keith Richards, Eric Clapton, and music historian Stephen LaVere.

Eric Clapton. *Me and Mr. Johnson.* 2004, Reprise, 48423-2.

Eric Clapton. *Sessions for Robert J.* 2004, Reprise, 48926-2.

Clapton pays tribute to his major source of inspiration and documents the recording sessions on video.

Walter Hill, dir. *Crossroads.* 1986, Sony/Columbia Pictures.

Ry Cooder. *Crossroads: Original Motion Picture Soundtrack.* 1986, Warner Brothers Records, 1-25399.

Ry Cooder's version of Robert Johnson's "Crossroads Blues" (not used in the film) is by itself worth the price of the album.

Chris Hunt, *The Search for Robert Johnson.* 1992, Columbia Music Video, CVD 49113.

Interviews with Johnson's contemporaries and with subsequent blues scholars. Narrated by John Hammond, Jr.

CHAPTER 3

The Campbell Brothers et al. *Sacred Steel—Live!* Arhoolie, (1999) CD 472.

A very good introduction to a distinctive musical tradition. The Campbell Brothers are the leading exponents of sacred steel guitar. They are recorded here live—in church, with guests including Robert Randolph.

Georgia Tom (Thomas A. Dorsey). *Complete Recorded Works in Chronological Order.* Vols. 1 and 2, Document Records/RST Records, BDCD 6021, BDCD 6022.

Georgia Tom Dorsey. *The Essential.* 2002, Classic Blues, B00006JMB2.

Thomas A. Dorsey. *Precious Lord: The Great Gospel Songs of Thomas A. Dorsey.* 1973, Sbme Special Markets, B0012GMVX0.

The remarkable career of bluesman Thomas A. "Georgia Tom" Dorsey, "Father of Gospel Music." The Essential *collection is focused on his hokum collaborations.*

Bob Dylan. "I and I," on *Infidels.* 1983, Columbia Records, QC 38819.

Al Green. *Anthology.* 1997, The Right Stuff/Hi Records, 72438-53033-2-6.

No artist traverses the divided territory of gospel and Rhythm & Blues as effortlessly and convincingly as the independent Memphis soul giant Reverend Al Green.

Howard Porter and Anne Elletson. *The Story of Gospel Music: The Power in the Voice.* 1996, BBC Video/Warner Brothers, E2108.

An excellent historical documentary with performance footage of Shirley Caesar, Reverend James Cleveland, the Fisk University Jubilee Singers, Tramaine Hawkins, Mahalia Jackson, and Sister Rosetta Tharpe. Highly informative commentary by Horace Boyer, Reverend Wyatt Tee Walker, and Charles Wolfe.

The Staple Singers. *Freedom Highway.* 1965, Sbme Special Markets, B0012GMY14.

The Staple Singers. *The Best of the Staple Singers.* 1990, Fantasy/Stax, B00000XGX.

Mavis Staples. *Have a Little Faith.* 2004, Alligator Records, ALCD 4899.

Mavis Staples. *We'll Never Turn Back.* 2007, Anti-Records, 88630-2.

Freedom Highway *represents the early gospel oriented work of the "First Family of Soul." The* Best of *collection represents the group's more "socially conscious" work at Stax, which Mavis Staples carries forward in her ongoing solo work.*

Stevie Wonder, "Superstition," *Talking Book,* 1972, Tamla/Motown, T319L.

CHAPTER 5

James Brown. *Star Time.* 1991, Polygram, STDB J BROWN.
James Brown. *"Live" at the Apollo, Volume II.* 1991, King Records, K2S 1022.

These two collections nearly encapsulate the music of the "Godfather of Soul" and inventor of funk. The Star Time *box-set is a comprehensive and well documented survey of the recordings. James Brown's live performances were legendary.* "Live" at the Apollo *documents the live show in the quintessential setting.*

Taj Mahal. *An Evening of Acoustic Music.* Ruf Records, (1996) Ruf 1009.

Taj Mahal gives his German audience a lesson on "the back beat."

CHAPTER 6

Mose Allison. *The Best of Mose Allison.* 2005, Rhino/Atlantic, B00123MBAG.

One of the greatest songwriters in the American songbook. There are dozens of compilations of Mose Allison's recorded work. All good.

Paul Butterfield Blues Band. *The Paul Butterfield Blues Band.* Elektra Records, EKS-7294.

Paul Butterfield Blues Band. *East-West.* Elektra Records, EKS-7315.

Paul Butterfield Blues Band et al. *What's Shakin'.* Elektra Records, EKL-4002.

The Butterfield Band with the original lineup as discussed in chapter 6. The follow-up album East-West *attempted to integrate elements of raga into a blues context. The* What's Shakin' *collection includes five tracks that didn't make the cut for the Butterfield Band's debut and three cuts of Eric Clapton and the Powerhouse—Clapton's first collaboration with Steve Winwood (before Blind Faith).*

The Electric Flag. *A Long Time Comin'.* Columbia Records, CS 9597.

Michael Bloomfield's ambitious, eagerly awaited, but ill-fated post-Butterfield project.

Buddy Guy. *Damn Right, I Got the Blues.* 1991, Silvertone, J2 1462.

Buddy Guy. *Slippin' In.* 1994, Silvertone, 01241-41542-2.

You want authenticity? Check out "Don't Tell Me About the Blues" on "Slippin' In," in which Buddy deflates blues pretension. Damn Right, I've Got the Blues *includes a memorial tribute to Stevie Ray Vaughan.*

CHAPTER 7

D. A. Pennebaker. *Monterey Pop.* 1968, Criterion, B00006JU7P.

The first and arguably the best rock festival, with stunning performances by Otis Redding, Ravi Shankar, and a then unknown Jimi Hendrix. The third disc of "Outtakes" (from the final cut of the film version) includes performances by Janis Joplin, the Byrds, Buffalo Springfield, the Butterfield Blues Band, the Electric Flag, Jefferson Airplane, and more.

CHAPTER 8

James Booker. *Junco Partner.* Hannibal Records, (1993) HNCD 1359.

Capturing the erratic Booker's genius was a challenge. This is the definitive recording. Booker's rendition of Chopin's "Minute Waltz" is priceless.

Niels Eje. *MusiCure 1–8.* Gefion Records, GFO 20147.

Designed music for therapeutic relaxation.

John Lee Hooker. *The Hook: 20 Years of Hits and Hot Boogie.* Chameleon Records/Vee Jay Hall of Fame Series, (1989) D2-74794.

John Lee Hooker. *The Healer.* Chameleon Records, (1989) D1-74808.

Therapeutic trance boogie from the legendary blues shaman.

Jelly Roll Morton. *The Complete Library of Congress Recordings.* 2005, Rounder
 Records, CD 11661-1888-2.

*The definitive interviews conducted by Alan Lomax; musically illustrated by Morton; pack-
aged with the definitive documentary materials, including Lomax's book* Mister Jelly
Roll.

Index